An Eye for An I: Living Philosophy

Robert Spillane

M
A
MICHELLE ANDERSON PUBLISHING
MELBOURNE

First published in Australia 2007
by Michelle Anderson Publishing Pty Ltd
PO Box 6032
Chapel Street North
South Yarra 3141
Melbourne Australia
Email: mapubl@bigpond.net.au
Website: www.michelleandersonpublishing.com

© Copyright: Robert Spillane 2007
Reprinted 2008
Cover design: Deb Snibson, Modern Art Production Group
Cover: Rene Magritte, The Difficult Crossing
Photo: © Erich Lessing/Eric Lessing Culture & Fine Arts Archives
        © Rene Magritte licensed by VISCOPY, Australia, 2006
Typeset by: Midland Typesetters, Australia
Printed and bound by Griffin Press, South Australia

National Library of Australia Cataloguing-in-Publication data

Spillane, Robert,
    An eye for an I: living philosophy.

    ISBN 9 780 85572 381 1

    1. Meaning (Philosophy) 2. Life. 3. Philosophers.
    I. Title

Contents

Acknowledgements   vii

Prologue: An Eye for an I   1

Living . . .

1   Heroically: Gilgamesh, Homer, Aeschylus,   11
Sophocles, Euripides

2   Rationally: Socrates, Protagoras, Plato,   38
Aristotle

3   Cynically: Antisthenes, Diogenes, Crates,   70
Peregrinus, Voltaire, Rousseau,
Bierce

4   Stoically: Zeno, Epictetus, Marcus   105
Aurelius, Ellis

5   Religiously: Frazer, Augustine, Aquinas,   131
Luther, Calvin, Weber

6   Politically: Machiavelli, Hobbes, Locke,   161
Burke

7   Mindedly: Descartes, Ryle, Mead, Szasz   187

8 Sceptically: Pyrrho, Timon, Bacon, Locke, 217
Hume, Russell, Popper,
Feyerabend, Stove

9 Romantically: Kant, Fichte, Friedrich, Stirner, 250
Schopenhauer, Nietzsche

10 Naturally: Eramus Darwin, Lamarck, 285
Charles Darwin, Wallace,
Malthus, Huxley, Butler,
Nietzsche, Hardy, Geertz

11 Existentially: Kierkegaard, Sartre, Beauvoir, 313
Camus

Epilogue: An I for an Eye 347
Index 357

For Rhiannon

'A philosopher is a sort of miser, secretly hoarding up the treasures of reflection which other people wear as the occasional ornaments of intercourse, or use as part of the heavier coinage of conversation. If, as a non-philosopher, you confine your reflections to moments, the result is perhaps a serious talk with a friend, or nothing more noteworthy than an occasional hour of meditation, a dreamy glance of wonder at this whole great and deep universe, with its countless worlds and wayward hearts. Such heart searchings, such momentary communings with the universe, such ungrown gems of reflection, would under other circumstances develop into systems of philosophy. If you let them pass from your attention you soon forget them, and may even fancy that you have small fondness for philosophy. But nonetheless, all intelligent people, even the haters of philosophy, are despite themselves, occasionally philosophers.'

(Josiah Royce)

Acknowledgements

This book owes its existence to my having been invited by the Art Gallery Society of New South Wales in Sydney to deliver two series of lectures in 2003 and 2004 – *The Mind's Eye: An Introduction to Philosophy*. The aim of the series was to personalise philosophy and so emphasise those ideas which enable people to gain insight into and mastery of themselves. I should like to thank Louise O'Halloran whose idea it was to have me to deliver the lectures and to those who so ably supported me – Judith White, Michelle Munro, Vanessa Herlihy, Craig Brush, Fran Hellier and Ian Shadwell.

I am grateful to Lenore Grunsell for allowing me to work from the unpublished lecture notes of her late husband and my friend and co-author, John Martin, whose ideas inform Chapters 5 and 10.

Thanks are also due to my publisher, Michelle Anderson, who encouraged me to write philosophy for a wider audience. When I could not see that audience I wrote for Joanna.

Prologue:
An Eye for An I

I am a philosopher although my philosophy does not allow me to say so. But a philosopher is what I am. I cannot say that I aspire to be a philosopher because I am one. Nor can I say that I am becoming a philosopher because I have arrived, so to speak. I think rather than feel philosophy but that is a philosophical matter. Whatever else I am becoming, I am a philosopher.

As a philosopher I should know better than to say I AM a philosopher because I am other things as well. Perhaps I should have started at the beginning (where else?) and announced grandly, I am I. Of that there can be no doubt. The move from 'I am I' to 'I am a philosopher' is a tricky one because philosophy is a war of isms – a war that I actively participate in. There is philosophy and there are competing philosophies, so to say that I am a philosopher leaves me open to the charge that I am not an I, but many I's. And this I readily acknowledge because I have chosen a philosophy that is not one – and it is definitely not an ism. My philosophy is not Philosophy – it is detached from Philosophy – but not from life. Or so I assert. You see philosophers usually argue, but I have to start somewhere – and I start with assertions. I assert and you may well ask, as many have, what it is that I assert. In my scientific moments I assert facts. But the postmodernists I meet at dinner-parties tell me that there are no facts. So, I assert, it is a fact that there are no facts. And where is to be found the person who will challenge this assertion? This assertion, (or is it an argument?) makes them angry, as indeed it is intended to. I am, after all, a man of paradox in an age of paradoxes. Well, if Donald is a duck . . .

I also assert values. One of my I's believes the value of values is that they are feelings and thus add a sentimental touch to the serious business of logical analysis. (Can I analyse without logic?). If values are mere explosions of feelings, then they cannot be deduced from facts (thankfully) because they are not facts. Another one of my I's believes that values are not feelings, but actions. Values are, therefore, the very stuff of philosophy. Of that I am certain – indeed it is a fact. I am my values because my values are my actions. They are decidedly not my feelings, although many people have told me that I have no feelings. I feel, think and value that is certain, but it is true that I have no such things as feelings, thoughts, or values. If my values are my actions then I am the sum of my actions and that is that. But if I am the sum of my actions where is the 'I' behind the actions? Where is the puppeteer pulling the strings of my actions? The simple answer: there is no 'I' behind the actions – there are only the actions themselves. How then can I assert, as is my wont, that I am a philosopher, or an I? Again the answer is simple: I am as many I's as their are actions. Whilst many subjects study human action – psychology, sociology, for example – it is the supreme task of philosophy to study all those I's that I am.

Some philosophers tell me that 'I' is a mere pronoun – an accident of language – and I need not waste my time contemplating it because to ask what 'I' is, is to treat 'it' as a noun. So the answer to the question: what is this thing called 'I'? is that it is a no-thing, a nothingness. Other philosophers with a spiritual bent, incline to the view that 'I' is a soul-like substance, given to us by god(s), which we use to think, feel and value, and which uses us when it becomes sick. There are many words for this ghost in the machine – soul, mind, psyche, ego, self, character, personality – and they all have their champions in philosophy. That strange German genius, Friedrich Nietzsche, asserted that 'I' is a multiplicity – many 'I's fighting with each other for supremacy. This is a dangerous view to assert in public since it is widely believed, especially in Hollywood, that I should have one strong I and those deviates with several I's – the three I's of Eve for example – are suffering from an illness of I, or mental illness. As an aside, Eve's problem was that she had only three I's and they didn't get along with each other.

In the chapters which follow, I introduce several I's – heroic, rationalist, cynical, stoical, sceptical, romantic, existential, and others. Since I am a philosopher rather than a Philosopher, I cannot be any one of these I's. For to commit myself unreservedly to any one philosophical ism is to disqualify myself as a critical thinker. A man of multiple I's moves easily between the various perspectives, happily embracing one today and another tomorrow. This may appear to some folk a perfect example of frivolity. But it can be seen as a way of remaining free from dogmatic commitments to one I in favour of a free play of conflict between many I's. But, as the man of many I's said, what doesn't destroy me makes me stronger, and the battle of the isms that is philosophy will have its winners and losers, which means that some of my I's are stronger than others. And that is as it should be for how, otherwise, would I be able to talk with myself?

Philosophy teaches me how to talk with myself and thus enjoy a high class of conversation. That little voice, so beloved of schizophrenics and deranged killers, is just philosophy in action. If philosophy is thinking about thinking, and thinking is talking to myself, and talking to myself involves an I that talks and a Me that listens, then a book of philosophy should enable readers to talk to themselves in different voices – to have various I/Me conversations. If I does the talking, I need several I's because one poor old unchanging I would be intolerably boring. Sartre said somewhere that people who eschewed philosophy were boring because they always spoke with the same voice, something we cannot accuse Sartre of doing. To speak with different voices to others and to my-self, is not to enter a schizophrenic world, but to participate in what Wittgenstein called an intelligent play of language games, which was for him the mark of the well-educated person.

Writing about the warring isms of philosophy has one important advantage. It gives me licence to interpret philosophers my way and not to bother with what they 'really meant'. This may seem self-indulgent, and indeed it is. But it enables my I's to interpret various philosophers, to allow an I to select those assumptions which are important, and thereby to construct from the skeleton of their writings a body of ideas which can provide one of my I's with a way of living. Whether I actually live the philosophy is of as little importance as is my name, or my preferences, although I will admit to envying squirrels. There are limits to my egocentricity, to be sure, but when I am engaging with philosophers I try to be free of constraints.

One egocentric philosopher, Max Stirner, founded his philosophy on nothing except himself, and thereby had a fascinating topic to think and write about. Is this what gives philosophy a bad name? Is this what happens when free spirits, for whom the only liberty is 'my power' and the only truth 'the splendid selfishness of the stars', read philosophers? Nietzsche, who so often sounds like Stirner, argued in this vein that if God really did exist how could I bear not to be him? And so he tried to become God. Is that what philosophers are trying to do when they claim to have discovered the truth of the world? Sartre claimed that he was totally free to create the person he wanted to be, and succeeded. So to enter the world of philosophy is a potentially hazardous exercise. It is like entering Virgil's Cave of Polyphemus, or a woman's handbag, in which people are seen to enter but never leave. In the case of philosophy, the journey is out of the light of the Me and into the darkness of I. We live between these two poles – talking and listening to ourselves. Philosophy teaches us how to talk to ourselves, and therefore how to live.

That philosophy is for the living is an ancient doctrine.

And when several of my I's embrace the ideas of the ancients, they are in no way strangers to the experience. The ancient thinkers are long dead (one of my I's loves tautologies) but their ideas are so refreshingly alive today that I can be as they were – a cynic, stoic or sceptic. None of their ideas is strange, even if some are eccentric. Their ideas are more than idle reflection to be occasionally practiced in the rarefied atmosphere of the academic study. Rather, they offer my I's the opportunity to shape and give direction to Me. I have found that each philosopher discussed in this book offers ideas of considerable force and fascination, and whilst a philosophy's ability to fascinate by presenting a dramatic picture of human existence is not a criterion of its truth, it certainly adds to its power to change my way of living.

Try as I may I cannot escape from philosophy because I philosophise when I reflect critically on how I am living. And living involves thinking (talking to myself), arguing, choosing and acting. The critical enquiry into what all this means is philosophy. Like the philosophers, I often wonder about living and the study of living, suitably elaborated, is philosophy. One way to evaluate a philosopher's ideas is to see whether I can live by it and this means I have to penetrate the illusions of appearances and the delusions of common sense. This is, I guess, what the ancients called wisdom: knowledge of what is true and right combined with responsible choice as to action. To choose a philosophy responsibly is, then, to base my choice on the truth or rightness of the ideas contained therein. To determine what is true and right is what my I's wrestle with, argue about with Me. And that means I have to act like a detective. My job is to uncover the philosophers' assumptions and compare them with my own.

One of my I's concluded long ago that what is important about any philosophy is not what it explains, but what it assumes. To uncover and analyse assumptions is the task of the educator, as Socrates realised, and most of my I's are inclined to agree with him. If it is the task of educators (in a world of trainers) to develop the intellectual, moral and aesthetic powers of individuals, then philosophy is not, like the study of Latin, an exercise in 'training the mind'. To train is to instruct, drill and subordinate individuals to practical routines and standards. That is not philosophy. Philosophers are educators because they prefer questions to answers, argument to instruction. Because philosophy is a critical enterprise – thinking about thinking – it is a subversive and liberating affair. Nietzsche understood this when he wrote that educators can be nothing more than liberators – this is the secret of all education.

Philosophers are educators because they question the assumptions on which all other subjects depend. It is a subversive activity because those imbued with the philosophical spirit are never satisfied with final answers. It is a liberating affair because it has the power to change lives, for better or for worse. I love the philosophers discussed in these pages because they are so politically incorrect, so confronting, so unconcerned with their reader's feelings that they say what they think, so unworldly, so virile. They are always challenging my I's with striking ideas, confronting them with their prejudices, and arousing curiosity, not satisfying it.

How my readers interpret my interpretations is up to them, not me. In these pages I have engaged with philosophers who represent diverse worldviews, or ways of living. I have placed them in various categories and called them 'living philosophies' because they are still alive for eleven of my I's. Perhaps the writers I have plundered would object to my doing so. But this is how I have used them, for my benefit. I have no time for party-lines since I am a philosopher and not a Philosopher, which means that I am not a theologian although I discuss religions critically – so this book is not for those who have found religious salvation since they have no need of philosophy.

In our age of relativism where seriously frivolous people believe in everything and its opposite, many turn to philosophy for religious salvation. But they do not find solutions. They find questions and arguments, negation, nay-saying, and nihilism. Philosophers spend much of their time just keeping their heads above the water that threatens to submerge them in negativity. They have invented such words as 'absurdity', 'contingency', 'nihilism' to account for the experiences which threaten to drown those who seek salvation. No, philosophy is not, as Socrates thought, a preparation for death. It is a quest for living a life of negation without despair, of looking without falling into the abyss, of laughing in the face of absurdity, of looking squarely at the brutality of humans and still loving some of them, of experimenting with the idea that 'hell is other people' but stopping short of killing them, of playing with the idea that people are basically rational and coping with the inevitable disappointments.

Philosophy has different descriptions for the human

animal, *homo natura* (natural man), *homo sapiens* (man the truth-seeker), *homo homini lupus* (man is a wolf to man), *homo economicus* (man the calculating machine), *homo faber* (man the maker). If I am a philosopher, I am all of these and more. If, however, I am frightened by my fellow creatures, if I shy away from unmasking their lies and prejudices and follow the path of political correctness, if I want final answers to questions of existence, I am not a philosopher. Since I am a philosopher, I therefore live in constant confusion, absurdly but willingly. It is the task of my several I's in these pages to pass along that confusion in the hope that others will become equally confused and so enjoy the delights of confusing friends with one's multiple I's.

So who am I? I am not just the person whose name appears on the cover of this book. He has to deal with the mundane world of academic politics, unstable relationships with colleagues and friends, the vagaries of publishers and the demands of audiences. He has, therefore, to be far more rational than I. He hopes that people will buy this book, praise him for writing it, and earn champagne money from it. He is a captive of his reputation (such as it is), a slave to convention, and so unable fully to engage with philosophers. He is too concerned with constructing elegant sentences, arguing validly, describing ideas accurately. In short, he is too logical, too rational, too inclined to take fools seriously, too concerned to use his intellect to avoid the abyss which beckons. He tries to maintain a consistent I for his students and friends (well two I's since he would not dream of talking to his friends the way he talks to his students). The challenge in writing this book is that he has to allow some of his other I's to emerge.

One of those I's (the one he works hard to conceal from friends for fear they will commit him to a mental hospital) has willingly and happily taken up residence in the abyss. That I reads philosophers to see what escape routes they offer, discovers interesting, desperate suggestions but finds none of them convincing because they assume that we can only live happily if we avoid, or escape from, the abyss. And so we invent religions, political systems and Philosophy to protect us from falling into nothingness. We erect philosophical safety fences so that we might live in communal happiness, untroubled by fear of the darkness. We even refer to the abyss as hell – a Dante's *Inferno* where poor sinners reside, or our everyday world where Sartre's 'others' threaten. But Dante and Sartre are wrong – hell is not in another world, nor is it 'other people'. I am the abyss – the abyss is I. And philosophy is the study of I – all else is secondary. A philosophy is an eye for an I.

S,
Sydney, 2007

1

Living Heroically

'Zeus, The chief of Grecian Gods, adored by the
Romans as Jupiter and by the modern Americans
as God, Gold, Mob and Dog.'

(Ambrose Bierce)

Some years ago a British sailor overturned his yacht and an Australian naval ship put to sea to rescue him. When the sailors returned to port, the newspapers hailed them as 'Our Heroes'. I have heard feminists assert that there are no heroes since the term is a dead white male anachronism, while other members of the sisterhood refer admiringly to such heroes as Joan of Arc and Simone de Beauvoir who were glorified by fire and autobiographies respectively. I have heard masculinists reserve the word 'hero' for footballers and cricketers. I have even heard business executives refer to their favourite management gods as 'heroes' although I am not sure they are serious.

There is something touching in the way heroes are applauded for their deeds even if today the deeds are not so great. If heroism entails a striving after something appallingly hard to obtain, then many of today's heroes do not deserve the label or the exaggerated applause. If, for example, I concern myself with the search for happiness, if I adopt the posture of the optimist, if I think that the world is wonderful, if I try to spend my life in Christian fashion, loving everyone, I disqualify myself from the possibility of living heroically. Because if 'heroism' is anything, it is a way of life and is not confined to occasional praiseworthy acts. If I prefer to concern myself with improving the 'quality of life' by placing pleasure at the top of my hierarchy of needs, I am not heroic. Not for me a life of hardship, struggle and overcoming; as a non-hero my preferences would be sentimentally tied to the modern obsession with rights rather than responsibilities, with pleasure rather than power. Is it possible today to give a coherent meaning to heroism as a way of life? I think so.

Ancient heroes lived and died for power and glory and thereby brought prosperity and honour to their families. If I prefer to live in a soft, hedonistic way, I cannot live heroically. In ancient times, heroism was a way of life; today it is sporadic and confined to specific situations. Ancient heroism was embedded in a results-culture where poor performance was not tolerated. Today's 'heroes' are often excused for poor performance and even attract sympathy when they fail. Ancient heroes expected to live short and glorious lives – the Irish hero, Cuchulain, said that 'If I achieve fame I am content though I had only one day on earth'. Today's heroes wish for long lives as celebrities.

For Homer's noble warriors in the *Iliad* to live heroically is to live honourably. The great warrior, Aias, emboldens his men: 'My friends, be men and think of your honour. Fear nothing in the field but dishonour in each other's eyes. When warriors fear disgrace then more are saved than killed. Neither honour nor salvation is to be found in flight.' And the heroic Nestor: 'Be men, my friends. Think of your reputation in the world. Remember your children too, and your wives, your property and your parents, whether they are alive or dead. For the sake of your absent dear ones I beseech you to stand firm and not to turn and run.' The noble Trojan warrior Hector emphasises the importance of glory: 'But if I hid myself like a coward and refused to fight, I could never face the Trojans and the Trojan ladies. Besides, it would go against the grain, for I have trained myself always, like a good soldier, to take my place in the front line and win glory.' And so it is for Sarpendon: 'Ah, my friend, if after living through this war we could be sure of ageless immortality, I should neither take my place in the front line nor send you out to win honour on the battlefield. But things are not like that. Death has a thousand pitfalls for our feet, and nobody can save himself and cheat him. So in we go, whether we yield the glory to some other man or win it for ourselves.'

A hero is a man of distinguished courage and performance admired for his noble qualities. He is to be found in *The Epic of Gilgamesh* (about 2300 B.C.), in Homer's great epic poem, *Iliad* (about 750 B.C.), in the Viking societies (7th to 11th Centuries), in the Irish and Celtic sagas (8th Century), in the Icelandic sagas (13th Century) and in Japanese Bushido of the Edo period (16th Century). Heroes in these societies are warrior chieftains of special strength, courage and nobility. They shared a worldview based squarely on power and glory. Those inheritors of the earth – the meek and the mild – are yet to make their appearance on the world stage. And when they arrive, the heroic worldview will receive its greatest challenge. Notions of nobility, courage and honour will be re-defined and combined with ideas about compassion, humility, truth and happiness, which are more familiar and comforting to the modern mind.

But that is to anticipate. I am concerned in this chapter to understand what it means to live heroically and to see how the philosophy of heroism was transformed in the classical age of Greece by philosophers and dramatists. Heroism will always be with us even if its philosophy today is less consistent and coherent than it once was. When in the 19th Century Nietzsche tried to effect another inversion of values, it was to Homer that he turned. But, inevitably, he returned to Homer through the lens of his time and so foisted on ancient heroism a modern face which emphasised the importance of the powerful, alienated individualist. Thus was created a modern view – heroic individualism – much favoured by Hollywood, where noble, strong individualists pit themselves against malevolent authorities. This makes for inspiring story-telling but it has little to do with ancient heroism, which would have regarded individualists as dangerous aliens.

The first reference to heroism in Western literature is to be found in *The Epic of Gilgamesh*, a story about the legendary king in Mesopotamia, a hero of the Kingdom of Uruk who fights with axe, sword and bow to win glory. The Gilgamesh poem – a tragic adventure story –

antedates Homer's epic poems by 1500 years – and it tells a rollicking story of heroic deeds in the face of great adversity. Underlying it all is the search for the secret of immortality.

The hero of the poem is Gilgamesh, who is two parts God and one part man, and the tension between the desires of the Gods and the fate of man constitutes the tragedy of the story. He is beautiful, strong, courageous, arrogant and lusty but he is, alas, human all too human as he confronts, at the end of his life, dashed hopes, lost opportunities and his pointless struggle with the inevitability of death. Gilgamesh's search is for an earthly immortality, that is, for a God-like glory on earth. But he eventually realises that he is 'searching for the wind'. He must come to accept the futility of struggling for what he cannot have. In that acceptance is a hero who has learned to stare death in the face and, if not laugh, smile.

A close and loving friend, Enkidu, interprets one of Gilgamesh's dreams thus: 'The father of the Gods has given you kingship, such is your destiny, everlasting life is not your destiny. Because of this do not be sad at heart, do not be grieved or oppressed. He has given you power . . . to be the darkness and the light of mankind. He has given you unexampled supremacy over the people, victory in battle from which no fugitive returns, in forays and assaults from which there is no going back. But do not abuse this power . . .'

If one cannot be a God one can at least be a hero and be talked about through the ages. So Gilgamesh shakes off his melancholy and announces: 'I will set up my name in the place where the names of famous men are written, and where no man's name is written yet I will raise a monument to the Gods. Because of the evil that is in the land, we will go to the forest and destroy the evil . . .' Inevitably, he goes to the forest to face a ferocious giant, Humbaba. His friend suffers doubts about the adventure but Gilgamesh utters words reminiscent of later heroic poems: 'Where is the man who can clamber to heaven? Only the Gods live for ever . . . but as for men, our days are numbered, our occupations are a breath of wind. How is this, already you are afraid! I will go first although I am your lord, and you may safely call out, "Forward, there is nothing to fear!" Then if I fall I leave behind me a name that endures; men will say of me, "Gilgamesh has fallen in fight with ferocious Humbaba." Long after the child has been born in my house, they will say it, and remember.' To be God-like, if not an actual God, is to live long and gloriously in people's memories.

To be a hero, then, is to be the main subject of noble tales handed down to children and passed on to students. For more than 2500 years educated people in the West studied admiringly the adventures of the great warriors. Above all, epic tales of heroism provide a table of values against which I can judge myself. For here can be found the challenges and dilemmas of human existence: courage and cowardice, love and loss, success and failure, honesty and betrayal, life and death, mortality and immortality. These dilemmas are not debated; they are embedded in the characters and I can evaluate them by what they do and say. Values in heroic society are not laid up in a God-created heaven. Rather, my values are judged by what I do. Gilgamesh and Enkidu are the sum of their actions and by their actions they shall be judged. This is especially true of the relationship between the sexes, then and now.

The Epic of Gilgamesh is not without its humour and insights into love and the relations between the sexes. When lovely Ishtar, Goddess of love, fertility and war, proposes marriage to Gilgamesh, he replies: 'If I take you in marriage, what gifts can I give in return? What ointments and clothing for your body? I would gladly give you bread and food fit for a God. I would give you wine to drink fit for a queen. I would pour out barley to stuff your granary; but as for making you my wife – that I will not. How would it go with me? Your lovers have found you like a brazier which smoulders in the cold, a backdoor which keeps out neither squall of wind nor storm, a castle which crushes the garrison, pitch that blackens the bearer, a water-skin that chafes the carrier, a stone which falls from the parapet, a battering-ram turned back from the enemy, a sandal that trips the wearer. Which of your lovers did you ever love forever?'

Ishtar was not pleased. Tearfully she runs to her father and begs permission to destroy Gilgamesh. The poor father points out that the citizens of Uruk will suffer if Gilgamesh dies. Ishtar, the woman scorned, is unmoved and plots her revenge. Foiled by Enkidu, Ishtar is determined that he too must die. Enkidu is thus struck down by a fatal illness and after twelve days of pain realises he will not die heroically in battle, but shamefully in his sick-bed. His end is doubly tragic for a man who has lived a life of heroic action. He dies in agony and Gilgamesh is devastated.

Bitterly Gilgamesh weeps for his dead friend and because Enkidu's death awakens in him his own fear of death, he begins his doomed search for everlasting life. On his travels he meets the divine wine-maker, Siduri, who tells him to eat, drink and be merry for tomorrow we may die. But Gilgamesh is not placated and cries: 'How can I be silent, how can I rest, when Enkidu whom I love is dust, and I too shall die and be laid in the earth.'

Clearly, knowledge of the inevitability of death can liberate or enslave us. In *The Epic of Gilgamesh* it encourages bold adventures, but it can also inhibit courageous action and lead to despair. At the end of this remarkable story I am left pondering the worth of human ideals – youth, friendship, love, status and eternal life. The ending, which has often been described as unsatisfying, teaches us that all must end with our deaths. As he approaches his own death Gilgamesh is told that, whilst death cannot be cheated and everlasting life is not the destiny of poor mortals, he should be proud that he has lived nobly and will be remembered as a hero. For despite its travails life can be more than an ignoble struggle in the dark. It was Gilgamesh's fate to die a tragic and flawed hero, because all human beings are flawed and life is fundamentally tragic.

The Epic of Gilgamesh teaches the higher truth that heroism entails tragedy – without tragedy there is no heroism. There is nothing especially heroic about a man who fights bravely and hopes to die so that he may travel to a heavenly paradise. Whilst we can admire the power of these warriors, they are not heroic unless they face the heroic paradox – the more they fight the quicker they expose themselves to an unwanted and painful death. To fight in the knowledge that one is thereby guaranteed an excruciating death and an eternity of misery is only possible if one defers to a table of values that renders one 'God-like' on earth.

And so Gilgamesh, noble and tragic hero, dies. To be remembered as a man of beauty, power and heroic deeds, who did not abuse his authority but used it to fight evil, should be enough to fill a man's heart.

Western literature, it is said, begins with Homer around 750 B.C., but this is not true. Because the clay tablets on which *The Epic of Gilgamesh* was written were not discovered until the 18th Century, it was Homer's epic poems that inspired readers for more than 2700 years. Homer's great heroic themes echo those of Gilgamesh, but go further to include anger and withdrawal of the hero from battle, fights to the death between great warriors, feudal loyalty and disobedience, revenge and its bloody realisation.

The central theme in heroic societies is power expressed through action. Whilst the *Bible* says that in the beginning was the word, heroic societies emphasise the deed. A man in heroic society is what he does; he is the sum of his actions. What a man does is defined by social roles, rules and rewards. In heroic society a man knows who and what he is by knowing his role and the rules which bind roles. When he knows his role – his place – he knows almost everything he has to know. He knows what he is owed and what he owes others. He knows what to do in the face of the enemy and how to relate to warriors and camp-followers. There is a clear understanding of standards and orders of rank. Without a role a man would not know who he is. In short, a man in heroic society is what he does and what he does is largely influenced by the role he occupies.

To say that a man is what he does may sound banal to modern ears. But in our day, most people disagree with the heroic view, believing instead that there lurks in humans a hidden source of actions – a puppeteer pulling the strings of action. We have diverse names for this actor – mind, soul, self, psyche, ego, character, personality. Yet, for Homer, there are no hidden depths, there is no puppeteer. He makes no distinction between actor and action in the same way in which we should make no distinction between the flash and the lightning (since the lightning is the flash). And so there is, for Homer, no mind, ego, self, psyche, character, personality or 'I', and so no psychology. Achilles is obviously different from Hector, and is so described, but neither is described in terms of an underlying personality, i.e. a quasi-mechanical force which compels them to act in their different ways. But neither is there any sense of free will in Homer's heroes who are fated to live a long life of security and mediocrity or a short career of danger and glory.

Clearly, Homer's characters do make choices even if Homer lacks a language of choice. If a hero is not treated like a hero, deprived of his just rewards for example – he is faced with the need to choose an appropriate course of action. This dilemma sets in motion the plot of the *Iliad* and gives it its dramatic tension. But this dilemma and its consequences for our understanding of the *Iliad* assumes that Achilles, who was deprived of his rewards by his commander-in-chief, Agamemnon, had a choice (in the modern sense of the term). Modern readers imagine Achilles struggling with his possibilities, overwhelmed by various alternatives which he must finally resolve by private, critical deliberation. But reading the *Iliad* it is clear that Achilles does not choose; he does what he must. The heroic code has been violated, he acts accordingly. Achilles is fated to fight and kill Hector after which he will himself soon die. The heroes of the *Iliad* accept their destiny and are ennobled by that acceptance. As Seneca was later to write: 'Fate leads you if you assert, drags you if you do not.'

Heroic life was a constant pursuit of *arete* – virtue, excellence, power, courage, nobility. Young men were expected to be impetuous and fiery; old men to be prudent and visionary; warriors to be courageous and self-reliant; women to be chaste and useful. Women, however, represent a 'problem' for warriors.

In the poignant scene with Hector, Andromache and their son, the dilemma of the warrior woman is beautifully and tragically outlined. Since a woman's status depends on her warrior husband, the possibility of his death looms large in her thinking, especially when battle awaits. Realising that Hector is fated to fight Achilles, Andromache understandably wants to hold Hector back from the fight and keep him in her world of comfort and security. It is clear that Homer believes it is typical of warrior women that, in the end, they want men to resist them and 'go out among the flying spears'. As Hector says, he would not be able to face his people if he refused to fight and seek glory. His social status (and that of Andromache's) depends on his status as a successful and brave warrior. Andromache upsets Hector but she does not really provide him with a moral dilemma. He will do what he must, or as Hollywood would say: 'A man's got to do what a man's got to do.'

Hollywood did, in fact, make a movie based on the scene between Hector and Andromache and transferred its location to the American wild west. Starring Gary Cooper and Grace Kelly, *High Noon* begins with Gary (a lawman) and Grace leaving a church after their wedding. Word arrives that villains are on their way to settle their accounts with the town and its lawman. Gary buckles on his guns to the chagrin of his bride who attempts to dissuade him from this potentially fatal course of action. She tells him in no uncertain terms that he has new responsibilities to her and so he should leave the townsfolk to their fate and travel to her world of comfort and security. This, of course, he cannot do. He cannot run from danger, abandon his fellow citizens, spend a life looking over his shoulder. He must stay and face the enemy because his reputation is founded on the moral code he lives by. His bride is unimpressed and gives him a choice: either come away with her or face the villains without her. He stays, she leaves. And we can leave the movie at this point because Hollywood takes over and the movie ends happily with the villains dead, the newly-weds re-united, travelling into the sunset.

Half way through *High Noon* Homer is left behind in his tent pondering the dilemma of the hero's loved ones who live with the fear that the heroic code, which gives them their status and wealth, will lead to their death.

Because the hero always strives to excel and cannot accept loss of face, he stubbornly risks his (and his family's) life to achieve glory. There is an inexorable tension between the necessities of battle and the welfare of the family because all parties know that this heroic determination to excel may do damage to friends and community. Heroic self-assertion is thus set against the well-being of society and it represents one of the main tragic themes in epic poetry. Heroes do not intend their loved ones to perish but they know that this can only be avoided by success in war. It is not their intentions that count, but their successful performance in battle.

Since Homeric heroes must be strong, brave and successful, intentions are irrelevant. Their worldview is calculative rather than intentional, powerful rather than just – might is right. Results count more than effort so that Homeric men are always under pressure to perform. They cannot trade on past successes: they must continue to fight successfully so that they are forever in a state of preparedness for battle. They are judged by others and are, accordingly, concerned about what others think of them. Since they can only please others by competitive excellence and warlike achievement, they set the judgements of their peers against estimations of themselves – what they do is, in the final analysis, what counts. And their actions must be successful because they adopt a 'win at all costs' philosophy. In such a worldview it is pointless to distinguish between a moral error and a mistake because both lead to failure. And failure will be met with disapproval whatever the cause. Such are the stresses of a results culture!

Homer compares his warrior heroes to a lion, wild boar, storm, river in flood, raging fire. Their eyes flash, fire beats in their breast, they are filled with fury as they leap at the enemy with a terrifying cry. And he describes dying in the most gruesome terms. One warrior lies in the dust with hands stretched out to friends shrieking; another bellows with pain clutching the bloody earth or biting the cold bronze which has severed his tongue, another has his brains spread over the face of a friend, another writhes like a roped bull about the spear, and another has his liver thrust out and watches his lap fill with blood. Life and death are contrasted in stark terms: alive a hero is full of vitality and splendour; dead there is nothing but horror and torment.

Homer does not glorify war. When a hero dies it is agonisingly painful and he travels to Hades which, unlike a Christian heaven or Islamic paradise, is not a place to look forward to. Faced with the knowledge that the more he fights the quicker he dies, and knowing that his death will be painful and that Hades is his eternal place of torment, the obvious question is: why do warriors continue to fight?

For Homer's heroes it was obvious that whether hero or coward, noble person or base, death awaits all. Life is therefore the standard of value and the way one acts in life is the standard against which one is judged. To understand that death lies ahead, that defeat not victory is the final outcome, is a virtue. All men must suffer – that is the way the Homeric Gods plan human life – and heroes are trapped by the logic of heroism. They strive to excel and cannot accept loss of face. They are stubborn and may wreak damage on foe and friend. All is subordinated to a noble death and the hope that a hero may become a god.

Ancient heroism is complicated by the presence of 55 gods who enter and leave the action unpredictably. But the gods serve many purposes. Warriors occasionally act wildly and defy the roles and rules which govern them. These 'aberrations' have to be explained and Homer resorts to explanations from without – the gods are responsible and intervene directly into human bodies. If I say: 'he has a job but his "heart" is not in it, and he lacks the "brains" to succeed and the "guts" to resign.' I am following Homer's practice of explaining human action by reference to bodily organs.

Homer's belief that human action is initiated through the body by the gods was to suffer a serious setback when, in the sixth century BC, 54 of his 55 gods were retrenched. The ancient Greeks then needed a different way of explaining human action, particularly those actions that violated the heroic code. If a warrior expressed fear in the face of the enemy, contrary to the dictates of his role, Homer assumed he lacked *menos* which could be corrected by the intervention of a god. But if the gods are subtracted from Homer's psychology, he is left with roles, rules and rewards as explanations of internal experiences, and these concepts cannot carry the burden placed upon them.

Rules, roles and rewards can 'explain' a lot, but they cannot help us understand feelings and actions that stand in opposition to them, such as a strong desire to run away from battle. With the removal of the gods from Mt.

Olympus, Homeric psychology had to change radically. The obvious solution to the problem was to reverse causes – human action is not externally caused, it is internally caused. This has led, in our time, to the popular view that my behaviour is caused by personality traits which reside in me. Whereas Homer might have said that Achilles was bothered by the (external) angers, I am tempted (though not for long) to say that I am angry because of an angry personality which I inherited. A moment's reflection reveals the circular reasoning involved in attributing angry behaviour to an angry personality. I am angry because of an angry personality; I have an angry personality because I am angry. Homer's gods have been removed from the mountain but they have taken up residence inside human beings as personality traits.

Reading the *Iliad* it is obvious that Homer's heroes are subject to violent changes in mood which would nowadays be called mental instability. The fiercest warriors weep openly before their colleagues, sometimes in rage, other times in sadness. They are quick to acknowledge their fears, worries and wishes. They live and fight intensely, the very opposite of modern movie heroes who stare unblinkingly at the danger that confronts them and have the emotional life of a machine. Living was an intense, emotional affair and those who failed to express appropriate emotion were regarded as incomplete human beings. It was to be several centuries before Plato would argue that Homer's characters were child-like because their emotions overpowered their rational faculties. But Homer does not have a language for rationality. His characters argue and debate but they do not think in terms of an overarching, superior standard of rationality. Their actions are judged pragmatically rather than rationally and their debates are conducted against the background of practical necessity. The forceful expression of emotions is an important aspect of this background because, in a world dominated by power, it is often necessary to intimidate enemies and colleagues alike.

Of course, this begs the question: where do the emotions come from? Since Homer did not use a language of 'psychological' causes, his machinery of gods vividly portrays the surging emotions of his heroes. Whilst it is true that he was not innocent of ascribing behaviour to bodily organs, he nonetheless avoided a language of mental events. He interprets the 'irrational' elements in human nature as an interference with human life by human-like gods who put something into a warrior and thereby influence his conduct and thinking. Hector confronts Glaucus who had suggested that he fight Aias with the following words: 'Believe me, fighting and the noise of chariots do not frighten me. But we are all puppets in the hands of aegis-bearing Zeus. In a moment, Zeus can make a brave man run away and lose a battle; and the next day the same god will spur him on to fight.' When Zeus heard this he said: 'Unhappy man! Little knowing how close you are to death, you are putting on the imperishable armour of a mighty man of war, before whom all others quail ... Well, for the moment great power shall be yours. But you must pay for it. There will be no home-coming for you from the battle, and Andromache will never take the glorious armour of Achilles from your hands.'

Homer's men and gods 'know' things. Achilles 'knows wild things, like a lion,' or the Trojans 'remember flight and forget resistance'. Now if character is knowledge, what is not knowledge is not part of character but comes to a hero from outside. So when he acts in a manner contrary to his dispositions which he 'knows', his actions are not his own but have been imposed upon him. What we should call irrational impulses are, therefore, not his but emanate from alien sources. Above all, Homer's characters 'know' that they cannot escape their fate. After listening to Lycaon beg for his life, Achilles says: '. . . Yes, my friend, you too must die. Why make such a song about it? Even Patroclus died, who was a better man than you by far. And look at me. Am I not big and beautiful, the son of a great man, with a goddess for my mother? Yet Death and sovran Destiny are waiting for me too. A morning is coming, or maybe an evening or a noon, when somebody is going to kill me too in battle with a cast of his spear or an arrow from his bow.'

Neither these alien sources nor *psyche* are spiritual. Homer's *psyche* is composed of material that resides in the body while the person is alive, and at death flies down to Hades through a bodily orifice. From there it may be summoned to address the living. *Psyche* has no mental function in the living person: it is simply that whose existence ensures that the person is alive.

Today 'I' is used to designate 'that which takes decisions'. But in Homer there is much less emphasis on 'I': words like *psyche* and *thymos* are used as sources of power. So Homeric characters act as their *thymos* directs them. A warrior's *thymos* tells him that he needs to eat, or slay the enemy, or it advises him on appropriate courses of action. Lacking the linguistic framework to distinguish between a psychological function and a bodily organ meant that *thymos* was felt as a hot sensation in the chest, a surge from within. If, on the other hand, Homeric man felt a backward impulse he might say that another *thymos* restrained him. *Thymos* is also associated with consciousness: it feels emotions and is conscious of that feeling. It is the *thymos* in which internal debates occur.

As he prepares to face Achilles in mortal combat Hector 'groaned at his plight and took counsel with his indomitable *thymos*'. In short, he debates with himself. 'If I retire behind the gate and wall, Polydamas will be the first to cast it in my teeth that, in this last night of disaster when the great Achilles came to life, I did not take his advice and order a withdrawal into the city, as I certainly ought to have done. As it is, having sacrificed the army to my own perversity, I could not face my countrymen and the Trojan ladies in their trailing gowns. I could not bear to hear some commoner say: "Hector trusted in his own right arm and lost an army." But it will be said, and then I shall know that it would have been a far better thing for me to stand up to Achilles, and either kill him and come home alive or myself die gloriously in front of Troy. I could of course put down my bossed shield and heavy helmet, prop my spear against the wall, and on my own authority make overtures to Prince Achilles . . . But why do I contemplate such a course, when I have every reason to fear that when I approach Achilles he will show no pity, nor any regard for my person, but will kill me out of hand like a woman, naked and unarmed as I should be? No; at this hour I cannot see Achilles and myself as a pair of trysting lovers, billing and cooing to each other like a lad and lass. Better to waste no time and come to grips. Then we should know to which of us the Olympian intends to hand the victory.' Here, in this poignant inward debate, we have the main heroic themes: courage, doubt, shame, virility, power, glory and fate.

It is clear that, judged by today's standards, Homer's language is different; some would even say it is primitive. Yet there is a beautiful simplicity in employing an action language stripped of dubious abstractions and the circular reasoning which says that a person acts aggressively because he has an aggressive personality. Homer describes the world in human terms; he does not concern himself with a mysterious inner world of mental events. But this was soon to change.

The dramatist Aeschylus was the first to show clearly that when a man acts some psychological process is involved. Aeschylus emphasises human 'choice', by which he means a deliberate act of decision. Homer does not speak of such a dilemma; his warriors merely know that it is their fate either to die as young men in a blaze of glory, or to live long and mediocre lives. Aeschylus is less interested than Homer in what his characters do because he believes that the essence of human action is to be discovered in the act of decision. Action involves a commitment to the future – it is more than a mere reaction to events. So when a man is about to act, he weighs alternatives and assumes the responsibility for his decision, and this is what gives the dramatic tension to Aeschylus's plays.

Aeschylus composes tales of what happens to a man when he makes a crucial choice. Not gods but man himself controls the significance of what happens. When Homer makes the meaning of human events depend upon the actions of gods, these deeds are unalterable facts in the face of which human choices are impotent. When I come to the world of Aeschylus, I am cut adrift from the power of gods and must take care of myself. But this new freedom is also a burden which I may find onerous. In Aeschylus's plays freedom wears people down and isolates them from the support of gods. This inexorable path to isolation and loneliness continues in the plays of Sophocles whose characters are already lonelier than those of Aeschylus.

In Sophocles *psyche* is 'I' – a living self – which has taken over the functions of Homer's *thymos*. *Psyche* now means 'life' or 'person' as contrasted with soma or body. We might say that *psyche* is the psychological correlate of *soma* which together make a complete human being. Sophocles' Oedipus refers to himself as *psyche* and *soma* where I might say 'I'. By the fifth century B.C. *psyche* is used to refer more to the emotional, than the rational, self – it is the seat of courage, passion, anxiety.

Euripides' characters continue the process of detaching themselves from the natural world. Like Aeschylus and Sophocles, Euripides attempts to understand the quint-essential nature of human beings – their motives and their capacity for choice. In Euripides' world, I am alone with my passions. And my passions are not easily tamed by reason. Indeed, Euripides thought that reason was rela-tively impotent in the face of strong passion and wondered whether any rational purpose is to be found in the world of human affairs. Good and evil are not god-given qualities assailing reason from without. Rather, they are part of the defining characteristics of human beings.

Euripides places the responsibility for good- and evil-doing inside me. Passion and knowledge are the two great determining factors; external factors are devalued as deceptive devices used to avoid confronting the sad fact that I am responsible, through my passions and inadequate powers of reasoning, for the good and evil I create. It is therefore important to study the internal workings of 'I' if I am to discover the motives which inspire good and evil deeds.

In Euripides' play, *Medea* (431 B.C.), two themes which loom large in the centuries ahead dominate – the qualities of women and the importance of human motives. In her attempt to win back Jason from another woman, Medea threatens, and then proceeds, to kill her children. While audiences are appalled by her actions, they strive to understand her motives. Medea, for all her crimes, is somehow more human than Homer's characters because she defies her biological and social conditioning. She rises above everyday feelings to achieve her goals and even though I might find her behaviour despicable, I cannot help but try to understand why she acted as she did.

Medea knows that she is at war with her irrational self. The tragedy of Medea is that she surrenders to the strength of her passion, knowing all the while that she can do otherwise. 'I understand the horror of what I am going to do; but anger, the spring of all life's horror, masters my resolve.' Referring indirectly to the Homeric sense of heroism, she says: 'A woman's weak and timid in most matters; the noise of war, the look of steel makes her a coward. But touch her right to marriage and there's no bloodier spirit ... We were born women, useless for heroic purposes but skilled practitioners in all kinds of evil ... Let no one think of me as humble or weak or passive; let them understand I am of a different kind: dangerous to my enemies, loyal to my friends. To such a life glory belongs.'

If I am defined by my ability to transcend my biological and social conditioning, I am very dangerous indeed. I might be saved from this danger if I could be sure that I could master my strong passions. But Euripides is not sanguine about this; he is convinced that humans can be relied upon to allow their passions to control and guide them on the important matters of living. So long as 'I' as *psyche* is granted the status of the emotional self and the cause of important actions, there seems to be little room for the 'rational man' who can, with education and intellectual discipline, tame his passions. This man was soon to appear on the world stage with Socrates/Plato, who took the crucial step of identifying *psyche* or 'I' with rational thinking, whose virtue is knowledge.

Through the exercise of rational thinking Medea's problems can be re-defined and managed and the tragic element in human affairs eliminated. This grandiose worldview, based on a newly-found intellectual optimism, was to wage war on Homeric heroism and consign it to an ignoble history.

The Homeric poems present us with a literature of noble action and emotion in a language which records what it is like to live in a 'results' culture. Since success is crucial and good intentions are of no importance, actions are evaluated in terms of matters external to one's self. There is, therefore, no need to postulate an 'I' as a cause of actions. And yet the unity represented in English by 'I' exists. We see this in Homer's allowing his warriors moments of self-doubt as they ponder their actions. In the end, they 'decide' to act in terms of how their actions will appear to others, and so no Homeric character can possess internal serenity because past successes have constantly to be replaced by suitably approved deeds. In this way, 'results' cultures involve their citizens in a strong sense of shame if they fail to perform well. And the phenomenon of 'shame' pre-supposes 'I'.

In the *Iliad* heroism does not produce happiness; its reward is fame. Yet there is no self-pity in Homer's heroes. They confront a world which is nasty, brutish and short courageously and without any sense of being depressed by a future which will end in pain and misery. They teach me how to live nobly in the face of adversity and death. If I cannot be immortal, I can at least live nobly and die well. Homeric man resists the impulse to invent another, perfect 'spiritual' world to house its heroes. Homer's is a realistic philosophy of life in which 'what you see is what you get' and nobility means confronting a brutal world without illusion. To confront and accept the tragic element in human life demands a worldview which does not excuse poor performance, or tolerate hand-wringing complainers.

Homer's men are hardy folk with strong bodies of

classical beauty. Their philosophy emphasises all the finer human emotions – love, chivalry, courage, virtue, excellence and justice. The warriors are lusty in company, fearless in fight and steadfast in friendship. They applaud excellence in battle and in oratory. After hearing Agamemnon suggest that they run unashamedly from impending disaster, Odysseus 'of the nimble wits' scowls: 'My lord, this is preposterous. What fatal leadership! You should have had a set of cowards to command, instead of leading people like ourselves, whose lot it is from youth to age to see wars through to their bitter end, till one by one we drop. So this is how you propose to bid farewell to Troy of the broad streets, for which we have undergone so many hardships! You had better hold your tongue, or the men may get wind of this idea of yours, which nobody with any sense in his head would ever have put into words, least of all a king with a huge army like yours at his command. You can have no brains at all to have made such a suggestion . . .' No mealy-mouthed subordinates in the world of heroes! Agamemnon replied: 'A harsh rebuke, Odysseus! But I acknowledge its force. Very well, I will not order the men to drag their ships into the sea against their better judgement. But now one of you must come forward with a sounder scheme than mine. Seniority does not matter – I shall be pleased to hear him.'

Faced with a cruel and short life, Homer reminds us that human existence can be more than an insignificant struggle, even though human life is governed by in-exorable conflict. A philosophy of glorious power is, therefore, an understandable consequence of the need to transform their intolerable, battle-bound lives into a spectacle. This philosophy did not require gods to offer them the prospect of ever-lasting happiness. Indeed, happiness is not a feature of heroic philosophy at all. Rather, they needed their reckless gods as a contrast to the nobility which they demonstrated in their lives. Homer's gods were so capricious and irresponsible that if I approach them with another religion, searching for charity and benevolence, I will be forced to turn away because there is nothing in them that suggests spirituality or duty. I cannot help but wonder how these high-spirited men could have found life so enjoyable. To be able to confront a brutal life without self-pity suggests a philosophical worldview which we would do well to study.

In *Culture of Complaint*, Robert Hughes argues that we live in a culture which screams for freedom without responsibility and happiness without pain. If so, then I must seriously ponder whether I can give a sense to the ancient idea of the heroic. If I pursue 'happiness' and 'quality of life' I disqualify myself from heroic status. If I submit to political correctness totalitarians and the demands of minority groups (paranoid and otherwise), I vote for a dubious democracy which has lost touch with the great aristocratic sentiments and standards by which greatness is achieved. If I, in my self-pitying haste, seek out counsellors for my ills, I deny the virtues of courage and noble action.

It is Homer's genius that he was able to describe the heroic worldview in a way that combined an emphasis on heroic self-assertion with a deep sense of the tragedy of human existence. Homer's heroes are alive for me today and deserve my respect because they looked squarely at the world and stood firm in the face of its terrors. They have never left Western consciousness and they stride across the stage of history as giants who bow their heads only to their mortality.

2

Living Rationally

'You, my friend, are you not ashamed of heaping up
the greatest amount of money and honour and reputation,
and caring so little about wisdom and truth and the
greatest improvement of yourself which you never
regard or heed at all? And if the person with whom
I am arguing says: Yes, but I do care; then I do not let
him go; but I proceed to interrogate and cross-examine
him, and if I think that he has no virtue in him,
but only says he has, I reproach him with undervaluing
the greater, and overvaluing the lesser.'

(Socrates)

Had I lived in the classical age of Greece – Plato's time – I would have confronted a new cultural hero – the philosopher-king. Homer's warriors no longer occupy the higher reaches of human achievement because men of action have been replaced in the heroic pantheon by men of thought. This period is characterised by the first great transformation in Western thought, or what Nietzsche called the 'genuine antagonism'. Had I been educated in Plato's *Academy* I would have been told to ignore Homer's *Iliad* and commit myself to Plato's Utopia (described in

The Republic). An odd development, one might say. And Nietzsche did say so, but that was over 2000 years later and most philosophers disagree with him in any case. Nietzsche thought that Homer was a glorifier of life and Plato a slanderer of life – a man who had to lie himself out of reality. Nietzsche was a naturalist and believed with Homer that there is only one world and this is it! Plato, like all religionists, believed in two worlds and therein lies a complicated story, and many fascinating philosophical problems.

Plato and his followers replace Homer's emphasis on physical prowess and heroic action with the importance of *logos* – thinking and reasoning about the world. Those who dedicate themselves to *logos* will be led to *sophia* – wisdom – and those who love (*philo*) wisdom are philosophers. Plato transcends Homer's world because he replaces *mythos* – thinking about a god-driven world – with *logos*. So the Homeric idea that man is *homo natura* is replaced by the idea that man is *homo sapiens* – man the knower, or man the truth-seeker. Plato creates a new cultural hero, replacing the sophisticated fighting animal with the truth-seeker. Virtue is transferred from the physical to the intellectual plane and the physical world is progressively devalued in favour of the spiritual world.

The first great transformation in Western thinking is a movement from one world to two – from this material world to a second, immaterial world. Something must have been in the air in the 6th Century B.C. because this is when the Buddha in India, Zoroaster (Zarathustra) in Persia and Isaiah in Palestine preach a philosophy of two worlds. The Homeric world was, as we have seen, a single, natural world in which Hades was simply the underworld – underground. After the 6th Century B.C. philosophers took seriously the idea that there are two worlds – a physical world accessible to the senses, and a metaphysical world accessible to the mind. Since the physical, everyday world is infected by sense-defeating illusions, the metaphysical world must be the 'real', true world. The mind is the key to penetrating this second world and so the mind is extolled in proportion as the senses are indicted. Here is the beginning of the Western rational tradition, and a libel on the natural world.

Philosophically this tradition begins with Thales (around 600 B.C.) who claimed that 'everything is really water'. Now it is obvious that the world of the senses does not lead me to conclude that the world is really water. So, philosophically, the most important of Thales' four words is 'really'. The world I perceive is characterised by considerable diversity (rocks, trees, people, mountains, lakes, etc), but the real world is uncontaminated by human perception – it is a single, metaphysical world. Since my everyday world of sense-perception is not the real world, it must be an apparent, illusory world, because in reality the world is one. So everything is really something else and not what it appears to be. A consequence of this reasoning is a devaluing of the natural, everyday world in favour of a private, mental world which is revealed by thinking. This private world is richer than the natural world because it enables me to build a bridge from mind to a supernatural world uncontaminated by the senses.

It was inevitable that Thales would be followed by

philosophers who agreed with him in principle but who disagreed with his conclusion that the world is really water. Anaximander said that everything is really primal being, Anaximines preferred quality, Pythagoras numbers, Heraclitus fire, Parmenides being (which is) and not-being (which is not), Empedocles love and strife, Anaxagoras *nous*, Democritus atoms. I am reminded of the various soapbox orators in *The Life of Brian* announcing the arrival, at different times and places, of the messiah.

With their emphasis on *logos* these philosophers generated more complicated forms of reasoning, such as the following teaser by Parmenides which religionists have been dining off for centuries:

If x can be thought, x can exist,
nothing cannot exist,
so if x can be thought, it is not nothing,
therefore it must be something,
so if x can be thought, it must exist.

By about 430 B.C., in what is known as the 'Athenian Period', some thinkers attempted to bring a halt to this orgy of philosophical speculation. 'When Zeus is toppled', wrote Aristophanes, 'chaos succeeds him and whirlwind rules'. Such sentiments found expression in the work of rhetoricians who were sceptical about absolute truths. Led by Protagoras (481–411 B.C.) and known as Sophists they quickly became the official opposition to the truth-seeking philosophers. The Sophists travelled from town to town arguing for one truth today and another tomorrow. (They were the first management consultants.) In some cases they argued against the possibility of arriving at the truth at all. Forsaking truth-seeking for power and persuasion, their motto was not *homo sapiens* but *homo mensura* – man is the measure of all things – a view which leads to subjectivity and scepticism with respect to truth, pragmatism with respect to life and relativism with respect to everything, except relativism. In our day, the only philosopher postmodernists bow their knee to is Protagoras, whose legacy could be seen on plaques which adorned the front doors of the trendies of the 1970s when postmodernism took hold: 'You are you, and I am I, and if by chance we meet, that's wonderful.' Was there ever any connection behind those doors?

It seems that Protagoras was the first Greek to maintain that there are two opposing sides to every question. He gave public readings for which he charged handsome fees and was never short of an audience. In his *Lives of Eminent Philosophers*, Diogenes Laertius says that Protagoras would begin his lectures by announcing: 'Man is the measure of all things, of things that are that they are, and of things that are not that they are not.' Even after such an auspicious opening, he would still have an audience. (I am now even more convinced he was the first management consultant.) He believed that the soul was nothing apart from the senses and as for the gods: 'I have no means of knowing either that they exist, or that they do not exist. For many are the obstacles that impede knowledge, both the obscurity of the question and the shortness of human life.' (Now this sounds far too sensible for a management consultant.) For these agnostic words the Athenians expelled him and burned his books in the market-place. He was the first to extol *carpe diem* (seize the day), to institute debating as an important cultural activity, and to teach rival pleaders the tricks of the trade. He seems to have been the inventor of the Socratic dialogue of questioning, answering and more questioning. When he asked a student for a fee, Euathlus said that he had not won his case yet. 'No', said Protagoras, 'if I win this case against you I must have the fee for winning it; if you win I must have it, because you win it.' (Definitely, a management consultant.)

The view that 'man is the measure of all things' leads easily to the pragmatic view that 'truth is what works.' This, of course, makes all religions, voodoo, Indian rain-dancing and countless other absurdities true because they all 'work' for true believers. Replacing logical and scientific truths with pragmatic truth is popular with the advocates of political correctness because if a true statement (that is, one that corresponds with the facts) offends a particular group, it clearly does not 'work' for them and so should not be uttered. That we have arrived at this state of intellectual affairs shows the influence of Protagoras and the Sophists who chime in well with the relativistic spirit of our times. After all, how can one give offence to another if the key question is not: 'Does it correspond with the (inconvenient, upsetting) facts?' but 'Does it work for you?'

Now the Sophists were not so naive as to believe that they could dispense with truth. But their influence did lead to a widespread scepticism about the capacity of humans to arrive at the truth. Gorgias, in the 5th Century, claimed to have 'proved' that (a) there is nothing; (b) if there were anything, no one could know it; (c) if anyone did know it, he could not communicate it. Such reasoning led many people to conclude that if one can 'prove' these propositions, then one can prove anything. In our time this form of pragmatism has led to what philosophers in the 19th Century called 'nihilism', and what I call postmodernism. The man who stood against the Sophists, relativism and lazy pragmatism, was Socrates (469–399 B.C.).

To say man is the measure of all things is saying very little if one does not know what 'man' is. To discover 'man' Socrates engaged people in conversation and encouraged them to argue rather than merely express their feelings. He worked with a hierarchy of language functions: the expressive function which is the most primitive and serves to express the feelings of the speaker; the descriptive function which describes states of affairs; and the argumentative function which serves to present and compare arguments in connection with questions or problems. These three functions constitute a logical hierarchy because when I describe I express, and when I argue it is about descriptions: I cannot argue about feelings. An argument serves as an outward expression of an internal state of a person. Insofar as it is about something it is descriptive. Since self-expression is revealing of feelings it is independent of truth or falsity; descriptions can either be true or false; arguments can be either valid or invalid. For example, a communication may hide or reveal the feelings of a speaker; describe a situation accurately; suppress rather than stimulate argument. Socrates encouraged people to pursue the higher functions of language because it is only by using the descriptive and argumentative functions of language that they can be said to be *homo sapiens*.

The purpose of Socratic dialectic is to move knowledge outward to objective definitions and inward to the inner person. Socrates searches for truth through argumentation and he presupposes an ability and willingness to work with the rules of logical validity. His project is based on the famous motto: 'the unexamined life is not worth living' and it owes much to the unique individual who was Socrates. Short of stature with a strutting gait, he was by all accounts an ugly, urbane, even-tempered man who loved debate, a good dinner and plenty of wine. Plato describes him as indifferent to pleasure and careless of dress, morally courageous as he was physically courageous on the field of battle, and intellectually honest. He surprised his colleagues by his powers of physical endurance and could stand for hours, apparently lost in mystical reverie: the most famous instance was when serving in the army and he amazed his comrades by standing lost in thought for a day and a night.

He delighted in engaging unsuspecting youths or retired military officers in conversation and quickly discovered that they did not know of what they spoke. When they used such words as 'justice', 'courage' or 'love' he would interrupt them with the question: 'Ah! but what is "courage"?' His interlocutors would give examples of Athenian courage, Trojan courage or Spartan courage and again Socrates would interrupt them: 'I did not ask you for a laundry list. I asked you what is the meaning of "Courage".' The usual response to such a challenge was to offer a definition which Socrates would throw back with the comment: 'But this leads to an infinite regress since you have to define every word in your definition ad infinitum.' The Platonic dialogues show us this dialectical procedure in action and it is clear that Socrates has the upper hand throughout because he asks unanswerable questions about the meanings of words. Indeed, he seems never to have accepted any answer to the question: 'What is the essential meaning of a moral concept, such as "justice" or "courage".'

One can imagine that after encountering Socrates, debating, dining and getting drunk with him, the youth of Athens would have run into difficulties with their parents. By arguing incessantly about the meaning or words, such as 'justice', 'courage', 'knowledge', 'beauty', Socrates showed his interlocutors that they used words without knowing what they 'really' meant and so they literally did not know what they were saying. When one's interlocutors are the sons of the rich and powerful, it is inevitable that he would fall into disfavour. Socrates must have been the subject of many animated discussions around Athenian dinner tables where there would be no shortage of people willing to criticise and punish him. He may have been a gadfly but many people came to regard his eccentricities as dangerously subversive. 'I am that gadfly which God has attached to the State, and all day long and in all places am always fastening upon you, arousing and persuading and reproaching you. You will not easily find another like me.'

It is obvious that Socrates had an enviable ability to argue his opponents into the ground. He would choose an appropriate victim, set the agenda, invite his opponent to speak his thoughts freely, and then counterpunch the poor fellow into submission. Lacing his attacks with heavy irony, sarcasm and personal insults he was not content until he had elicited from his hapless victim a public confession of utter bewilderment. He would then propose that, after heavy debate and heavier drinking, they take to their beds and resume their battle another time. But, unsurprisingly, he never had a second dialogue with the same person. And many of those who had suffered at his hands and by his words turned against him. A gadfly he was, but he was also a cool, ironic, thorn in the sides of his powerful contemporaries. He tried to teach the Athenians the virtues of wisdom, courage, love and justice in the midst of corruption and cowardice. Such men are likely to come to grief.

In 399 B.C., he was charged by the Athenian democracy with corrupting the youth of Athens (he was) and introducing false Gods to the community (he was not). Tried and sentenced to death for his refusal to compromise his intellectual integrity, he died a martyr to the truth. He lived and died arguing and his martyrdom is the best argument for argument in the Western rational tradition – a tradition named after him.

Accounts of his trial, speech to the jury and last days on earth are to be read in Plato's *Euthyphro*, *Apology*, *Crito* and *Phaedo*. These works live as unparalleled tragic drama and it is difficult to read Socrates' farewell to his friends in the *Phaedo* without emotion. When asked by his friend, Euthyphro, what charges have been brought against him by the Athenian democracy, Socrates ironically replies:

'What is the charge? Well, a very serious charge, which shows a good deal of character in the young man (Meletus who charged him), and for which he is certainly not to be despised. He says he knows how the youth are corrupted and who are their corrupters. I fancy that he must be a wise man, and seeing that I am the reverse of a wise man, he has found me out, and is going to accuse me of corrupting his young friends. And of this our mother of the State is to be the judge . . . He brings a wonderful accusation against me, which at first hearing excites surprise: he says that I am a poet or maker of Gods, and that I invent new Gods and deny the existence of old ones; this is the ground of his indictment . . . I have a benevolent habit of pouring out myself to everybody, and would even pay for a listener, and I am afraid that the Athenians may think me too talkative. Now if, as I was saying, they would only laugh at me, as you say that they laugh at you, the time might pass gaily enough in the court; but perhaps they may be in earnest, and then what the end will be you soothsayers only can predict.'

The charge of corrupting the youth was a serious one; yet he never denies it. He argues against Meletus that either he does not corrupt the youth or he corrupts them unintentionally. He asks Meletus to call several witnesses to testify on his behalf, but the closest he comes to denying the charge is his admission that his project in life is to urge men to pursue virtue: 'If in saying these things I corrupt the youth, that would be harm indeed.' For a man who lives by argument and is sensitive to the difference between logic and rhetoric, Socrates does a particularly poor job in defending himself. Rather than engage in the type of dialogue for which he has become justly famous, he descends to rhetoric and most of his famous speech to the jury is directed, not towards the indictment, but towards the lies and prejudices he has suffered at the hands of 'the old accusers'.

Socrates' rhetorical speech to the court appears in the *Apology* – the only one of Plato's works which is not a dialogue. Socrates begins his speech to the large jury by telling them that, unlike poets and politicians, he has a special sort of wisdom – he is wise because he knows that, with respect to philosophical matters, he knows nothing, and that is more than they know. 'At last I went to the artisans. I was conscious that I knew nothing at all and I was sure that they knew many fine things; and here I was not mistaken, for they did know many things of which I was ignorant, and in this they certainly were wiser than I was. But I observed that even the good artisans fell into the same error as the poets; – because they were good workmen they thought that they also knew all sorts of high matters, and this defect in them overshadowed their wisdom; and therefore I asked myself, whether I would like to be as I was, neither having their knowledge nor their ignorance, or like them in both; and I answered myself that I was better off as I was . . . This inquisition has led to my having many enemies of the worst and most dangerous kind, and has given occasion also to many calumnies. And I am called wise, for my hearers always imagine that I possess the wisdom which I find wanting in others: but the truth is, O men of Athens, that God only is wise; and by his answer he intends to show that the wisdom of men is worth little or nothing.'

Socrates will not agree that he is a curious evildoer who searches into things under the earth and in heaven, and he makes the worse appear the better cause. He claims he has nothing to do with physical speculations, and does not teach for money. 'Although, if a man were really able to instruct mankind, to receive money for giving instruction would, in my opinion, be an honour to him.' Rather Socrates admits to acquiring enemies because of his want of diplomatic hypocrisy. After talking with a politician who had a reputation of wisdom, Socrates says: 'When I began to talk with him, I could not help thinking that he was not really wise, although he was thought wise by many, and still wiser by himself; and thereupon I tried to explain to him that he thought himself wise, but was not really wise; and the consequence was that he hated me, and his enmity was shared by several who were present. So I left him saying to myself: Well, although I do not suppose that either of us knows anything really beautiful or good, I am better off than he is – for he knows nothing, and thinks that he knows; I neither know nor think that I know. In this latter particular, then, I seem to have slightly the advantage of him. Then I went to another who had still higher pretensions to wisdom, and my conclusion was exactly the same. Whereupon I made another enemy of him, and of many others besides him.'

It was the custom in Socrates' time to propose to the jury a penalty for his 'crime'. Socrates proceeds thus: 'And what shall I propose on my part, O men of Athens? Clearly that which is my due. And what is my due? What returns shall be made to the man who has never had the wit to be idle during his whole life; but who has been careless of what the many care for – wealth, and family interests, and the military offices, and speaking in the assembly, and magistracies, and plots and parties. Reflecting that I was really too honest a man to be a politician and live, I did not go where I could do no good to you or to myself; but where I could do the greatest good privately to everyone of you, there I went, and sought to persuade every man among you that he must look to himself, and seek virtue and wisdom before he looks to his private interests . . . But I cannot in a moment refute great slanders; and, as I am convinced that I never wronged another, I will assuredly not wrong myself. I will not say of myself that I deserve any evil, or propose any penalty. Why should I?'

After the good democrats of Athens condemned Socrates to death, he addressed them: 'I am speaking now not to all of you, but only to those who condemned me to death . . . (I was convicted) because I had not the boldness or impudence or inclination to address you as you would have liked me to do, weeping and wailing and lamenting, and saying and doing many things which you have been accustomed to hear from others, and which, I maintain, are unworthy of me. I thought at the time that I ought not to do anything common or mean when in danger: nor do I now repent of the style of my defence; I would rather die having spoken after my manner, than speak in your manner and live.'

He then concludes with addresses to his murderers and to his friends. 'I prophesy to you who are my murderers, that immediately after my departure punishment far heavier than you have inflicted on me will surely await you. Me you have killed because you wanted to escape the accuser, and not to give an account of your lives. But that will not be as you suppose: far otherwise. For I say there will be more accusers of you than there are now; accusers whom hitherto I have restrained: and as they are younger they will be more inconsiderate with you, and you will be more offended at them. If you think that by killing men you can prevent some one from censuring your evil lives, you are mistaken; that is not a way of escape which is either possible or honourable; the easiest and the noblest way is not to be disabling others, but to be improving yourselves.'

To his friends Socrates points out that death is not to be feared, but welcomed. Either death is like an eternal peaceful sleep and therefore not to be despised, or death is a journey to another place where all the dead live, in which case it represents a fascinating journey for all of us. 'What would not a man give if he might converse with Orpheus and Musaeus and Hesiod and Homer? Nay, if this be true, let me die again and again. I myself, too, shall have a wonderful interest in there meeting and conversing with (any ancient hero) who has suffered death through an unjust judgement; and there will be no small pleasure, as I think, in comparing my own sufferings with theirs. Above all, I shall be able to continue my search into true and false knowledge; as in this world, so in the next; and I shall find out who is wise, and who pretends to be wise, and is not . . . In another world they do not put a man to death for asking questions: assuredly not.'

We might, however, ask at this point: Why did not Socrates defend himself better? Did he want to die by effectively committing suicide? He did not try to present himself as a man of character, nor did he try to put the audience into a receptive mood. Indeed, he seems deliberately to have antagonised them by attacking politicians, poets, playwrights and craftsmen for claiming knowledge of matters of which they are ignorant. In short, he told his audience that they and their rulers are ignorant. If he did this to them, what then did he do to the youth of Athens? In lacing his speech with heavy and ironical rhetoric, instead of appealing to his audience in plain educated speech, Socrates was identified with the excesses of the Sophists and it is understandable, therefore, why he was brought to trial and why he was convicted. But it does not explain why he conducted his defence so ineptly. The answer in Plato's *Apology* is simple: Socrates sought neither conviction nor acquittal because to achieve the latter he would have had to humble himself before the audience and speak in a language he found abhorrent. He could not bring himself to produce the kind of speech that was expected of a defendant. Rather he chose to remain true to his life's project – to urge men to pursue virtue. His project required that he tell the truth and act virtuously and this is what he believed he was doing before the jury. He would accept the consequences, even death. Because he claimed that he knew nothing, he was accused of dishonesty. But his ignorance was heartfelt and the foundation of his teaching. He aimed for enlightenment but he was accused of arrogance.

Though it was not his wish to be hated, Socrates made many enemies. People do not like to be bettered in argument and Socrates was a formidable debater, so vehement in argument that men would set upon him with their fists or tear his hair out. Widely despised and laughed at, he bore it all with extreme patience so much so that when he had been kicked he said: 'Should I have taken the law of a donkey, supposing that he had kicked me?' He exercised his body to keep fit, prided himself on his plain living, and was obviously a man of strong 'I', which helped him survive several plagues in Athens. When asked in what consisted the virtue of a young man he replied: 'In doing nothing to excess.' And when asked whether one should marry or not, he quipped: 'Whichever you do you will repent it.' (He had two 'difficult' wives – Myrto and Xanthippe.) When he was told that someone had spoken ill of him he said: 'True, for he has never learnt to speak well.' To one who said: 'Don't you find so-and-so offensive?' he replied: 'No, for it takes two to make a quarrel.'

Socrates spent his last day talking with his wife, Xanthippe, who was holding their child in her arms. Phaedo tells us that 'when she saw us she uttered a cry and said, as women will: "O Socrates, this is the last time that either you will converse with your friends, or they with you".' Socrates turned to Crito and asked him to take her home and she was led her away, crying and beating herself. After a lengthy discussion about the immortality of the soul (in which Socrates believed and so must have made it difficult for his friends to argue against), Socrates drank the hemlock. His friends all burst into tears and one, Apollodorus, 'broke out in a loud and passionate cry which made cowards of us all.' Socrates alone retained his calmness: What is this strange outcry? he said. I sent away the women mainly in order that they might not misbehave in this way, for I have been told that a man should die in peace. And so Socrates wrapped his head in his cloak and died peacefully among his friends, believing he was going to a better world in which he would, at last, discover the truth and rightness of existence. At his passing Phaedo remarked: 'Such was the end, Echecrates, of our friend; concerning whom I may truly say, that of all men of his time whom I have known, he was the wisest and justest and best.'

After he died the Athenians soon felt such remorse that they closed the training grounds and gymnasia, banished the other accusers but put Meletus to death, and honoured Socrates with a bronze statue.

Socrates lives today as a legendary figure who lived and died for the truth. But in a world which no longer values truth as he did, he is now regarded as something of a relic. His dialogues are widely regarded as 'difficult', boring and pointless. Since the 1970s and the rise of the postmodern world, thinking has been largely replaced by feeling – I feel, therefore I exist. Argument is now widely regarded as aggressive, rude and confronting. So we have to endure conversations laced with 'in my opinion', 'it seems to me', 'I feel', 'subjectively speaking' and such other phrases as enable people to pretend they are well mannered by not causing offence to others. What these phrases actually do is protect their users from criticism. Feeling statements cannot be true or false since no one can know another's feelings. To immunise oneself against criticism, then, one has only to use these apologetic phrases to disarm one's opponents. Socrates was not interested in how people feel, but in the truth of their descriptions and the validity of their arguments. He would be appalled that 2400 years on we lack the courage to submit ourselves to debate for fear that we will offend others. And so he went out of his way to offend others because he believed that argument is the vehicle by which we arrive at the truth, and the truth should be acknowledged no matter who it might offend. Today's political correctness guardians do not respond warmly to Socrates. I suspect they would gladly put him on trial all over again because in following the truth wherever it led him, he offended many people. His view was that a truth unuttered is a crime against philosophy and humanity and if people did not like to hear truths expressed, too bad. But he was surrounded, as I am, by people who fear freedom of expression and seek to prohibit it. Consequently, the great age of Greek enlightenment was also characterised by many trials for 'corrupting the public' and Socrates and Protagoras were two of many who were found guilty and severely punished. Very little has changed over the centuries.

Of those who succeeded Socrates, the most famous is Plato (427–347 B.C.) who was too distressed to be with his mentor on his last day. Plato was greatly influenced by Socrates' obsession with the meaning of moral concepts. In his famous parable of the cave he asks me to imagine being a member of a group of people chained together and able only to face a wall. Behind me is a source of light and between me and the light something moves, thus throwing shadows on the wall of the cave. When asked questions about the 'real' world the only possible answers are 'shadowy' because the shadows represent the world of the cave-dwellers. I am released from bondage, find an escape route, climb a tunnel and escape into the sunlight. The sun is too bright and there is a strong temptation to return to my friends in the safety of the cave. I have spent considerable energy in climbing out of the tunnel (the hard work of training) and exposure to the sun is tiring and painful. However, I persevere and eventually find comfort and rewards in the sun – I have become enlightened. As a member of a community my duty is now to return to the cave and pass on my knowledge to the other cave-dwellers. This is a dangerous enterprise because I now speak a different language and introduce new, strange images and ideas to my colleagues. My likely fate is death and so it is prudent to keep the cave-dwellers chained until they too 'see the light' and in their turn enlighten others.

Teachers have learned to follow Plato's advice and endeavour to keep their students chained – by examining them – which doesn't seem unreasonable although many students believe that the exams are unreasonable and that their (low) grades are unfair because they are based on their teachers' feelings. It has to be said that teachers brought this upon themselves with the popular belief that education should be free of competition and stress, and that students should be seen as customers who demand and should therefore receive appropriate service – that is, they should pass their subjects. And so it is today suggested (half-jokingly) that students should not be failed on the grounds that this discriminates against those with low ability. Socrates would have appreciated the half-joke; Plato would not.

Enlightenment is intimately connected in Plato with his Theory of the Forms. Whilst we can conjecture about images, have beliefs about objects, understand concepts, it is through pure reason that we have knowledge of the Forms. The Forms (or objective ideas) are universals such as justice, courage, love and beauty. Perfect, adamantine, unchanging, such universals exist on their own unmixed with time and space or each other. So no particular action can be called truly courageous: only 'courage' is really courageous. Whilst Plato maintains that the Forms are external to the individual, it is plain that since they are spaceless and timeless, they cannot be said to be anywhere. In short, they are everywhere and nowhere. Nonetheless, if through philosophical reflection, I can entertain some notion of, say, 'courage', I am in a better position to act rationally and wisely with respect to courageous action. I can be trained to act courageously, but I cannot 'know' courage thereby. Really to know courage I need to be educated and this requires at least some knowledge of moral concepts. Since education is concerned to draw out the innate knowledge which resides in the mind, Platonic education is governed by the rules of deductive reasoning and based on the practice of dialectic.

In one of Plato's later dialogues, *Parmenides*, Socrates encounters the venerable Parmenides and discusses with him the Theory of the Forms. Parmenides replies with a devastating critique of the theory and reduces Socrates, for the first time in Plato's dialogues, to despair. There are three difficult questions to be answered before the Theory of the Forms can be accepted. First, are there Forms of everything? Socrates is sure that there are Forms of justice, beauty and goodness. But he suffers doubts about whether there are Forms of mud, hair and dirt. Second, are Forms thoughts in the mind? Socrates argues that Forms do not exist independently but are only thoughts in the mind, while Plato emphasises their objectivity. Parmenides objects that thoughts are of real things and so cannot merely be thoughts in the mind. Third, are the Forms cut off from the world? Since knowledge must be of real things, it is difficult to see how one can know the Forms, which are by definition unreal because they are universals. Furthermore, how is it possible to talk about Forms? If we say that a painting is beautiful we imply that the painting partakes of the Form of beauty. But if we say with Plato that the Form of beauty is eternal, we seem to be saying that the Form of beauty partakes of the Form of eternity. And this appears to mean that the Forms communicate with each other, which Plato denies.

Socrates offers no convincing answers to Parmenides' challenges but this is attributed to his insufficient education which, when improved, may enable him to save the theory of Forms. They have not been saved although they have been modified by generations of spiritualists and religionists.

Education is, for Plato, the noblest profession since it helps others climb the greatest of human heights. At the summit, people will come to understand the true meaning of moral concepts and so will have acquired wisdom through rational means. And since rational people are wise – they cannot engage in evil intentionally – they should be the rulers of Plato's ideal society outlined in *The Republic*. Unlike Homer who thought that the best warriors should be rulers, Plato prefers philosopher-kings, because they think rationally and act wisely. Warriors are well-trained but ill-educated. Rulers must be trained and educated – they must be philosophers.

Plato realises, however, that warriors are disinclined to accept their exclusion from rulership. In his attempt to address and correct this dilemma, Plato is led into an apparent paradox when he argues that since philosophers are those who love truth, rulers must nonetheless lie so that they may gain the acceptance of warriors and workers. 'It is the business of the rulers of the city if it is anybody's to tell lies deceiving both its enemies and its own citizens for the benefit of the city and no one else must touch this privilege . . . If the ruler catches anyone else in a lie . . . then he will punish him for introducing a practice which injures and endangers the city.' Plato goes even further and asks himself: 'Could we perhaps fabricate one of those very handy lies? With the help of one single lordly lie we may if we are lucky, persuade even the rulers themselves'. The lordly lie is that some people are born gold – born to rule and it has been accepted by many rulers who see it as the perfect justification for legitimating power.

Plato's influence has been immense. He is the father of ancient philosophy and after his death a story was current in Athens that he was divine, born of a virgin and a son of Apollo. In the 20th Century, Karl Popper scandalised a large part of the philosophical world with his attack on Plato in *The Open Society and its Enemies*. Popper charged Plato with being the spokesman for a closed society ruled by totalitarian gangsters. He argued that, unlike Socrates, Plato compromised his integrity with every step he took. He was opposed to free thought and the pursuit of truth, and defended lying, superstition and brutal violence.

Yet Plato challenges me to understand what he called Forms, or what philosophers call the problem of universals. What, for example, do I mean when I talk of ideals – ideal justice, ideal courage, ideal beauty? Are they mere abstractions – nothing more than words? Or am I able in some imperfect way to come to an understanding that beyond the data of my five senses there is a 'world' of perfection against which I judge myself and others. When I strive for excellence, what do I strive for? Is there some eternal, unchanging ideal standard of excellence which I dimly apprehend and which guides me through life? To be sure, only a few people can gain an imperfect appreciation of ideals, but does that invalidate their existence? As Whitehead rightly says, Plato asks fascinating and important questions to which we still strive to find answers. In this sense, all Western philosophy is but a footnote to Plato.

Plato believes that reason should guide and control the feelings which sabotage our quest for truth. If I am well-educated and pursue a rational approach to life, I will act wisely. I should have a physician of the body to cure my physical problems, and a physician of the 'soul' to cure my psychological problems. He invented 'I' as soul for the practical purpose of helping people live in truth. But in arguing that people who act 'irrationally' are suffering from illnesses of the soul, he fathered the mental illness industry. Plato's views, therefore, encourage those in power to act against people like Socrates, because they are 'mad'. He starts out lamenting the fate of Socrates but he ends with a philosophy which has encouraged totalitarians down the ages to incarcerate or kill those who argue against them – either by indicting them for a crime or by depriving them of their liberty by labelling them as 'irrational' or mentally ill. It was this paradox that worried Plato's most famous pupil – Aristotle.

Close to Plato in spirit, Aristotle developed a theory of body, *psyche* and mind which informs his influential theory of ethics. He believes that philosophy begins with a sense of wonder before the world of nature and concludes that the best and happiest people spend as much time as possible in philosophical activity, using their reason to govern their actions and thinking.

Aristotle was born in 384 B.C. in northern Greece. His father was court physician to the king of Macedon. At the age of 17 he studied at Plato's Academy in Athens where he remained for 20 years until Plato's death in 347 B.C. He confidently expected to replace Plato as head of the Academy but the job went to a justly forgotten opponent. He then worked for a philosopher-king in Sicily after which he tutored the young Alexander (the Great). Aristotle's influence on Alexander, is unknown but it must have been quite a challenge for a philosopher to teach an arrogant, drunken, cruel, vindictive, superstitious tyrant.

Aristotle returned to Athens in 336 B.C. and founded his own academy – the *Lyceum* (discovered by archaeologists in 1996). More scientific institute than philosophical academy, it reveals Aristotle's interest in empirical research. Alexander's unexpected death in 323 B.C. saw Aristotle, like Socrates before him, charged with impiety.

Unlike Socrates, Aristotle prudently went into voluntary exile saying that he wanted to 'prevent the Athenians from committing a second sin against philosophy,' but sadly his exile took him away from his philosophical friends and he soon died at age 62 leaving an impressive body of work.

Aristotle is widely regarded as a philosopher of common sense – Plato diluted by common sense as Bertrand Russell quipped. He is difficult because Plato and common sense do not mix easily. In contrast to the idealistic Plato he is more of an empiricist with a strong scientific bent. He is not so distrustful of the evidence of the senses as was Plato preferring theories of the natural world to metaphysical speculation. Whilst he respected Plato he could not accept his eternal, unchanging world of Forms. Rather, he thought of the Forms as metaphors that distract us from the empirical study of the natural world and the relationships between people therein. Yet, he could not entirely abandon Plato from whom he took the view that reality lies in form.

He has two questions for Plato: (a) if the Forms are essences of things, how can they exist separated from things? (b) if they are the cause of things, how can they exist in a different world? Aristotle concluded that Plato's theory of two worlds was an intellectual disaster and that Forms are not separate entities but are embedded in particular things. They are in the world, not separated from it. Consequently, they are singulars, not universals. Forms are in a body and matter is what is unique to the object. All trees have the same form but no two trees have the same matter.

Aristotle was also critical of Plato's inability to explain motion and change. Unsurprisingly, Plato regarded change as a feature of the perceived world and permanence as a feature of a transcendental world. Aristotle argued that Plato could not account for the causal relationships between the two worlds. Indeed, this problem bedevils all two-world theories: how does one world interact with the other? Nor could Plato's Forms account for motion and change since the former are timeless and spaceless. So Aristotle renounced them, laughing: 'So goodbye to Plato's Forms – they are no more meaningful than singing "la la la".'

But now Aristotle faced the problem of how to introduce notions of stability into his philosophy. His answer involved a distinction between actuality and potentiality. Matter and form are represented by potentiality and actuality, as we can see in the example of an acorn. The acorn's matter contains the potentiality of becoming an oak tree which is the acorn's actuality.

Nature is, for Aristotle, a teleological system which strives towards perfection (rather than towards Plato's transcendental 'Good'). Aristotle suggests that perfection must exist in the *telos* towards which things strive. This he calls the *Prime Mover* and it is the only thing in the universe with no potentiality – it is pure actuality. The nature of things consists of an innate tendency to develop in a certain direction that demands an external cause. The only unmoved mover is the *Prime Mover* who is immaterial and pure actuality. The *Prime Mover* is engaged in eternal thought and so is a pure mind whose only object of thought is himself.

When Aristotle returns to mere mortals he struggles mightily with the concept of *psyche*. Since, in his way of thinking, 'perfect' precedes 'imperfect', so *psyche* is a product of the perfect mind. *Psyche* is, however, inseparable from the human body – *psyche* is form, body is matter. All the powers of *psyche* (except *nous* – the power of abstract thought) have bodily organs. Aristotle ridicules those who characterise *psyche* as immaterial. He argues against Plato's widely held view of the *psyche*, which involves the absurd idea of a *psyche* placed in the body and no explanation of how they interact. So, for Aristotle, possessing a *psyche* is like possessing a skill – *psyche* cannot be separated from the body.

Furthermore 'mind' and *psyche* are different. Mind is an independent, indestructible substance implanted within a *psyche* which moves the body and perceives – *psyche* is characterised by self-nutrition, sensation, feeling and motivation. Mind, on the other hand, has the higher function of thinking and has no relation to the body and the senses.

There is in the *psyche* one element that is rational and one that is irrational. The life of the rational *psyche* is contemplation. Individuality is connected with body and *psyche*. But when we think correctly about, say, logic, there is no difference between people. It is the irrational that separates us; the rational unites. We partake of the divine through rational thought and if we are successful, we eliminate our individuality.

In *The Nicomachean Ethics* Aristotle emphasises his distance from Socrates: 'Our object is not that we may know what virtue is, but that we may become virtuous.'

Humans are political animals, and whilst self-sufficiency is an important human achievement, it must be embedded in a web of social and political obligations since man is born for citizenship.

Humans are teleological creatures – their acts are performed for some purpose. The ultimate goal of human life is happiness and our function is 'to engage in an activity of the *psyche* which is in accordance with virtue and which follows a rational principle.' Virtue takes two forms: intellectual and moral. A character is morally virtuous if it moves towards a 'golden mean of moderation'. For example, when facing danger I can act in either of two extreme ways: in a cowardly or foolhardy fashion. The mean of moderation would be to act courageously. I learn to act courageously by the exercise of choice and trial and error elimination. Intellectual virtue derives from inheritance and education and the highest virtue is associated with the exercise of pure reason which is achieved through disinterested thought, the goal of which is philosophical wisdom. Since we are political animals we need to combine theorising with practical matters. Here Aristotle anticipates Kurt Lewin's famous quip: 'there is nothing so practical as a good theory'.

Sadly there are obstacles to the achievement of happiness. Before we can pursue happiness through philosophical activity we need: good friends, riches, political power, good health, good birth, good children, good looks and we should not have to engage in manual labour – 'no man can practice virtue who is living the life of a mechanic.' Whilst he acknowledges that there are alternatives to the philosophical life, Aristotle clearly favours a life based on a rational 'I'. We may, for example, pursue a life of pleasure and amusement (like children, animals, women), or we may pursue a life of virtuous public service. He discounts the life of pleasure and amusement because it fails to elevate men above the animals (or above women) and thus denies what is quintessentially human. He respects those who choose a life of virtuous public service but praises above all else the philosophical life because it informs the life of public service. It is difficult to see how a life of public service informs philosophy.

I reveal myself by the way of life I choose. My choices should be based on careful deliberation and not on desire or impulse. I reveal my character by what I voluntarily do and for which I am responsible. My virtue is especially revealed by my rational control over my irrational emotions. If I cannot control my emotions I am immature and morally weak. (Aristotle thought that moral weakness was generally to be found 'among foreigners' and was caused by disease, madness or bad habits, e.g. cannibalism, ritual murder, cruelty, chewing nails/raw meat/coal, effeminate homosexuality and fear of mice).

In *The Nicomachean Ethics* Aristotle has much to say about the qualities of noble men. If I am a noble man I am good in the highest degree, because I deserve more than the average person. I aspire to greatness in every virtue and so it is hard to be truly noble and impossible without goodness of character. I am pleased at honours that are conferred by good men, but I despise honour from unimportant people and on trifling grounds, since I deserve better. I face dangers, and when in danger I am unsparing in my life, knowing that there are conditions in which life is not worth having. I am the sort of man to confer benefits, but I am ashamed of receiving them; for the one is the mark of a superior, the other of an inferior. And I am apt to confer greater benefits in return; for thus the original benefactor will incur a debt to me. I ask for nothing but to give help readily, and to be dignified towards people who enjoy a high position but unassuming towards those of the lower class. I am open in my hate and in my love, for it is cowardly to conceal my feelings. I speak my thoughts because I tell the truth except when I speak in irony to the vulgar. I do not gossip, for I will speak neither of myself nor about another, since I care not to be praised nor for others to be blamed. I am one who possesses beautiful and profitless things rather than profitable and useful ones. It is my duty to promote logic and noble rhetoric which seeks to perfect men by showing them better versions of themselves, whereas base rhetoric influences people in the direction of evil. Such then is my noble I; the man who falls short of me is unduly humble, and the man who goes beyond me is vain.

Aristotle's description of the noble man applies to aristocrats and some philosophers, but not to the majority of people. Modern critics ask whether we can regard as morally satisfactory a society that confines the best things in life to the few. Plato and Aristotle say: 'Yes'. Stoics and Christians disagree arguing that virtue is for all people, and democrats agree although they want to add qualifications about power and property. Aristotle was clear: the aim of the State is to promote and produce 'cultured, noble gentlemen'. After the French Revolution of 1789, industrialism, universal education, the World Wars of the 20th Century, modernism and postmodernism, the days of the 'cultured, noble gentlemen' have, for good or ill, passed.

3

Living Cynically

*'Other dogs bite their enemies, I bite my friends
for their salvation.'*

(Crates)

I have never understood the force of the objection to cynicism. Why does cynicism have such a bad reputation? Is it because the cynic delights in exposing naked emperors, or in showing that there are no emperors? Is it that cynics are professional nay-sayers to convention and thus upset those who seek balance and harmony in their relationships? Do cynics have a bad reputation because, like Diogenes, they deface the currency, mock, tease and upset others? A day that passes without upsetting somebody is a bad day for a cynic.

For 800 years the Cynics – the dogs – roamed the streets of classical Greece and Rome, defacing the currency, upsetting their colleagues and unsettling customs and conventions. In modern times, however, the word 'cynic' has a different connotation. Today a cynic is a person who behaves unethically, dishonestly and sarcastically, and distrusts all human motives. Hypocrisy, deceitfulness, unrestrained egoism, rampant materialism and Machiavellian ruthlessness characterise modern cynics. Yet it was not always so.

The man who inaugurated the ancient school of Cynicism was Antisthenes (446–366 B.C.), an Athenian and pupil of Gorgias, the rhetorician. After encountering Socrates he was so impressed that he advised his pupils to debate with him. From Socrates he learned his frugal way of living, including his disregard of feeling. He went so far as to demonstrate that pain is a good thing and often stated that he would rather be mad than feel pleasure. When a pupil asked him what sort of wife he should marry, Antisthenes replied: 'If she's beautiful, you'll not have her to yourself; if she's ugly, you'll pay for it dearly.' When a priest spoke glowingly about the delights of Hades, he asked: 'Why, then, don't you die?'

He was a stern teacher and when asked why he had so few students, he replied: 'Because I use a silver rod to eject them.' He was particularly suspicious of flatterers remarking that it is better to fall in with crows than with flatterers; the former devour you when you are dead, the latter when you are alive. And when applauded by thieves, he said, 'I am horribly afraid I have done something wrong.' When asked what is so good about a life of philosophising he replied: 'The ability to talk with myself.' He was critical of Plato who, in turn, regularly slandered him. He taunted Plato with being conceited and when he visited his sick-bed, he pointed to the basin into which Plato had vomited and said: 'The bile I see, but not the pride.'

Antisthenes believed virtue can be taught; nobility belongs only to the virtuous; virtue is sufficient to ensure happiness; virtue is an affair of deeds rather than words;

if I am wise I am self-sufficient and will be guided not by the laws of the land but by virtue; I will marry in order to have children from union with a beautiful woman; if I am wise I know who is worthy of love and make friends of men who are brave and just; I pay attention to my enemies because they are the first to discover my mistakes; I acknowledge that virtue is the same for women as for men; I count all evil as alien and believe that wisdom can neither be removed nor betrayed.

When he lay dying of consumption his friend, Diogenes, responded to his cries of pain by drawing his dagger. Antisthenes replied, 'I want relief from pain, not from life.' This story, from Diogenes Laertius, is important in the history of Cynicism because it suggests an apostolic succession – a symbolic handing over of the keys of the cynical kingdom. Antisthenes the old dog hands over the secrets of the cynical way of life to the young pup Diogenes, a 'Socrates gone mad', as Plato called him.

Cynicism, then, was a school of philosophy founded by Antisthenes and developed by Diogenes (404–323 B.C.) who chose to live like canines. As Diogenes often said, 'I am called a dog because I fawn on those who give me anything. I yelp at those who refuse, and I sink my teeth in rascals.' He held up the life of animals as a model for humankind, advocated free love and did in public what is normally done in private – and even what is not done in private. He adopted a vagrant, ascetic life, attacked established values and used satire to entertain and educate.

Diogenes was forced into exile when his father adulterated the State's money. This act of defacing the currency became his philosophical motif since he saw himself as the architect of demolition. On reaching Athens he met Antisthenes and after being rejected suggested he strike him with his staff: 'Strike, for you will find no wood hard enough to keep me away from you, so long as I think you have something important to say.'

He took a fiendish delight in pouring scorn on his famous contemporaries, especially the school of Euclides which he called bilious, and Plato whose lectures he considered a waste of time. When he saw philosophers and physicians at their work, he deemed man the most intelligent of all the animals; but when he saw interpreters of dreams and diviners and those who believed in their nonsense, he thought no animal more silly.

When Plato invited him to his home for dinner, Diogenes wiped his dirty feet on Plato's carpet saying: 'Thus, I trample on Plato's pride', to which the ever-sharp Plato replied, 'Yes, Diogenes, with pride of another sort.' As Plato was conversing about his famous Forms and using the abstract nouns 'tablehood' and 'cuphood' Diogenes said: 'Table and cup I see; but your tablehood and cuphood, Plato, I cannot see.' 'That's readily explained,' said Plato, 'for you have the eyes to see the visible table and cup; but not the understanding by which ideal tablehood and cuphood are discerned.'

He loved witty repartee and was quick with humorous replies to the constant stream of questions put to him.

Why do you eat in the marketplace? That is where I feel hungry.

What have you gained from philosophy? To be prepared for every fortune.

Where do you come from? From the cosmos.

Why are you drinking here? Well, I get my haircut in a barber's shop.

What can you do as a slave? Govern men.

How do you wish to be buried? Face down because soon down will be up.

How can I begin the study of philosophy? Carry a cheese around the market square.

What are you doing with a lamp in the daylight? Looking for a real man.

Do you believe in Gods? Yes, when I see a God-forsaken wretch like you.

Your people exiled you? And I them to home-staying.

What creatures' bite is the worst? Of those that are wild a sycophant's, of those that are tame a flatterer's.

Why is gold pale? Because it has so many thieves plotting against it.

Why do you not drink from a cup? Because I have two good hands.

Who will bury you? Whoever wants my house.

Why did you remove from your door the inscription 'Let nothing evil enter'? How then should I get in?

Was it right for Plato to call you a dog? Yes, for I come back again and again to those who have sold me.

What is the proper time for lunch? If a rich man, when you will; if a poor man, when you can.

What do you think of the demagogues? They are the lackeys of the people.

What did you say to Phillip when he asked who you

were? A spy on your insatiable greed.

Do you feel guilty about begging for money? No, it is repayment of my due.

What did you do when a group of boys threw bones at you? I pissed on them.

What do you say to those who complain of people annoying them? Don't hang out a sign of invitation.

With one blow I will break your head! And with one sneeze I will make you tremble.

Why are athletes so stupid? Because they are built up of pork and beef.

What is wretched in life? An old man destitute.

What do you think of ingratiating speech? It is like honey used to choke you.

Do you think I am beautifully dressed? If it's for men, you're a fool; if for women, you're a knave.

What do you think of blushing? It is the hue of virtue.

What is the best wine to drink? That for which other people pay.

How do you feel when people laugh at you? Well, I am not laughed down.

Why do people give to beggars but not to philosophers? Because they think they may one day be lame or blind, but never expect that they will turn to philosophy.

What is your reaction to people who respond slowly to your begging? My friend, it's for food, not for funeral expenses.

Were you not wrong to deface the currency? That was the time when I was such as you are now; but such as I am now, you will never be.

What do you think of fat people? Let us beggars have

something of their paunch; it will be a relief to them and we shall get an advantage.

Does it bother you that most people laugh behind your back? And so very likely do the asses at them, but as they don't care for the asses, so neither do I care for them.

What do you think of libertines? They are like figtrees growing on a cliff: whose fruit is not enjoyed by any man, but is eaten by vultures.

What do you think of beautiful courtesans? I compare them to a deadly-honeyed potion.

Do you really know anything? Even if I am a pretender to wisdom, that in itself is philosophy.

Why do you go into a theatre when others are coming out? This is what I practice doing all my life.

What do you say to one who rejects philosophy? Why then do you live, if you do not care to live well?

What do you say to one who despised his father? Are you not ashamed to despise him to whom you owe it that you can so pride yourself?

What is your opinion of lovers? They derive their pleasures from misfortune.

Is death an evil thing? How can it be evil, when in its presence we are not aware of it?

What is education? A controlling grace to the young, consolation to the old, wealth to the poor, and ornament to the rich.

What is an example of madness? That men choose to be miserable.

What, above all else, do you prefer? Liberty.

Why do you not pursue wealth? Because I prefer courage.

Why do you not express your feelings more? Because I prefer to express my reason.

What is the right time to marry? For a young man, not yet; for an old man, never.

Is life evil? Not life, but living ill.

What is the most beautiful thing in the world? Freedom of speech.

There are two stories of his death. One has it that he was bitten on the foot by a wild dog who was competing for his food. The other is that he died at a grand old age by holding his breath. After his death it was written of him:

'That famous one who carried a staff, doubled his cloak and lived in the open air. But he soared aloft with his lip tightly pressed against his teeth and holding his breath withal. For in truth he was rightly named Diogenes, a true-born son of Zeus, a hound of heaven'.

At his grave in Athens was inscribed:

'Time makes bronze grow old: but your glory Diogenes
All eternity will never destroy
Since you alone did point out to mortals the lesson of self-sufficiency and the noblest path of life.'

Diogenes is not a 'cynic' in the modern sense – he sought virtue and moral freedom in liberation from desire. To this end he rejected social and religious conventions – manners, dress, housing, normal food, decency, patriotism. By declaring that 'I am a citizen of the world', he coined the word 'cosmopolitan'. The general attitude towards him was one of amused tolerance. He lived for some time in a wine vat and perfected the art of begging. When the great Alexander came to visit and asked him what he wanted, his immortal reply was: 'Get out of my sunshine.'

The most important disciple of Diogenes is Crates (360–280 B.C.) who renounced a life of wealth in favour of practical asceticism. Known as 'the Watchdog' and 'the Door-Opener' he was warmly received as a man of honourable wisdom, even acting as an umpire of family quarrels. He was revered as a household deity and was favourably compared to Heracles the slayer of wild beasts: Crates overthrew anger, lust, envy and greed in men's hearts – from such pests as these he freed men. Plutarch says of him: 'He passed his whole life jesting and laughing as though on perpetual holiday.'

Unlike Diogenes, Crates did not beg and even more surprisingly, married. A rich and beautiful young woman, Hipparchia, fell in love with the disfigured 60 year-old Crates and threatened to kill herself if he did not marry her. The girl's parents were horrified and appealed to Crates to dissuade her from marriage. This he attempted but failed to convince her whereupon he took off his clothes and said: 'This is the bridegroom, here are his possessions; now make your choice. You will never be my mate unless you share my pursuits.' Even this desperate manoeuvre failed and the girl had her way. They married around 300 B.C. and the union seems to have been one of the few marital successes in the long history of philosophy. They had two children, a boy and a girl, and it was rumoured that they were conceived and born in the style of the Cynics, in public. Hipparchia became famous as a

Cynic and was fondly called 'the female philosopher'. Sadly, she fades from history after Crates' death in old age.

The Stoic Epictetus argues in his *On the Calling of the Cynic* that marriage distracts Cynics from their calling and may even be inconsistent with it. If a Cynic marries he will be caught in the trivia and compromises of domestic life. 'What then will become of the Cynic whose duty is to be overseer to the rest of mankind – who have married, who have children, who quarrel? See to what straits we are reducing our Cynic, how we are taking his kingdom away from him.' The Cynics replied: 'Yes, but Crates married'. Epictetus: 'You are talking of passionate love: besides, you are assuming another Crates in the person of the woman.'

Crates was obsessed with the philosophical life. Upon hearing that Diogenes was dying he advised Hipparchia to return quickly to Athens so that she may find Diogenes alive although near the end of his life, and learn from him how much philosophy can achieve even in the most terrifying circumstances. And in another letter he tells his wife and fellow philosopher that it is not because they are indifferent to everything that others have called their philosophy Cynic, but because they robustly endure those things which are unbearable to others who are effeminate and subject to false opinion. Stand firm therefore, he instructs Hipparchia, and live the Cynic life, (for females are not by nature inferior to males, as female dogs are not by nature inferior to male dogs), in order that she might be freed even from nature, since all are slaves either by law or through wickedness. Reaffirming their commitment to the philosophical life Crates warns his wife about the dangers of 'womanly behaviour'. He returns the tunic that she wove because those who live a life of perseverance are forbidden to wear such things, and he returns the gift so that he may cause her to desist from this task which she has undertaken with much zeal so that she might appear to the masses to be someone who loves her husband. Now, Crates says, if he had married her for this reason, she would certainly be acting properly. But since he married her for the sake of philosophy, for which she herself yearned, she should renounce such pursuits and try to be of greater benefit to human life through philosophising. This is the lesson of Diogenes and Crates – reason is a guide to the good life, and the greatest good to men. So he tells her to seek how to acquire reason for herself for then she will secure a happy life. And she should seek wise men, even if she has to go to the ends of the earth. He tells his wife that because she cares for him, he approves of her, but because she is still uneducated and not practicing the philosophy for which he has tutored her, he censures her. He advises her to give up her womanly tasks and endeavour to do those things for which she wanted to marry him. She can leave the wool-spinning, which is of little benefit, to other women who have aspired to none of the things she does.

On hearing of the birth of his son Crates wrote to his wife that he had heard that she had given birth quite easily. He congratulates her for believing that hard work is the cause of her not having to work hard at giving birth. He opines that she would not have given birth so easily unless, while pregnant, she had continued to work hard as the athletes do. Most women, however, whenever they are pregnant, are enfeebled; and when they give birth, those who happen to survive bring forth sickly babies. Having shown that what had to come has arrived, he tells her to take care of 'this little puppy of ours'. And he is in no doubt that she will take care of him, if she enters into child rearing with her usual diligence. Therefore, he advises, his bath water should be cold, his clothes should be a cloak, his food should be milk, but not to excess. When he is able to speak and walk, he should be dressed, not with a sword, but with the uniform of the Cynic – a staff, cloak and wallet – with which to protect him better than a sword.

Crates tells me that I should proceed toward happiness, even if it is through fire, and shun not only the worst of evils – injustice and self-indulgence – but also their causes, pleasures. Rather I should pursue self-control, perseverance and hard work. If I am a Cynic I toil according to this philosophy, and to be a Cynic is to take a short cut in doing philosophy. Living philosophy is more important than talking or writing philosophy. I should be judged by what I do so that a philosophy is judged by how I live. As a person of character I live my philosophy without compromise – I am the sum of my actions. Consequently, Crates tells me neither to fear the name of Cynic, nor to resent being called bad. In short, I should not be bothered by or enslaved to the opinion of others and should not allow their name-calling to have any adverse effect on me for they are only 'mere shadows'.

Cynicism faded when the centre of philosophy shifted from Greece to Rome. Its practical asceticism was not to the taste of Republican Romans and so it survived as a quaint literary phenomenon. It later fused with Stoicism, revived in the first century A.D. and faded again in the 6th Century after it turned increasingly pessimistic and misanthropic. The story of the self-immolation of Peregrinus at the Olympic Games of 165 A.D. added to its reputation as a dangerous philosophy for the masses.

As a youth Peregrinus was involved in many love affairs with men and women for which he paid heavily. He was accused of strangling his father to relieve him of the pain of old age. Travelling in Palestine, he fell in with the Christians and was entranced by 'people who worship a crucified sophist'. He immersed himself in Christian cult worship and soon became a head of their cult in Palestine before being thrown into prison by the Romans. The Christians rallied to his defence and virtually worshipped him as a God. In relating the story of Peregrinus, Lucian who was an educated pagan, notes that the Christians are a strange sort of folk for they have persuaded themselves that they are immortal and are ready to die for their beliefs, and following the teachings of their crucified leader, insist on dealing with one another as if they are brothers and sisters.

Freed by the Romans, Peregrinus travelled to Parium where the strangling of his father was held against him. He appeared before his accusers dressed in the cloak of the Cynics and offered to yield his possessions to the people. Impressed by his Cynical appearance they shouted: 'He is truly a philosopher who stands side by side with Diogenes and Crates!' He returned to Palestine where he continued to exploit the Christians until finally they expelled him. He travelled to Rome and abused the Stoic philosopher/

emperor, Marcus Aurelius, who banished him from the city. He removed to Athens and abused and insulted everyone in authority. This was too much for the good people of Athens who attempted to stone him to death. He then conceived a plan to burn himself four years later during the Olympiad of 165 in the presence of the thousands of spectators who would be there for the games. He was true to his plan. At midnight he jumped into a burning pyre shouting to the spirits of his mother and father: 'Receive me with favour on the other side!' I wonder how the spirit of his strangled father did, in fact, receive him.

Cynicism revived in the period of the high Renaissance, and was adapted for political purposes by Machiavelli. After being driven underground in the periods of the Protestant Reformation and Catholic Counter-Reformation, it revived in the era of the French enlightenment and fed into the ideas so well represented in their separate ways by Voltaire and Rousseau.

The debate between Voltaire and Rousseau is the debate between the French Enlightenment and early Romanticism, and both are influenced by Cynicism. Voltaire called for positive action against monarchical and religious despotism even though he maintained that the human world was infinitely evil. Rousseau, on the other hand, argued that individuals must submit to a general will; only thus can sovereignty be just and directed to the common good. Citizens must be 'forced to be free'.

Francois Marie Arouet (1694–1778), known as Voltaire, was a brilliant young satirist – too brilliant for his time since he was banished from Paris several times, exiled in Holland and England, and imprisoned twice in the Bastille. He was a member of the French Enlightenment, so named because of the insistence of the intellectuals of the day that everything be viewed in the light of reason. This meant that political relationships should be argued to their rational conclusions, which would end in a defence of and commitment to liberalism. Voltaire became, therefore, a promoter of an English-style liberalism derived from the enlightened philosophy of John Locke. Lockean liberalism was clearly more open to freedom of speech and non-conformity than the political systems of Europe and so Voltaire wittily prosecuted the liberal cause through plays, novels, pamphlets, biographies, histories, letters and reviews.

Voltaire had read Locke and Newton with admiration and remarked that they would have been persecuted in France, imprisoned at Rome and burned in Lisbon. After falling out of favour with Frederick the Great in 1752 Voltaire set up house near Geneva. In 1758 he acquired a property at Ferney near the border so that he could change countries when danger threatened (from either side). Here he wrote the works for which he is famous: *Candide* (1759); *Treatise on Tolerance* (1763); the *Philosophical Dictionary* (1764); *The Ignorant Philosopher* (1766). When he finally returned to Paris in 1778 he was treated as an all-conquering hero, and it killed him.

The full force of Voltaire's cynicism is revealed in his brilliant satire, *Candide* in which the quantity of evil vastly exceeds the quantity of good and so renders its subtitle – *The Optimist* – rather poignant. The story begins in the castle of Baron Thunder-ten-tronckh. The Baron has a wife who weighs 350 pounds and is, therefore, greatly respected, a son and a plump and tempting young daughter, Cunegonde. The house philosopher is Dr. Pangloss who teaches metaphysico-theologo-cosmolonigology. He insists that there is no effect without a cause and that, in the best of all possible worlds, the Baron's castle is the most beautiful castle and its mistress the best possible Baroness. Candide, the simple-minded son of the Baron's sister, believes everything Pangloss tells him. He also falls in love with Cunegonde but is not bold enough to tell her.

While out walking, Cunegonde comes across Pangloss in the bushes giving a lesson in experimental physics to her mother's pretty maid. This so inspires Cunegonde that she lures Candide into kissing her with trembling knees and wandering hands. When the Baron unexpectedly observed this cause and effect, he expels Candide from the castle.

After wandering in the snow, Candide stops at an inn where he is removed to a Bulgarian regiment, whipped and given the option of running the gauntlet of 2000 men or taking 12 bullets in the brain. He protested that men's wills are free and he wanted neither one nor the other, but he had to make a choice and so he chose to run the gauntlet. When the King of the Bulgarians learned that he was a young metaphysician very ignorant in worldly matters, he generously pardoned him.

Candide now takes part in a battle against the Abarians in which 6000 men perish in the opening salvos, then the musketry kill 10,000 rascals from the best of all worlds; the bayonet accounts with sufficient reason for many thousand more. Candide, who trembled like a philosopher, hid himself from this heroic butchery and determined to escape. Arriving in Holland he gives his money to a beggar who is, in fact, Pangloss and who is obviously no longer in the noblest of castles. Pangloss tells Candide that Cunegonde is dead – raped and disembowelled by Bulgarians – and her parents murdered. Pangloss has succumbed, through love, to syphilis caught from the pretty maid, who caught it from a learned monk, who caught it from an old Countess, who caught it from a cavalry captain, who owed it to an aristocrat, who got it from a Jesuit who caught it from one of Columbus's crew. Candide believes that the devil is behind these illnesses but Pangloss does not compromise his principles – syphilis is a necessary ingredient in the best of worlds for if Columbus had not introduced syphilis to the old world, we should not today have chocolate. He also notes that the disease is peculiar to the European continent, like theological disputes, although there is sufficient reason why other peoples will succumb sooner or later.

A friend who has taken Candide and Pangloss to Lisbon drowns in a tidal wave which precedes the Lisbon earthquake. Pangloss, who has been cured of syphilis at the cost of an eye, an ear and the tip of his nose, proves that Lisbon Harbour was designed for their friend to be drowned in it. While he was proving this *a priori*, the boat sank under them and everyone drowned except Pangloss and Candide and a murderous sailor. After the earthquake, Pangloss consoled his neighbours by assuring them that things could not be otherwise and that all this is for the best; for if there is an earthquake at Lisbon, it cannot be anywhere else; for it is impossible that things should not be where they are; for all is well. One of his listeners, familiar with the Inquisition, accuses him of denying original sin, for if everything is for the best, the fall and its punishment cannot have taken place. Pangloss's claim that man's fall enters necessarily into the best of possible worlds provokes the charge that he denies man's freedom. His attempt to argue that we are necessarily free is terminated and he is sentenced to be hanged and Candide is sentenced to be whipped for agreeing with him. After the earthquake which destroyed three-quarters of Lisbon, the wise men of the town decided that the sight of several persons being slowly burned in great ceremony is an infallible secret for preventing future earthquakes. And so while a few hapless souls were burning, Candide was flogged and Pangloss hanged. Sadly, the same day the earth shook again. Candide, terrified and bewildered asks: 'If this is the best of all possible worlds, what are the others?

Candide's flogging is witnessed by Cunegonde who had been sold to a rich man and lives in a country house which she shares with the Grand Inquisitor. Candide is taken to Cunegonde by an old woman who is a daughter of a pope and princess, has lost a buttock which was eaten by soldiers, and suffered countless other horrific misfortunes. Reunited in blissful love, Candide and Cunegonde are surprised during love-making by the patron and the Inquisitor and Candide kills both of them. They flee to the new world but are betrayed by a Franciscan's theft of Cunegonde's jewellery. Orders are issued for Candide's arrest and he abandons Cunegonde to the governor of Buenos Aires and sets out with Cacambo to fight for the

Jesuits. But he discovers that the commander is Cunegonde's brother who welcomes him warmly until Candide declares his intention to marry Cunegonde. Infuriated he strikes Candide who sticks his sword in the Jesuit's belly.

After diverse adventures, including an encounter with savages who refrain from eating him only when they learn he is not a Jesuit, Candide and Cacambo discover the paradise of El Dorado. But Candide wants to be with Cunegonde and soon leaves with his pockets filled with diamonds. Along the way he meets Martin whose misfortunes are so great that he has become a Manichean who believes, contrary to Pangloss, that everything is for the worst. He tells Candide: 'I confess that when I consider this globe, or rather this globule, I think that God has abandoned it to some evil creature. I have never seen a town which did not desire the ruin of the next town, never a family which did not wish to exterminate some other family. Everywhere the weak loathe the powerful before whom they cower and the powerful treat them like flocks of sheep whose wool and flesh are to be sold. A million drilled assassins go from one end of Europe to the other murdering and robbing with discipline in order to earn their bread, because there is no honester occupation; and in the towns which seem to enjoy peace and where the arts flourish, men are devoured by more envy, troubles, and worries than the afflictions of a beseiged town. Secret griefs are even more cruel than public miseries.' Candide asks whether Martin believes men have always massacred each other? Have they always been liars, cheats, traitors, brigands, weak, flighty, cowardly, envious, gluttonous, drunken, grasping, and vicious, bloody, backbiting, debauched, fanatical, hypocritical and silly? Of course they have and will continue, like the animals, to follow their natures. Candide is not convinced and replies that the difference between men and the animals is free will.

Candide exercises his free will by travelling to Paris where he is cheated at cards and is unfaithful to Cunegonde with a woman who robs him of his diamonds. He arrives in melancholic England in time to see the English carrying out their custom of executing an admiral to encourage the others to kill more men. Candide moves on to Venice where he encounters the maid who had given Pangloss syphilis. Candide is told that Cunegonde has grown very ugly and Cacambo is a slave of a Turkish sultan. Candide ransoms Cacambo and Pangloss who is a galley slave. It seems that Pangloss's hangman was incompetent and he recovered from his ordeal when a barber was dissecting him. The barber sewed him up and he was re-arrested and condemned to the galleys for returning a corsage to a lady in a mosque.

When Candide is re-united with Cunegonde he discovers she has indeed grown so ugly that he does not want to marry her. Candide and Cunegonde stay together, however, while Candide debates with his philosophers. After many intellectual discussions he decides to emulate the local fruit-grower, care nothing for public affairs and work his property. Although Cunegonde has become ugly, she is at least a good cook. Pangloss says to Candide: 'All events are linked up in this best of all possible worlds; for if you had not been expelled from the noble castle by hard kicks in your backside for love of Mademoiselle

Cunegonde, if you had not been clapped into the Inquisition, if you had not wandered about America on foot, if you had not stuck your sword in the Baron, if you had not lost your riches in El Dorado, you would not be here eating candied lemons and pistachios.' 'That is all very well,' replies Candide, 'but we must cultivate our gardens'.

In *The Social Contract* Jean-Jacques Rousseau (1712–1778) committed himself to the view that society was a corrupting influence over human nature. 'Man is born free; and everywhere he is in chains.' This philosophical stance may have sprung more from passionate reaction to the oppressive aspects that Rousseau found in the society of autocratic France than from a conscious choice of assumptions. Once committed to it, however, he worked it through until its assumptions stood out explicitly. They then provided the basis for a further set of arguments about the direction change should take, especially in education.

Rousseau set up a theoretical antithesis between a state of nature and a state of civilisation and took it as his thesis that primitive man was the ideal. This 'noble savage' was clearly stated to be not a fact of history so that it is idle to criticise Rousseau as historically inaccurate or to produce examples of primitive savagery to refute him. The concept he uses is closely related to that of Adam before the fall – innocent, noble and free to develop without the distortions of character brought about by guilt, shame and mutual exploitation. Two centuries earlier, Calvinism had declared both man and the world to be corrupt. Now Rousseau was declaring that only the world was corrupt;

far from being a vehicle of original sin, man was the vehicle of natural virtue. At the beginning of *Emile* he says: 'God makes all things good: man meddles with them and they become evil.'

Rousseau does not explain how a naturally virtuous creature could create an evil society. This is not surprising since it is a blatant contradiction in terms and probably was meant to be read as hyperbole. But what he considers as evil is clear. It is exploitation of one person by another. The beginnings of private property mark the beginning of the fall, for at this point one man begins to interfere with the free development of another. From then onwards, the element of social compulsion increases until men are little more than slaves to the 'general will'. Because Rousseau holds that evil is a result of society's distortion of human nature, he undermines the doctrine of personal responsibility that informs all conservative political and religious institutions. Because he lauds freedom and denigrates constraint, he elevates the person to the premier place in the scheme of things. Thus Rousseau's proto-Romantic doctrines are often credited with being an important factor in giving direction to the popular dissatisfaction that culminated in the French Revolution.

The revolution that Rousseau really tried to bring about was in education. His theoretical work, published as *The Social Contract* in 1761, was undertaken in order to work through the dilemma created by the fact that while he was convinced society was corrupt, he also came to admit that it was inevitable. There was no way that the human race could get back to natural freedom and natural virtue; so that the only course was to discover a form in which society could exist without destroying man's natural goodness. Society is, he thinks, based on a contract between people and their chosen leaders. As the various clauses of the contract are detailed, however, it becomes clear that what is in view is nothing less than a complete inter-penetration of person and society, so that there is really no longer any problem concerning the relationship between person and group. They melt into each other. The outcome is that people put themselves under the supreme direction of a general will that is just and aims at the public good.

Rousseau thus introduces a quasi-spiritual entity that transcends individuals. To alienate one's individual rights and one's freedom to this transcendent common will is to advance from a spurious freedom to a superior status in which one's faculties are developed. Thus the problem of the relationship between person and society is to be resolved by bringing about full concordance between them and the possibility of this hinges on the contract entered into by the person voluntarily and universally. In the process of his argument, however, Rousseau has come to mean something unusual by the term 'society'. He has ceased to think about it in terms of institutional behaviour and has come to think of it as a 'group will'. There is a semi-mystical element in maintaining that a complete union with the 'will' of society represents the ultimate in liberty for person. Admittedly, there is a kind of joy in feelings of community; liberty, say some, is a beloved discipline. But it becomes uncommonly hard to see how I am to convince the person who has to clean sewers that his freedom is enhanced, ideas extended and soul elevated by acknowledgement of the general will that this must be done. Education must be the answer, as Rousseau sees it.

Emile appeared in the year following *The Social Contract*. It was a novel in which Rousseau expounded his ideas on how education could produce the right sort of society. Since he thought of the good qualities of man as developing naturally in children he argued that children should be society's first consideration, i.e. they should be assisted to develop to their fullest their natural capacities. Although this does not sound revolutionary now, it was considered so at the time, for it implied that society should be so organised as to give the freest possible expression to the natural potentialities of children.

Every part of this thesis was thoroughly antithetical to the accepted policies of the time. Traditionally, education was a process of moulding children to meet social standards that were regarded as fixed, and in which the religious and political establishment had a vested interest. Rousseau wished to turn this attitude on its head and quickly aroused powerful opposition. Religious institutions were still the chief agents of education and religious educators saw themselves as expunging tendencies towards original sin and inculcating the morally good in their place. And environmentalists were not particularly willing to give up the congenial belief that they were inscribing good and useful things on all the blank tablets placed before them.

The immediate result of the publication of *Emile* was a warrant for Rousseau's arrest. He escaped to his birthplace Geneva whose noble citizens rejected him. He lived for a while in Neuchatel, then went to England where he lived with the Scottish philosopher and historian, David Hume. Here his paranoia took a new turn and he became convinced that Hume, rather than society, was his persecutor. Eventually he died in France.

The long term effects of *Emile* have been happier. It is the original of all treatises on permissive education about which it contains a host of practical suggestions. Many of these are in accord with what later liberal educators and psychologists have advocated, e.g. the concept of stages of readiness to learn, the practice of learning through play, the necessity to expose children to conditions in which their senses will be directly exercised by the environment, and the value of learning practical skills as a way of becoming an independent person. These suggestions are not direct derivatives of his original assumption of natural virtue that in effect merely serves to neutralise the opposing and popular doctrine of the necessity to suppress original sin. The more constructive propositions are really based on the voluntarism that informs *The Social Contract*. The non-explicit assumption is that the person is purposeful by nature. As the child comes to experience, one by one, the purposes and desires common to human life, the teacher who offers the knowledge necessary for their accomplishment will find it absorbed without difficulty. So far as instruction in the means for accomplishing ends is concerned, this is a tenable position. But as Rousseau's opponents saw, people frequently adopt purposes that involve the destruction of others, so the moral problem remains. The suggestion that it has been solved is false.

Voltaire and Rousseau are great contributors to the

Enlightenment, even if their contributions were often regarded as dangerously cynical. There is no doubt they were influenced by the ancient Cynics, and especially Diogenes. The Enlightenment thinkers agreed with the Cynics' emphasis on: freedom from prejudice, religious dogma and political power, and freedom of the individual. But Diogenes also represents sarcasm and this makes him (along with Voltaire and Rousseau) a target for Enlightenment criticism. Like Diogenes, Rousseau believed that the human will was basically good but was too easily led into corruption. In fact, Rousseau briefly adopted the pose of a Cynic, which was really foreign to his character. In his *Confessions* he wrote: 'For shyness I became a Cynic and mocker, and I pretended to scorn deeply the good manners I had been unable to acquire.' But this condition did not last and he soon reverted to his Spartan character claiming, typically, that others had 'pushed him into Cynicism' – a Diogenes without the lantern.

Voltaire occasionally played at being an 18th Century Diogenes although he loved culture, the sciences and the arts. To criticise these civilising achievements seemed to him childish and absurd. Yet, he was sarcastic and biting in his mockery. Consequently, he was reviled by the Counter-Enlightenment as a malicious and dangerous cynic in both the classical and modern senses. De Maistre criticised Voltaire as a perverted cynic; Voltaire criticised Rousseau as a false Diogenes claiming that whilst other cynics aimed at virtue, Rousseau threw himself into filth and wallowed in it. By driving his imagination to the point of hellish enthusiasm, he leads himself to the outermost boundaries of evil.

Though in their different ways defenders of human liberty, it was inevitable that Voltaire and Rousseau would quarrel. When Rousseau sent his *Discourses on Inequality* to Voltaire he was stunned by the reply. Rousseau had argued that 'Europe is the unhappiest Continent' and 'to undo the evil, it is necessary to abandon civilisation, for man is naturally good, and savage man, when he has dined, is at peace with all nature and the friend of all his fellow-creatures.' Voltaire replied: 'I have received your new book against the human race, and thank you for it. You will please mankind to whom you tell a few home truths but you will not correct it. You depict with very true colours the horrors of human society which out of ignorance and weakness sets its hopes on so many comforts. Never was such a cleverness used in the design of making us like animals. One longs, in reading your book, to walk on all fours. But as I have lost the habit for more than sixty years, I feel unhappily the impossibility of resuming it. Nor can I embark in search of the savages of Canada, because the maladies to which I am condemned render a European surgeon necessary to me; because war is going on in those regions; and because the example of our actions has made the savages nearly as bad as ourselves.'

By the 20th Century cynicism, if not Cynicism, had become a mass phenomenon. Modern cynicism is an urban phenomenon – only in a city can cynicism truly flourish, because there are so many targets that invite mockery. I think of Oscar Wilde: 'I am not at all cynical, I am only experienced – that's pretty much the same thing.' Or Anton Chekhov: 'No cynicism can outdo life.' And

Peter Sloterdijk, in his *Critique of Cynical Reason*, argues that the discontent in our culture is a universal, diffuse cynicism based on an 'enlightened false consciousness.' Followers after naïve ideologies, modern cynics believe in everything – and therefore nothing. The ancient world knew the Cynic as a provocative, biting moralist 'who acts as though he needs nobody and is loved by nobody because nobody escapes his crude unmasking gaze uninjured.' Today the cynic stands before us as a mass figure.

One man who wrote for those masses, while despising them, was the American soldier, journalist and essayist Ambrose Bierce (1842–1914). Bierce fought with distinction in the American Civil War where he saw enough human cruelty and bureaucratic stupidity to cure him of any optimism he may have entertained about *homo sapiens*. His unrelieved pessimism about human beings and their pathetic attempts to civilise themselves found expression in his short stories, journalistic articles and letters. Bierce's cynicism is brutal and nihilistic, although he would disagree with the latter description, having defined a nihilist as a Russian who denies the existence of everything except Tolstoy. The leader of the school is Tolstoy.

He has been described as Voltaire with stomach ulcers, an inaccurate characterisation since Voltaire did suffer from stomach ulcers. But like his French predecessor he savagely attacked the religious establishment, corrupt lawyers and politicians and the pretensions of the literary and artistic worlds. Lawyers he considered to be skilled in circumvention of the law whilst politicians are eels in the fundamental mud upon which the superstructure of organised society is reared. When they wriggle they mistake the agitation of their tails for the trembling of the edifice. As compared with statesmen, they suffer the disadvantage of being alive. Politics is a strife of interests masquerading as a contest of principles, and the conduct of public affairs for private advantage. As for art, the word has no definition, though artlessness is a certain engaging quality to which women attain by long study and severe practice upon the admiring male, who is pleased to fancy it resembles the candid simplicity of his young.

In the 1880s he started writing *The Cynic's Word Book* which appeared in expanded form as *The Devil's Dictionary* in 1906, a collection of 1000 satirical definitions which continue to offend serious-minded people and confirmed his reputation as a man who had no affection for any living human being. The corrosive definitions of this witty book continue to appeal to cynics and those who are sympathetic to the black humour of our time. Bierce's humour is indeed black and it appeals to those who have no faith in religion, politics or progress. However the good folk of the American mid-West thought its author an extreme cynic – a scoundrel whose faulty vision sees things as they are, not as they ought to be, and hence the custom among the Scythians of plucking out a cynic's eyes to improve his vision. Unlike Voltaire he was not moved to fight for grand causes preferring to snipe away at the stupidities of human beings from his study. He considers the average human being to be an idiot – a member of a large and powerful tribe whose influence in human affairs has always been dominant and controlling. The Idiot's activity is not confined to any special field of thought or action, but pervades and regulates everything. The Idiot has the last word on every subject; his decision is unappealable. He sets the fashion of opinion and taste, dictates the limitations of speech and circumscribes conduct with a dead hand. Sadly, education cannot help since it is that which discloses to the wise and disguises from the foolish their lack of understanding.

He had a difficult and tragic life losing two of his children (who died) and his wife (who left him). I am surprised that his wife lasted with him as long as she did since his views on love and marriage do not augur well for easy companionship. A female, he regarded as one of the opposing, or unfair sex. Woman is an animal usually living in the vicinity of Man, and having a rudimentary suscep-tibility to domestication. It is credited by many of the elder zoologists with a certain vestigial docility acquired in a former state of seclusion, but naturalists of the postsu-sananthony period, having no knowledge of such seclusion, deny the virtue and declare that such as creation's dawn beheld, it roareth now. The species is the most widely distributed of all beasts of prey, infesting all habitable parts of the globe. The popular name (wolf-man) is incorrect, for the creature is of the cat kind. The woman is lithe and graceful in its movements, especially the American variety ('Felis pugnans'), is omnivorous and can be taught not to talk. Love is a temporary insanity curable by marriage or by removal of the patient from the influences under which he incurred the disorder. It is sometimes fatal, but more frequently to the physicians than to the patient. But marriage will be a Pyrrhic victory because it is the state of a community consisting of a master, a mistress and two slaves, making in all two. A bride is a woman with a fine prospect of happiness behind her and the wedding is a ceremony at which two persons undertake to be one, one undertakes to be nothing, and nothing undertakes to be supportable. Bierce can be charged with misogyny so long as we acknowledge in fairness to him (not that he would care about fairness) that he is profoundly misanthropic – he hates men as much as women. He defines a male, misogynously, as a member of the unconsidered, or negligible sex. The male of the human race is commonly known (to the female) as Mere Man. The genus has two varieties: good providers and bad providers. He defines man, misanthropically, as an animal so lost in rapturous contemplation of what he thinks he is as to overlook what he indubitably ought to be. His chief occupation is extermination of other animals and his own species, which, however, multiplies with such insistent rapidity as to infest the whole habitable earth and Canada.

Bierce believed that Western civilisation was moving rapidly towards its demise and that our minds are darkening in proportion to our loss of faith in ourselves. As we look into each other's eyes with fear and hatred, even the most optimistic folk will find it difficult to draw comfort from the idea of human progress. The light of reason will go out and decadence will be the order of the night. New philosophies of violence and nihilism will appear, and among them Ambrose Bierce may be exhumed. He is best remembered for *The Devil's Dictionary* in which he appears as a man of philosophical wit, a cynic who mocks a cruel and indifferent world. He is so politically incorrect that he must be saying important things. He lived much of his life alone, that is, in bad company. Here are some examples of the writings of one who loved to be called a bad man, a non-conformist of the first order. He is more than that.

Bore: A person who talks when you wish him to listen.

Cartesian: Relating to Descartes, a famous philosopher, author of the celebrated dictum, 'cogito ergo sum' – whereby he was pleased to suppose he demonstrated the reality of human existence. The dictum might be improved, however, thus: 'cogito cogito ergo cogito sum – 'I think that I think, therefore I think that I am'; as close an approach to certainty as any philosopher has yet made.

Duty: That which sternly impels us in the direction of profit along the line of desire.

I is the first letter of the alphabet, the first word of the language, the first thought of the mind, the first object of affection. In grammar it is a pronoun of the first person and singular number. Its plural is said to be 'We', but how there can be more than me myself is doubtless clearer to the grammarians than it is to the author of this incomparable dictionary.

Innate: Natural, inherent – as innate ideas, that is to say, ideas that we are born with, having had them previously imparted to us. The doctrine of innate ideas is one of the most admirable faiths of philosophy, being itself an innate idea and therefore inaccessible to disproof, though Locke foolishly supposed himself to have given it a 'black eye'. Among innate ideas may be mentioned the belief in the greatness of one's country, in the superiority of one's civilisation, in the importance of one's personal affairs and in the interesting nature of one's diseases.

Logic: The art of thinking and reasoning in strict accordance with the limitations and incapacities of the human misunderstanding. The basic of logic is the syllogism, consisting of a major and a minor premise and a conclusion – thus:

Major premise: Sixty men can do a piece of work sixty times as quickly as one man.

Minor premise: One man can dig a hole in sixty seconds; therefore

Conclusion: Sixty men can dig a hole in one second.

Mad: Affected with a high degree of intellectual independence; not conforming to standards of thought, speech and action derived by the conformants from study of themselves; at odds with the majority; in short, unusual. It is noteworthy that persons are pronounced mad by officials destitute of evidence that they themselves are sane. For illustration, this present (and illustrious) lexicographer is no firmer in the faith of his own sanity than is any inmate of any madhouse in the land; yet for aught he knows to the contrary, instead of the lofty occupation that seems to him to be engaging his powers he may really be beating his hands against the window bars of an asylum and declaring himself Noah Webster, to the innocent delight of many thoughtless spectators.

Me: The objectionable case of I. The personal pronoun in English has three cases, the dominative, the objectionable and the oppressive. Each is all three.

Mythology: The body of primitive people's beliefs concerning its origin, early history, heroes, deities and so forth, as distinguished from the true accounts which it invents later.

Newtonian: Pertaining to a philosophy of the universe, invented by Newton, who discovered that an apple will fall to the ground, but was unable to say why. His followers and disciples have advanced so far as to be able to say when.

Optimism: The doctrine that everything is beautiful, including what is ugly, everything good, especially the bad, and everything right that is wrong. It is held with greatest tenacity by those most accustomed to the mischance of falling into adversity and is most acceptably expounded with the grin that apes a smile. Being a blind faith, it is inaccessible to the light of disproof – an intellectual disorder, yielding to no treatment but death. It is hereditary, but fortunately not contagious.

Pessimism: A philosophy forced upon the convictions of the observer by the disheartening prevalence of the optimist with his scarecrow hope and his unsightly smile.

Philosophy: A route of many roads leading from nowhere to nothing.

Pyrrhonism: An ancient philosophy, named for its inventor. It consisted of an absolute disbelief in everything except Pyrrhonism. Its modern professors have added that.

Reality: The dream of a mad philosopher.

Revolution: In politics, an abrupt change in the form of misgovernment. Revolutions are usually accompanied by a considerable effusion of blood, but are accounted worth it – this appraisement being made by beneficiaries whose blood has not the mischance to be shed.

Sophistry: The controversial method of an opponent, distinguished from one's own by superior insincerity and fooling. This method is that of the later Sophists, a Grecian sect of philosophers who began by teaching wisdom, prudence, science, art and, in brief, whatever men ought to know, but lost themselves in a maze of quibbles and a fog of words.

Soul: A spiritual entity concerning which there has been brave disputation. Plato held that those souls which in a previous state of existence (antedating Athens) had obtained the clearest glimpse of eternal truth entered into the bodies of persons who became philosophers. Plato was himself a philosopher. The souls that had least contemplated divine truth animated the bodies of usurpers and despots. Dionysus 1, who had threatened to decapitate the broad-browed philosopher, was a usurper and despot. Plato, doubtless, was not the first to construct a system of philosophy that could be quoted against his enemies; certainly he was not the last.

Truth: An ingenious compound of desirability and appearance. Discovery of truth is the sole purpose of philosophy, which is the most ancient occupation of the human mind and has a fair prospect of existing with increasing activity to the end of time.

4

Living Stoically

'A man undisciplined in philosophy blames others in
matters in which he fares ill; one who begins to be
disciplined blames himself; one who is disciplined,
neither blames others nor himself.'

(Epictetus)

Stoics, who argue that freedom means becoming relatively indifferent to stress, upset postmodern sensitive
souls by arguing that people who pursue a stress-free life
are 'poor in spirit'. Postmodern society is still living with
the legacy of Freud who described the first half of the 20th
Century as a time of 'civilised nervousness' and its
dominant expression is the complaint about the stresses of
life. He should know. The popularity of his invention –
psychoanalysis – is testimony to the ubiquitous nature
of complaining about the moral dilemmas that define
human existence.

The institutionalisation of complaining has been
combined with a modern obsession with rights. Taken
together and ignoring issues of personal responsibility a
social movement has been built around a set of decidedly
unstoical attitudes to the experience of stress. Stress is no

longer regarded as an important and inexorable part of life. Rather, it is a 'condition' to be treated, a 'symptom' of malaise, an infringement of one's rights, an assault on one psyche, a 'psychological' injury, a reason to litigate, an example of coercion and harassment, an excuse for early retirement from work and life. Coupled with the assertion that we live in a rapidly changing world in which technology has overpowered defenceless folk, the stress movement has grown to uncontainable dimensions.

Since being stressed is one thing and doing something about it is quite another, I can follow the Stoics in appreciating the difference between stress and stress behaviour. I can be stressed and not complain, I can complain and not be stressed. I can claim that I'm sick (depressed) when I'm really faced with a moral dilemma (should I leave a marriage?). I have heard of people who, after gambling their salary away, claim they have a medical condition called 'compulsive gambling' (a condition only suffered by losers). I have heard women who beat their children claim they are not responsible because they were suffering from PMT. I have been tempted in my time to claim (as a joke) I am not responsible for abusing my students because I suffer from 'academic disorder', now regarded as an official mental disorder.

The willingness to dignify moral dilemmas with the status of medical conditions points to a wider issue – the medicalisation of moral conflicts. Whereas gambling and child-beating were once regarded as moral activities (since one knew the rights and wrongs of the matter and acted accordingly), gambling and child-beating are nowadays regarded as mental disorders, often caused by stress.

Defining moral dilemmas as medical conditions avoids the troublesome issues of right and wrong since the gambler/child-beater (i.e. patients) cannot be held responsible for their behaviour because they are ill. And should you, dear reader, suffer doubts on this matter there is a psychiatric bible, *Diagnostic and Statistical Manual of Mental Disorders* (DSM IV TR), (with over 700 pages of 'mental disorders'), to 'prove' it.

Some people have a well-practised ability to upset themselves and others. The ability to make oneself depressed or others angry was recognised long ago by Epictetus who argued that it is not what happens to me that upsets me, but how I take it. He knew of what he wrote since he was a slave of the Romans who respected his exemplary behaviour and courage in the face of adversity and freed him.

Stoicism has always been a refuge from the stresses of life. Yet it will surely be objected that in our democratic world no person should be a slave and so the need for stoicism evaporates. But how can this be true while people believe they are victims – of their genes, brain chemistry, childhood, parents, peer groups, teachers? Many people today are indeed slaves though the chains that bind them are philosophical rather than physical. What would the Stoics say to those who thrive on their self-acquired victim status? Would they maintain control when confronted with people who refuse to accept that they have choices and the responsibilities that irritably accompany them?

We can get an indication of an answer to these questions if we read the works of such modern stoics as Bertrand Russell in philosophy and Albert Ellis in psychology. Both have acknowledged their debt to the Stoics – the followers of Zeno (who was influenced by Crates), Seneca, Epictetus and poor old Marcus Aurelius. Stoic philosophy owes much to the life and work of Socrates, very little to Plato, and a lot to the Cynics. In recent times, the Stoic philosophy re-appeared in psychotherapy – no mean feat in an age of self-indulgent hedonism and victimhood – in the work of Albert Ellis whose stoical control is compromised by his New York manner and colourful language. His response to those who admonish him would, no doubt, be along the lines of 'tough shit'.

Stoicism gets its name from Zeno (336–263 B.C.) who lectured from a portico or 'stoa'. So Stoicism could have been called 'portism'. Zeno greatly admired Socrates for his strength of character and believed that Crates the Cynic (rather than Plato) was the thinker who most resembled him. When one day in his thirtieth year he sat in a bookshop and asked where were men like Socrates to be found, the bookseller pointed to Crates who was passing, and said: 'Follow that man.' And so he did for the next twenty years. Zeno became one of Crates's most famous pupils although his modesty prevented him from acting in the shameless manner of the Cynics. Crates tried to cure him of this inhibition by using what Albert Ellis was to call, 2300 years later, shame-attacking exercises. Crates made Zeno carry a pot of soup through the market-place and when he saw he was embarrassed and attempted to keep it out of sight, Crates broke the pot with his staff. As Zeno ran off screaming with the soup running down his legs Crates called out: 'Why run away, nothing terrible has befallen you.'

The people of Athens held him in high esteem and flocked to hear him lecturing, pacing up and down in the painted colonnade. But he disliked people getting too close to him and never walked with more than three people. He had an aversion to groups and when his admiring followers came too close he would disband them by asking for money for his friend Crates. His life was devoted to inquiry and he was a masterful reasoner and valued highly the study of logic. If he decided to engage another in argument he would present his case concisely, not emotionally, and keep his interlocutor at a distance. After noticing a vain youth picking his way across a water course he remarked: 'With good reason he does not look at the mud for he can't see his face in it.'

Zeno was a misanthropic character who was thought mean and austere. When a Cynic declared he had no oil in his flask and begged some from him, Zeno refused to give him any. As the man departed grumbling, Zeno asked his student to consider which of the two was the more impudent. To the question 'Who is a friend?' his answer was 'A second "I".' When chastising a slave for stealing, the slave pleaded that it was his fate to steal, 'Yes, and to be beaten too,' replied Zeno. When a student asked: 'Why am I the only pupil you do not correct?' Zeno's reply was: 'Because I mistrust you.' Like Socrates and Diogenes, he showed the utmost endurance and lived a life of admirable frugality. He was ninety-eight when he died and had enjoyed a life of good health without an ailment to the last. His manner of death is in the tradition of the Cynics. He tripped, fell and broke his toe. Striking the ground with his fist he said: 'I am coming anyway, why do you call for me?' and died, like Diogenes, by holding his breath.

Stoics rejected Plato's and Aristotle's Forms, preferring to return to pre-Socratic sources, especially the materialism of Heraclitus. For Zeno the end of life is to live 'in agreement with nature'. The virtuous life is one lived towards goals to which nature guides me because my individual nature is part of the nature of the whole universe. I am obliged, therefore, to live according to my rational human nature. If, through reason, I possess one, I possess all and this is what is meant by 'character'. As a man of character I do not allow myself to fall victim to such self-defeating emotions as sorrow, depression or anxiety. Such emotions are irrational judgements and should be eradicated by the power of reason. Whilst I am externally determined by the conditions of nature, I am internally free to choose my emotions, and, if I am rational, I will not choose sorrow, depression or anxiety. The Stoics agreed with Socrates that virtue is knowledge but, unlike him, they believed that as a rational person I will choose to free myself from worldly demands, negative emotions and pleasure-seeking.

Virtue is a harmonious disposition, worthy for its own sake, and not from hope or fear or any external motive. So it is in virtue that happiness consists. The cardinal virtues are: moral reason, self-control and justice whilst the good is defined as 'the natural perfection of a rational being'. Like Aristotle, the Stoics believed that the good is acting in accordance with my character. Since reality is perfection I should live in accordance with the perfect plan of reality which can be comprehended by reason and make my desires identical with that plan. Fools try to impose their own ideas on reality and come to grief. Unhappiness and unfreedom are the inevitable result of allowing my egoism to flout the dictates of reality. So freedom is will and the ability to want what the universe wants. I should not wish for desires; I should desire what I get.

Stoics believed that only individuals exist and our knowledge is of particular objects that make impressions on the mind. They invented the idea of the mind as a 'tabula rasa' (blank slate) on which experiences leave their mark. This view anticipates British empiricists, such as John Locke, although the Stoics also (inconsistently) believed in innate ideas that Locke (consistently) rejected. 'I' is composed of the five senses, the faculty of speech, the intellectual faculty deviation from which produces 'perversions' yielding in turn passions. Passions are defined by Zeno as irrational and unnatural movements in 'I', or excessive impulses. The most universal and destructive passions are grief (pity, envy, jealousy, rivalry, annoyance, distress, anguish); fear (expectation of evil, terror, shame, panic, guilt): desire (want, hatred, anger, love, wrath, resentment); and craving for pleasure (ravishment, malice, delight). The three emotional states which are good are: joy, caution and wishing because they are rational states in that they are self-promoting.

Of the three kinds of life – the contemplative, the practical and the rational, Zeno believes that I ought to choose the last because as a rational person I have been created by nature for contemplation and action. The universe is governed by reason and fate and I am so governed. The highest achievements of life are to be found in the exercise of my reason and the calm acceptance of my fate. These ideas were to have a great impact on the Roman Empire through the writings and teachings of Seneca, Epictetus and Marcus Aurelius.

Epictetus (50–138) was a Greek slave who was set free by Nero and became his minister. He lived and taught in Rome until he fell foul of the emperor and was exiled. Although he is one of the most widely read philosophers, little is known of his life, and that which is known derives from his famous *Discourses*. Born into slavery, lame and rheumatic, he suffered stoically at the hands of cruel masters. After his release from bondage he worked as Nero's secretary in charge of receiving petitions and later similarly served Domitian who, in 94, issued a decree expelling all philosophers from Rome. Epictetus wryly noted that this was an understandable act given the number of philosophers in Rome who were able 'to look tyrants steadily in the face.' Epictetus took himself off to Nicopolis and established himself as a teacher of philosophy. He lived and taught there until the end of his life. Like many of his predecessors he lived simply and taught passionately and thought himself fortunate to be paid for working at his hobby.

Like Socrates whom he greatly admired, Epictetus wrote nothing – his teaching was oral, delivered as lectures to his students. Thanks to one of his students – Flavius Arrianus – notes of his master's teachings have survived. He shared Socrates' contempt for the human body and respected his adherence to principle in the face of adversity. Also like Socrates he tried to live his philosophy and demonstrate its timeless truth. Clearly, he borrows heavily from Zeno and the Stoic philosophy of Greece, but he is also original and thus worthy of independent scrutiny.

Philosophy begins with the observation of how people contradict each other and how they search for the causes of these contradictions. Of things that exist, some are in my power (opinions, impulses, pursuits, avoidances), some are not in my power (body, possessions, reputation, authority). The things that are in my power are naturally free; the things that are not in my power are alien to me. 'Remember, then, if you hold things by their nature subject to be free, and things alien to be your proper concern, you will be hampered, you will lament, you will be troubled, you will blame the Gods and men. But if you hold that only to be your own which is so, and the alien for what it is, alien, then none shall ever compel you, none shall hinder you, you will blame no one, you will not do the least thing unwittingly, none shall harm you, you shall have no foe, for you shall suffer no injury.'

Like all Stoics, Epictetus makes much of the distinction between that which is within my power and that which is not. What, then, is in my power? My judgement of affairs and my will are within my power, and education consists in attaining true judgement and a right will. The essence of good and evil lies in an attitude of the will. Since this will lies within our power, we can conquer it but nothing external to us can conquer it.

Epictetus teaches that I have the capacity for virtue, the means of becoming happy, and self-control. 'What then is man's nature? To bite, to kick, to throw into prison, and to behead? No, but to do good, to cooperate with others, to wish them well.' I need therefore, to will virtue and so achieve victory over the problems of living. 'You must exercise your will and the thing is done, it is set right; as on the other hand relax your vigilance and all is lost, for from within comes ruin and from within comes help.' It is the task of every right-thinking human being to overcome the self-imposed limits to virtue. 'You must talk to yourself. You will be most easily persuaded; no one has more power to persuade you than you yourself.'

There are three divisions of philosophy – three steps to perfection – in which I must exercise myself if I want to be wise and good.

1. I will teach myself to order my pursuits and avoidances.
2. I will teach myself to rank my desires in accordance with right-thinking reason, freeing myself from self-defeating emotions.
3. I will teach myself to avoid delusion, hasty judgement and other defects of reason.

Of these the chief and most urgent is that which concerns the passions, which arise because of my failure to achieve or avoid something. Since I upset myself, not by things themselves, but by my opinions about them, Epictetus invites me to inspect my powers of reason for in these lie my abilities to keep passions at bay. This is not to suggest that I should be passionless, like a statue. Rather, I should cultivate self-promoting passions which will help me maintain appropriate social relations. From a basis in proper social behaviour I can move on to seek not to have things happen as I choose them, but rather choose them to happen as they do, and so I shall live prosperously. Such things as diseases are hindrances of my body, not of my will, unless the will consents. Lameness is a hindrance of the leg, not of the will. 'And this you may say on every occasion, for nothing can happen to you but you will find it a hindrance not of yourself but of some other thing.' I is will.

What then are the things that perturb and oppress me? In a word, they are 'opinions'. 'Now little children, if they cry because their nurse has left them for a while, straightaway forget their sorrow when they are given a small cake. Will you be likened to a little child? No, for I would not be thus affected by a little cake, but by right opinions.' And what are these opinions? 'A man should study all day long to observe – that he be not subject to the effects of anything that is alien to him, neither of friend, nor place, nor exercises; not even of his own body, but to remember the Law, and have it ever before his eyes. And what is the divine Law? To hold fast that which is his own, and to claim nothing that is another's; to use what is given to him, and not to covet what is not given; to yield up easily and willingly what is taken away, giving thanks for the time that he had it at his service. Do this – or cry for your nurse and mother.'

Finally, Epictetus tells me about living philosophy. I should choose for myself a certain type of conduct (Socratic, for instance) which I shall maintain with others and even when alone. I shall speak only when necessary, shall not engage in gossip or idle chat (about the weather, food, drink). When I speak I shall draw my colleagues towards that which is good and avoid blaming, praising or comparing others. I shall not laugh too often or loudly (if only patrons of restaurants would oblige) and never laugh to feign happiness. I shall shun dinner parties given by strangers and by the vulgar, but if I find myself in attendance I shall avoid descending, for reasons of political correctness, to their level by remaining above their conversation and raucous laughter. I shall pay special attention to my body – to cleanliness and providing for its basic needs. And when I visit the rich and powerful, I shall assume that he is not at home, that I will be shut out and the door slammed in my face, or that he will take no notice of me. And if I am in the presence of such people, boring as they are, I shall bear all that happens, and I shall never say to myself 'It was not worth it'. There is much to be learned by studying, though not arguing with, the fools, the pretentious and the pompous, so long as I do not become foolish, pretentious or pompous. Among such people I shall not proclaim my allegiance to philosophy but demonstrate my commitment through my actions. I shall not, for example, philosophise about food while eating, but eat as I ought. But if I am drawn into philosophy by the uninitiated who want to know what and why I believe this or that maxim, I shall answer in the broadest terms since there is a great risk that I shall vomit up what I have not digested. And when the great unwashed tell me that I know nothing, and it does not affect me, then I know that I have truly begun my life of philosophy.

Philosophy is, for Epictetus, what I need in order to become truly myself, to fulfil my potentialities, to achieve happiness and to become wise and good. Philosophy teaches me how to live well, how to talk to others and to myself. Philosophy is 'the art of life', but it is not for the masses because it requires a discipline and commitment to rationality that is beyond most people. To a rational person the only unbearable thing is irrationality, but a reasonable thing is quite bearable. Hanging, for instance, is not unbearable by nature. 'Whenever someone has the feeling that it's reasonable, he goes off and hangs himself! In short, by paying attention we shall discover that nothing distresses our species as much as irrationality, and that, conversely, nothing appeals to it so much as reasonableness.' This is the voice of an optimistic rationalist who believes that human beings have a natural capacity for thinking correctly on matters, a natural love of truth, a natural desire to argue validly, natural preferences and motivations. 'Just as it is every soul's nature to assent to truth, dissent from falsehood, and suspend judgement in relation to uncertainty, so it is its nature to be desirously motivated for the good, aversely motivated for the bad, and neutrally motivated for what is neither good nor bad.' Such sentiments may strike those who have lived after the carnage of the 20th Century as unduly naive and sentimental. But Epictetus would reply that such a charge against him ignores his injunction that it is not world events, such as wars, that make me unhappy, but how I take them. And if people were willing to think and act rationally, there would be no wars.

A philosopher who knew about wars was the Roman emperor, Marcus Aurelius (121–180), and he needed all that Stoicism had to offer in order to endure the plagues, famines, floods and Barbarian invasions that dominated his reign. After joining his legions on the Danube, Marcus composed his melancholic *Meditations*. Sadly, he did not learn the Stoic philosophy well enough, or at the very least, he failed to apply it. His mood swings – from hope to depression – and his obsessive longing for sympathy and affection would not have pleased Zeno or Epictetus. His meditations are gloomy, self-pitying and betray the feelings of a man who bows his knee to his duty whilst wanting to be somewhere else. As his job becomes more onerous, as the sight of blood nauseates him, as the deaths of his colleagues depress him, he withdraws more and more into himself and attempts, through Stoicism, to understand and master himself.

The second book of the *Meditations* starts with: 'Begin each day by telling yourself: today I shall meet with interference, ingratitude, insolence, disloyalty, ill-will, and selfishness – all of them due to the offenders' ignorance of what is good and evil. But for my part I have long perceived the nature of good and its nobility, the nature of evil and its meanness, and also the nature of the culprit himself, who is my brother (not in the physical sense, but as a fellow-creature endowed with reason and a share of the divine); therefore none of these things can injure me, for nobody can implicate me in what is degrading. Neither can I be angry with my brother or fall foul of him; for he and I were born to work together . . .' He tells me that I should resolve hourly to fulfil my tasks with dignity, humanity, justice and independence. 'This you can do if you approach every task as though it were your last, dismissing the wayward thought, the emotional recoil from the commands of reason, the desire to create an impression, the admiration of the self, the discontent with your lot.'

As for living philosophy, Marcus advises me that it is out of the question to claim that I have lived as a philosopher all my life, or even since adulthood; philosophy is still beyond me no matter how long I have engaged with it. Consequently, 'I' remains in a state of confusion and grows no easier with the title 'philosopher'. When I grasp this, I shall banish from my thoughts any concern about how others see me and rest content if I can make the remainder of my life what nature would have it to be. I must learn to understand Nature's will – in that will lies the secret to happiness. The search for the good life proceeds by doing what nature wills – by adopting strict principles for the control of impulse and action. Of any action I should ask: 'What will its consequences be to me?' and apply the maxim that nothing can be good for me unless it helps me to make myself just, self-disciplined, courageous and independent. And so I shall keep an untroubled I and look things in the face and know them for what they are. I shall do what nature demands without flinching and I shall say what seems to me just with courtesy, modesty and sincerity. I shall not blame others for their deficiencies. 'If the choice is yours, why do the thing? If another's, where are you to lay blame for it? On Gods? On atoms? Either would be insanity. All thoughts of blame are out of place. If you can, correct the offender; if not, correct the offence; if that too is impossible, what is the point of recrimination? Nothing is worth doing pointlessly.

The Stoic philosophy generally, and Epictetus's philosophy specifically, lives on today in many guises – religious, philosophical and psychological. In the field of psychotherapy it has found a receptive audience among those who practice 'cognitive-behaviour therapy' which became increasingly popular in the second half of the 20th Century. Arguably, the best known and most influential of cognitive-behaviour psychotherapists is New York psychologist, Albert Ellis. Originally trained in psychoanalysis, Ellis reacted against passive forms of therapy in favour of a more active, rational approach. Influenced by Epictetus, Marcus Aurelius and Bertrand Russell, Ellis developed what he called *Rational Therapy*, later known as *Rational-Emotive Therapy* and then *Rational-Emotive Behaviour Therapy* (REBT) to emphasise the positive emotions involved in a rational life.

According to Ellis, I respond to my practical problems with constructive attitudes which lead to motivation, or destructive attitudes which lead to distress. And so it follows that I have considerable powers to cope with and largely eliminate distress from my life so long as I am prepared to understand and accept responsibility for my self-created distressing feelings and irrational actions. Ellis is not impressed by those who believe that stress causes distress, nor with the belief that distress can be changed only by removing stressors from the environment. He believes, rather, that my attitudes cause distress and while these attitudes are influenced by environmental stressors, I have the power to change them. The elimination of distress will not necessarily lead to happiness but it does lead to motivation to change conditions for the better, or to accept those conditions that cannot be changed. Much that is called 'motivation' actually involves such negative feelings as frustration, concern, regret, determination, irritation. While these feelings are 'negative', they are motivating because they provide me with the energy to move towards desirable goals or away from undesirable outcomes. It is appropriate to feel sad at the death of a loved one; it is inappropriate to feel depressed. It is appropriate to feel concern at possible danger; it is inappropriate to feel anxious in its absence. It is appropriate to feel irritation at a friend's unreasonable behaviour; it is inappropriate to feel hostile.

REBT encourages the discovery and expression of emotions and emphasises the inter-relationship of thinking, feeling and behaving. Ellis claims that REBT can help me: 'think creatively about my emotional upsets; obtain emotional self-mastery; and channel energy into whatever endeavours I choose, so that my upsetting emotions do not interfere with my creative ability to solve problems'. REBT is based on the idea that anxiety, guilt, depression and hostility stem from my self-defeating attitudes and from faulty social learning experiences. By learning to alter the attitudes which create my upsetting emotions, I can develop greater capacities for dealing with my problems and live a freer and more emotionally satisfying life. The basic assumption of REBT is the principle formulated by Epictetus: 'Men are disturbed not by things, but by the views they take of them.' In other words, I face practical problems in living and sometimes upset myself about them – I create psychological problems about practical problems. And I have the power to eliminate my psychological problems.

Ellis studied people suffering from a range of emotional problems and he found that when the so-called traumatic events of his clients' early lives were investigated in detail, the events were really minor upsets and frustrations which they viewed as being catastrophic and hence made traumatic. His major finding was that emotionally upset people interpreted their early frustrations in exaggerated ways. They, therefore, 'invented' most of the traumata they claimed to have experienced. Ellis concluded that it is my unique way of interpreting the world (past and present) and the people around me that influences what happens to me and what I become.

The following ten clusters of beliefs are, according to Ellis, the major contributors to distress, neurosis, faulty human relationships and poor performance. They can be challenged and eliminated by vigorous debate as shown by the following examples, adapted from Ellis's *Reason and Emotion in Psychotherapy*.

1. *Irrational beliefs*: 'I need the approval of others for everything I do. When I don't receive this approval I feel rejected, anxious and angry. It is very important what others think of me. I need the support of others.'
   Rational beliefs: 'It is pleasant but not necessary for me to have the approval of others. It is better to win my own respect than others' approval. It is more desirable to stand on my own feet than depend on others. I am disappointed when I fail to get the acceptance of others, but that is a fact of life. The best way to get approval is sincerely to give it.'
2. *Irrational beliefs*: 'I must be competent and intelligent in all possible respects if I am to be considered worthwhile. When I act incompetently I feel depressed and

worthless. I should severely blame myself for my mistakes and shortcomings. When I fail to achieve my goals I feel inadequate and wish I were someone else.'

Rational beliefs: 'It is better to focus on doing than on doing well; to accept myself as an imperfect person who has definite limitations and fallibilities and to consider myself worthwhile whether or not I act competently. I can accept my mistakes and use them as guides for self-improvement. Punishing myself for my errors will sabotage action necessary to eliminate them. Failure merely motivates me to try harder.'

3. *Irrational beliefs*: 'Certain things my friends say and do are unbearable. They should not be that way and they should be blamed and punished for their behaviour. I get annoyed when they make mistakes and act inefficiently. Even though I criticise them and point out the error of their ways, they stubbornly refuse to change and that makes me so angry.'

Rational beliefs: 'Some of the things my friends say and do are inappropriate and when they act in these ways they are behaving ignorantly or ineffectively and it is desirable that I help them change by moving them towards more positive goals. Blaming or punishing people for their shortcomings is neither just nor effective. Getting upset about other people's errors and stupidities will not help me or them. I do not have to make myself angry about their behaviour.'

4. *Irrational beliefs*: 'It is terrible when things go wrong, when things are not the way I would like them to be. Problems should be easier than they are. My friends should make things easier for me and help me with

123

difficult problems. I can't stand difficult problems and I should be able to live without unexpected difficulties.'

Rational beliefs: 'It is unfortunate when things go wrong or are not the way I would like them to be. Problems are often difficult but challenging. There is no reason that it should be any other way. I can try my best to solve difficult problem. If this is impossible I had better resign myself to the way things are and stop telling myself how awful and terrible they are. I can stand what I don't like.'

5. *Irrational beliefs*: 'When things go wrong I can't help but get very angry or upset in some way. Anger and upset are externally caused; they are forced upon me by external people and events. I have little control over my emotions and cannot help feeling badly on many occasions, particularly when I fail at an important task.'

Rational beliefs: 'I have enormous control over my destructive emotions if I choose to work at changing the dogmatic attitudes which create them. Most human unhappiness is caused and sustained by the view one takes of experiences rather than by the experiences themselves. I have the power to develop those emotions that are positive, motivating, and help me lead an enjoyable life. I refuse to let others upset me. I take the credit for creating my place in the world.'

6. *Irrational beliefs*: 'If some aspect of my life is threatening, difficult or too challenging, I should worry about it; worrying about the threat may help ward it off.'

Rational beliefs: 'If something is or may be threatening I had better face it and try to render it unthreatening. If that is impossible I will focus on other things and stop telling myself what a terrible situation I am in. Worrying about a threatening situation will rarely ward it off and often will prevent me effectively counteracting it.'

7. *Irrational beliefs*: 'I need someone stronger than myself on whom to rely when making decisions. I should act cautiously when I have to make decisions or when there is no-one to guide me.'

   Rational beliefs: 'It is better to take the risks of thinking and acting independently if I am to succeed in life. Whilst I am prepared to seek out the advice of others, it is better to stand on my own feet than to depend on others. I accept the fact that in some essential respects I am alone in the world. I can accept help from others when it is needed but in the end I am responsible for my decisions.'

8. *Irrational beliefs*: 'Many difficulties I have in life are due to past experiences and these problems will be with me indefinitely. Because something once strongly affected my life, it will indefinitely affect it. Because society raised me to accept certain traditions, I must always accept them. Because society has done things in a certain way, I have to follow these procedures without deviation.'

   Rational beliefs: 'I can learn from my past experiences but I do not have to be overly attached to or prejudiced by them. Although it is true that, as a result of the past, I may find it difficult to change in some ways, it is irrational to believe that it is impossible for change to occur. Even though I once acted in a particular way, I no longer have to act in that way. I am able to consider and question alternative models of behaviour rather than act in a purely traditional manner.'

9. *Irrational beliefs*: 'It is easier to avoid than to face my responsibilities. The best action is often inaction. I frequently refuse to do unpleasant tasks or to take unpleasant decisions.'

   Rational beliefs: 'The so-called easier way of avoiding problems and decisions is usually the much harder way in the long run and the only way to solve difficult problems is squarely to face them. Inertia and inaction are generally unnecessary and relatively unpleasant. Humans tend to be happiest when they are absorbed in creative pursuits. I am prepared to do unpleasant tasks without complaining or rebelling.'

10. *Irrational beliefs*: 'There is invariably a right solution to human problems and it is terrible and awful if this solution is not found. There is a secret to it all and it is important for people to discover the truth.'

    Rational beliefs: 'We live in a world of probabilities, not certainties, and I can still enjoy life despite this. I do not need certainty, indeed life would be boring if this certainty were available. The challenge of living is to find solutions to difficult problems while recognising that my solutions will be tentative. Even when my solution appears to be the right one, it is only right on this occasion and will probably be modified for new problems. Life, thankfully, is not static. It is dynamic and challenging. I am not a 'true believer'. I do not need guarantees in life. The challenge of life is to live constructively in an uncertain world.'

These ten clusters of beliefs can be reduced for therapeutic purposes to three beliefs by which I sabotage myself: (1) 'shoulds', 'musts' and 'needs' which reflect unreasonable demands on problem solving; (2) 'awfulising' statements which exaggerate the negative consequences of a problem; (3) irrational valuation of myself and others which implies that some people are worthless and should be damned for their behaviour.

The characteristics of irrational thinking include oversimplification, overgeneralisation, exaggeration, illogic. By learning to dispute my irrational beliefs, functional behaviour will follow. In this respect, REBT is an extension of the scientific method to human existence. Humans, for biological and social reasons, tend to think unscientifically about themselves and the world generally. In science I am taught to develop hypotheses, to look for evidence to confirm of falsify my hypotheses, question and challenge them before accepting them as truths. REBT teaches me to question scientifically and to dispute my own unscientific, 'superstitious', self-defeating beliefs. Example:

A. ACTIVATING EXPERIENCE: My partner breaks the news that she is going out with another man and therefore wishes to break off the relationship with me.
B. BELIEF ABOUT THE EXPERIENCE: 'This is awful. Everything happens to me! That rat! She shouldn't be that way. I can't stand the world being so

unfair.' And/or: 'I really must be a worthless man. I'll never find another woman like her. She doesn't want me; therefore no one could possibly want me.'

C. UPSETTING EMOTIONAL CONSEQUENCES: Hostility and/or depression.

D. DISPUTING OF IRRATIONAL IDEAS: 'Why is it awful that I'm not getting what I want? Why shouldn't the world be full of injustices?' and/or 'Where's the evidence that because this woman wants to end our relationship that I am a worthless person; or that I'll never be able to have a really good relationship with someone else, or even that I couldn't be happy alone?'

E. NEW EMOTIONAL CONSEQUENCES: Annoyance: 'It's annoying that she was seeing someone else but it isn't awful or intolerable.' and/or 'Well, we did have a nice relationship, and I'm sorry to see it end, but it did have its problems and now I can go out and find a new friend, or live happily alone.'

Here, in summary, are examples of destructive self-talk and their constructive alternatives:

It is awful	vs	It is unfortunate
I have to/must do	vs	I had better do
I am worthless	vs	I behaved poorly
I can't do	vs	I won't do
It is impossible to	vs	It is difficult to do
It/you made me angry	vs	I made myself angry
Who am I?	vs	What do I want?
I am a failure	vs	I am failing at this task
He/she is crazy	vs	He/she behaves crazily

I hate myself	vs	I don't like some of my actions
I need	vs	I want
I should be rewarded	vs	I have earned this reward
I can't stand failure	vs	I don't like to fail
I will never master this	vs	I have not mastered this yet.

Rational-Emotive-Behaviour therapists offer various techniques to overcome distress: (1) admit to distress; (2) acknowledge that distress is self-created; (3) take risks; (4) adopt a philosophy of adventurous life; (5) adopt a philosophy of uncertainty; (6) don't take life too seriously; (7) use empowering imagery; (8) engage in shame-attacking exercises.

REBT promotes a stoical approach to human thinking, feeling and behaving and encourages me to adopt a critical attitude to my problems by uprooting my irrational, dysfunctional beliefs. But what is the difference between rational and irrational beliefs? According to Ellis, a belief is rational if it is self-promoting and can be supported by empirical evidence; a belief is irrational if it is self-defeating and cannot be supported by evidence. Ellis's insistence on the dogmatic nature of irrational beliefs encourages me to dispute and surrender them, by actively employing the critical method of science, which requires that all beliefs are treated critically, including rational beliefs. If a Rational-Emotive-Behaviour therapist demanded that I accept the truth of rational beliefs, he would extol the very attitude he means to indict. It is therefore important to establish REBT's position on the old problem of the rationality of beliefs because the identification of irrational beliefs presupposes a theory of their rational alternatives. If I adopt an irrational attitude to my new 'rational' beliefs, REBT would be guilty of encouraging a dogmatic, rather than a critical, attitude. So Ellis consistently emphasises the possibility that rational beliefs may be false. Here Ellis follows the philosopher of science, Karl Popper, who argues that it is 'rational' for me to suspend beliefs because all beliefs remain hypotheses to be tested against reality. Ellis's war is waged against those who hold irrational beliefs dogmatically. His critical attitude is consistent with Popper's critical attitude and this is, in turn, inconsistent with those psychologies which elevate irrational thinking to the level of personal truth.

The positive value of argument and critical thinking has been insufficiently stressed by psychologists. But if Ellis's (and Popper's) conjectures are accepted (critically), the argumentative function of language becomes the vehicle for self-development. REBT is one of the few psychotherapies which emphasises and actively promotes a therapeutic style which acknowledges this, and therefore remains within the spirit of the ancient Stoic philosophy.

5

Living Religiously

'Religion: The daughter of Hope and Fear, explaining to Ignorance the nature of the Unknowable.'
(Ambrose Bierce)

This chapter represents a special problem since none of my I's is religious. The words of the gods have fallen on deaf I's and so the tone of this chapter is less personal. One of my I's is, however, interested in and amused by magic which is a good place to start a discussion on religion.

How does religion differ from magic? This question poses special problems because if I fasten my attention on the behaviour of the practitioner alone, religion and magic are indistinguishable. The difference, therefore, turns on ascertaining something about the beliefs of the practitioner. If the practitioner believes he is establishing a relationship with supernatural beings, then he is practising religion. If he believes he is controlling some aspect of the universe by a series of acts, then he is performing magic. But this second definition allows the term 'magic' to cover all operations performed on the natural world and having real effects – e.g. the navigation of a ship, turning water into wine or bending spoons. These activities form a part of our scientific command of the world, but are not examples of magic, even though they may seem magical to the preliterate when they first encounter them. Consequently, this distinction between religion and magic forces a further distinction between magic and science. Both of these depend on perceptions of cause and effect and on the belief that it is possible to manipulate causes in order to produce effects, but they should not be regarded in the same light.

Both magician and scientist must demonstrate their mastery of causes by producing effects on demand. The magician gives ocular proof of his being seized by demons when he falls into a fit, and proof of his powers by drawing a stone from the body of his victim, who sometimes recovers. This evidence will be accepted by some observers, rejected by others. The scientist gives a similar style of proof of his powers. He produces tangible effects by the manipulation of causes, but differs from the magician in limiting his claims to what can be done in principle by anybody. In religion, the priest claims to communicate with supernatural beings to whom the whole cause-effect system is subordinate. These beings can manipulate causes in ways which are beyond human ken, or can reverse or suspend the normal cause-effect sequence. This claim cannot be submitted to the same kind of empirical tests as apply to magic and science, because it is essentially a claim that cause-and-effect does not account for everything. It is a denial of universal determinism, and the only pertinent test would require us to show that determinism is universal. The hypothesis of universal determinism is widely held (on logical grounds) to be unprovable, and if it is indeed so, no refutation of the religious claim will ever succeed.

In religious activity the claim of contact with the supernatural is always open to challenge because it is never susceptible to proof in the usual empirical way. Max Weber cites this fact to explain why the priesthood is not the ruling class in society, as it would be if it could demonstrate irrefutably that it had assured access to the panoramic intelligence and omnipotence attributed to supernatural beings.

The notion that science could supersede religion was argued by Sir James Frazer, who in his 1932 classic *The Golden Bough: A Study in Magic and Religion* put forward his own theory of the origins of religion. Magic comes first. It requires only the assumption that there exist laws governing the world, and this assumption can readily be generated from the ordinary perception of cause and effect. Since there are such causal relationships, the magician who knows them can control events. What the magician is doing is analogous to what everybody does in the ordinary course of living. The magician is simply held to have more knowledge than others. Despite this confidence, magic is subject to repeated failure because the particular causal connections assumed are, in fact, invalid, and gradually it becomes evident that there exist in the world powerful forces over which man has no control. When this occurs and man recognises his own impotence he becomes capable of awe, and it is then that true religion begins to appear. Religion is, by this account, much more complex psychologically than is magic or science because it involves more than just the assumption that the world is governed by causal-type laws.

Frazer's view of religion matches well with the distinctions proposed between magic, science and religion. But Frazer's suggestion that religion will eventually be replaced by science no longer seems plausible, for with greater experience of science we have realised that it is concerned exclusively with extending our technological power, and not at all with helping us decide how this power shall be used. In fact a strong counter-argument can be put against Frazer's suggestion, to the effect that scientific progress makes moral progress more important then ever in human destiny. Furthermore, we like to think science places the individual in a position to control society, whereas some, if not most, religions place the individual in a subservient position.

Ancient Judaism is the prototype of all Western religious creeds that place man in a subservient position as regards society. The main lines of the creed are simple enough. It declares that there is one God, this God having a special covenant with the group. This covenant requires that the group should obey certain commandments – made known by God to one of the prophets – in return for his favour. The individual's relationship with the group is therefore governed by the much closer relationship between the group and God. God is omniscient, all powerful and jealous that the law be kept. Transgression of the law means that the group will suffer, for God punishes evil.

Parallel with this ideology is a model of man which is dovetailed into it nicely. I am made of spirit, soul and body. Spirit is what permits the consciousness of God, so prophets have more of this than lesser men, like me. Soul is that which permits self-conscious life, especially the consciousness of good and evil. This consciousness of moral values is rationalised in the myth of the Fall, when man eats of the fruit of the Tree of Knowledge – an obvious metaphor for becoming aware of good and evil – and so against God's original wish, ceases to be innocent. Thereafter I am compelled to know about values, and can no longer pursue what I find desirable without some regard for the effect my actions may have beyond the immediate gratification of my appetites. I must be aware that my actions can have worthy or unworthy results, and be responsible for them. The third part of me is body, which is comparatively unimportant except that it is the seat of the appetites, and these might lead me astray if blindly pursued.

Spirit and soul are attributes which set me apart from all other animals. Animals cannot have souls because they cannot take the step of defying God as implied in the myth of the Fall; they remain innocent about the worth of the effects they produce. Not so me, who must struggle between good and evil. Lucky animals!

At first sight this leaves it entirely up to me to make my own judgements about what is good and evil. By asserting the knowledge of good and evil the legend of the Fall appears to place on me a formidable responsibility – that of making all my own value judgements in a world lacking rules. It is therefore desirable that this responsibility should be circumscribed, the problem ameliorated and reduced to manageable proportions by the provision of general rules for conduct. These general rules are the Ten Commandments. So far as these sacred rules apply there is a strict obligation to renounce personal judgement – this is why they are called the Ten Commandments and not the Ten Suggestions.

God is, of course, for good and against evil. What is evil is defined in the manner of case law in the religious writings with the Commandments as a base line. What is defined as good is directly related in a practical way to the advancement of an ordered society, specifically the society of the Chosen People – but potentially applicable to any social group. What is evil appears to be that which is likely to lead to disruption, destruction and a failure to expand the race. The aim was to establish social cohesion as a basis for the development of social power, the power itself being necessary to resist oppression by other powerful groups. The maintenance of social cohesion, however, also requires that certain kinds of behaviour likely to stimulate internal conflict be discouraged. It is behaviour of this kind which is specifically named and proscribed by the Ten Commandments.

Prophets continued working on this religion for thousands of years. But there are two problems which it fails to meet. The most obvious one arises because a very general set of rules like the Ten Commandments does not cover all the disputes that arise. Those who worked from this perspective elaborated the system of rules until it applied to even the minutiae of behaviour, such as what to eat and how to dress. In justification of this appeared the belief that a complete code of laws was attainable, such as would promote complete social harmony. The rise of doctrinaire groups (e.g. the Sadducees and the Pharisees), for whom the ideal was meticulous regulation by sacred law, was one aspect of that development. Law therefore retained its religious flavour, with little distinction between sacred and secular rules and became even more restrictive. Society remained closely identified with God and the constraints on the individual tended to become more precise and numerous.

The second problem lay in the position of the person regarding retributive justice. Because the system employed the tribal notion of blood brotherhood and common responsibility, punishment for transgressions might be visited on one person even though the offence was committed by others of whom the sufferer knew nothing. Protest about this begins to be heard in the later books of the *Old Testament* with Job being the most vocal in claiming that he did not deserve his boils. He seeks a representative for the person in the courts of the Lord, where up till then only the voice of the group had been heard.

The hard-won solidarity of the group depended on this special relationship between God and the group. To allow the person to go directly to God with his troubles would be to risk social disintegration. Not only that, but it would impugn the authority of the priestly profession by allowing the person to go over its head to the supreme authority. The prophets therefore had no solution to Job's dilemma. They remain silent for the five centuries preceding Jesus. The Christian outbreak, in which God is declared to be an individual, and chooses to reveal himself to men as such, is the most poignant expression of the dilemma and its most radical answer.

Among those creeds which assert the independent existence of the person, Christianity has had a dominant place in Western culture. It arose as a reaction to an emphasis on the importance of the group, which was not only a central characteristic of Judaism, but also a feature of the ethos of Rome. In these two systems, although the idea of the person might be said to have a place, that place made him definitely subordinate to the social group. The interests of the group were paramount, and if serving them meant submission to laws which intruded upon personal autonomy, this was not a sufficient reason for questioning them. The interests of the group took absolute precedence over any right to independence of the person. Both groups assumed what amounted to an absolute right to punish the erring or non-conforming member, and reduced members of all out-groups to an inferior status, indicated by the use of a single category with perjorative overtones – barbarian in the Roman case, Gentile in the Jewish case – to cover anybody not of the in-group. From the perspective of the in-group members these others are not of fully human status.

In ancient Jewry the right to punish the transgressor was religiously based and stemmed from the covenant by which God gave his approval to the society on condition that certain laws were obeyed. Social sanctions, then, had divine warrant in that they supported divine statements of law. There was one God only, so that no disputation was possible. The law had to be obeyed.

Christianity contains a radical re-assessment of the nature of God, since it places great emphasis on a particular aspect of his nature – mercy, and the readiness to forgive. This had been canvassed from time to time by the prophets, but not fully incorporated into active doctrine. The change forced into prominence a difficult element of complexity in God's nature in the sense that he became both merciful and punitive at once. Consistent with this, the new doctrine asserted that I am not finally damned so long as I am repentant and desire reform. Repentance and rehabilitation take their place alongside retribution as ways of promoting rectitude, and the force of the demand that I must conform totally to the institutionalised ethics of the day is slackened. The same creed revealed a new aspect of the question of personal responsibility by asserting that I can choose whether to be redeemed or damned. This assertion finally stamped Christianity as a revolutionary notion for it stripped from society the divine warrant to damn the transgressor. Punishment would have the divine approval only if those at whom it was directed were unrepentant. Since both Jewish and Roman society had been working towards a totally law-bound life and a rigid application of the law, Christianity was disruptive. It allowed the individual to criticise the social order without denying God (providing his intentions were good), and even if crucified for his trouble, he died virtuous.

Christianity is credited with having had a much more powerful solvent effect on Rome than on Judaism itself, which it left largely intact. Rome was a society openly organised to generate and exert power on its neighbours and saw the extension of civil order as the justification for forceful subjection of the barbarians. It also greatly relied on the use of power to maintain internal order. Its best known response to the heretical and non-conforming

Christians in its midst was to destroy them by force, hoping thus to do away with their ideas. But to destroy an unresisting person for his beliefs is to martyr him, and martyrdom is the ultimate kind of evidence for the claim that the person can preserve his autonomy against all odds. This is to provide the most convincing support for the idea on which the Christian creed was based.

Roman law was avowedly secular, its administration bureaucratic, its religion polytheistic, and it was concerned with the extension of civil law to a wide variety of colonised peoples. These are some reasons why Roman culture was one under which demands for justice to the person might have had more effect than under Judaism, where the foundation for authority and social cohesion was moral and religious; rooted in monotheism and a sacred pact between God and the group. In any event, it is a historical fact that Christian divines eventually reached a position from which they were able to criticise the Emperors of Rome and have those criticism attended to. This is to objectify the principle that the exercise of power is subject to moral direction.

A convenient place to begin a potted history of the rise of Christian authority is that era when Christianity, with its main body of adherents in Rome, found itself cut off from Judaism as a result of the sacking of Jerusalem by the Romans. Christianity's spirit was then individualistic, its political stance anarchistic, and its authority charismatic. Movements of this kind, lacking a stable structure of rules, seldom endure for long. They tend to perish when the special insights on which they are based become realised or superseded, and the zeal of the followers fades. But

Christianity must have been a special case, for its central problem – the question of the rights of the individual over against what is due by the individual to the group – is not resolvable in any final way. Perhaps, because of this, Christianity was able to continue as a radical movement long enough for an institutional form to be worked out to embody its problem.

Not until Augustine (354–430) did the main lines of the institution of Christianity emerge. The fundamental problem for the movement was how the notion of individual could be held to apply to everybody without putting everyone in the position of being able to deny that he owed anything to any group whatever. To endorse that kind of denial would be to destroy the possibility of social organisation altogether, for any form of social organisation requires the sacrifice of individual whims in the interests of regular cooperation.

The solution was to emphasise the hypothetical construct of I-conscience. This brings into prominence the process of evaluation of 'I', a process which can be made more objective if a fixed standard is provided by a social agency – the Church – through its representatives who undertook to supply this standard, using the personal characteristics of its founder as both model and warrant. At this point, then, the person is seen as being divided into I-conscience (self-evaluative side), and the actor (executive side). The background is, of course, original sin.

In accordance with this model of the person Augustine proposed a theory of authority. This is contained in his *City of God* where he describes two cities, the heavenly and the earthly, these being metaphors for the Church and the

State. Men, he claims, owe allegiance and obedience to both, but the Church or Heavenly City, always takes precedence over the State or Earthly City. The functions of the State take the instrumental form – it is the executor. Its actions are directed at the achievement, in the mundane sphere, of the aims for humanity formulated in the sacred sphere of the Church. The State is therefore the Church's instrument, and the most important of its functions is to suppress those kinds of behaviour declared morally objectionable by the Church.

According to this arrangement the Church could pronounce, through its representatives, on the worthiness of the actions of anybody, including the most powerful temporal rulers. Augustine himself did not hesitate to rebuke the Emperor of Rome when that worthy trans-gressed, and moreover had his rebuke heeded. All rulers also had the spiritual duty of ensuring that their followers obeyed the injunctions of the Church.

Immanent in this theory is a distinction between authority and power which was carried into the real world – to make it objective in the manner of a self-fulfilling prophecy – by allocating all power to the temporal rulers but making this power subject to moral direction. Many philosophers, including Bertrand Russell, see the working out of this theory to be deeply implicated in European social history. There is, of course, a flaw in it. If it should happen that the practical desires of the temporal ruler run counter to what the Church declares to be moral, conflict appears. The temporal ruler, having at his command considerable power, may choose to achieve his desires at the cost of severe disagreement with the Church. The consequences of such defiance are spiritual and certain – but in the after-life. That is, the form of control available to the Church in the present, although it takes the objective form of persuasion or threat, is ultimately psychological. Real disputes of this kind between princes and popes were common enough. They provide an exact parallel for the struggle which is said to take place internally when a person's desires conflict with his conscience.

The authority of the Church never went unchallenged for any length of time. Powerful princes were always at loggerheads with popes. And because of the particular distribution of authority this reacted continually on the individual. There were always two formidable claimants for his allegiance. Every time there was a disagreement between pope and prince, the vassals of the prince had a choice forced upon them. This struggle between Church and State remained an underlying feature of the society for 900 years and during that time was always breaking out into the open. Such competition for the loyalty of the individual, covering so many successive generations, could not help but confirm his importance and establish his freedom.

Change came to the theory because of a complex chain of circumstances. The fall of Constantinople resulted in numbers of scholars taking refuge in Italy and bringing with them knowledge of classical Greek thought – views on philosophy and mathematics which had not until then been much considered in Christian teaching – in particular the thought of Aristotle. This material found its way into the educational institutions of Christendom – all

Church sponsored – and so became accessible to the educated minority who were almost exclusively churchmen. Aristotelian thought acted as a leaven in this milieu. The scientific strain in Greek thought made it possible to perceive nature as something which might work on principles quite independent of humankind – cause and effect for example.

The scholar-priest Thomas Aquinas (1225–1274) set about re-working Christian social theory to incorporate the Aristotelian notion of the State. Aristotle believed that men were social animals with potentialities that could only be brought to fruition and expressed in social interaction, which implies common interests. Aquinas saw that authority which concerned itself with practical affairs was necessary if these common interests were to be served. Therefore the problem was to devise a form of government and establish a form of authority devoted to such practical affairs. Aquinas separated secular and ecclesiastical authority, providing each with its own separate hierarchy except that the Pope held the apex of both. This came to be known as 'the medieval synthesis'.

The 13th Century saw the emergence of autonomous nation states in Europe, some with organised bureaucracies exercising control over local affairs, centralised administrations for law and finance, more systematic taxation, and paid armies. A trend appeared in which authority over and responsibility for practical affairs outside the spiritual realm began to be assumed by local rulers.

Also during the 12th and 13th Centuries Europe

produced inventions based on the dawning perception of cause and effect in nature. Europe was moving, or rather stumbling, towards awareness of the potentialities which lie in material. The demand for such inventions as clocks and compasses gave rise to the great craft guilds of the Middle Ages. Many of them fitted quite neatly into the task of fulfilling the community's material needs which Aquinas's theory assigned to the local leaders, because they increased the power to meet such needs. They were what we would call today capital equipment. But they were capital of a different kind from most of what had previously been regarded in that light, which was land, for they were man-made.

Such historical developments are ponderous, especially at a time when communication over distances is poor. The fact remains that there were appearing in Europe a number of novelties, both in ways of thinking and in material goods, and these were setting the stage for the Reformation, the scientific revolution and eventually the Industrial Revolution. Some of these items were material: the introduction of gunpowder; the invention of the printing press; the devices for navigation; a host of items of capital which could be made, and therefore which could be had without robbing others. Others were ideas, some of which were intimately related to the material objects, and some being relatively independent of material conditions because they sprang from a new way of looking at the world.

Throughout the Dark Ages (500–1200) Christianity emphasised the importance of the conscience, which requires the practice of regular I-examination which, in turn, implies the possibility of insight and of personal responsibility. The conscience model allowed Christians to differentiate humans from the rest of nature since 'examining one's I-conscience' entails that one can distinguish between events which would not have happened if one had not acted as one did, and those events which would have happened anyway, and one can scarcely imagine any other form of life having such an ability. Furthermore, any examination of I-conscience draws attention to the fact that many events occur regardless of the wills of men. As Aristotle had noted long ago, the causes of many deplorable events lie outside the individual. So if such deplorable events, as say poverty, persist in occurring, and blame cannot be sheeted home to the activities of any individual, then it is not possible to prevent them by moral authority being applied to individuals. The logical conclusion is that if every action by every person were well intentioned and morally unobjectionable, events damaging to humanity would not be eliminated. So a world of morally good action does not produce a world good for all. This was the weak spot in the medieval parallel between the individual and moral authority. It remains so for all moral codes.

The many strands in the Reformation make it a complex social phenomenon, but they all rest on the common feature of challenge to the Catholic Church's claim to authority. The Protestant Reformation was, in effect, an attack on the 'middle man'. Martin Luther (1483–1546) nailed his 95 theses to the church door in 1517, putting forward the proposition that the individual could generate I-conscience in consultation with God through the scriptures, God being the only supreme authority. Since what God had said on the matter could be read in the *Bible*, no priest was necessary as intermediary. Once it is accepted that God is the only entity to which all human beings are of absolute value, then reliance can be placed on him for directions as to how one might behave. No college of cardinals, no human group, no matter how select or how superior the reasoning powers of its members, could possibly know better than God what was best for humanity.

This kind of argument has a highly solvent effect upon the readiness of the less privileged to accept the direction of their spiritual and temporal masters. It freed the I-conscience by invalidating the scale of religious values from which the establishment derived its legitimacy. Consequently, it released a storm of anarchism in Europe and there followed a series of bloody conflicts between rebellious peasants and established powers, and when the former were put down Luther, who did not support the peasants, came close to being executed. This might be seen as history's prompt reply to Luther's claim that men could be trusted to generate their own I-consciences in direct consultation with God's word. It implied that men had better have a cultivated I-conscience, no matter who did the inculcating. Anarchistic individualism simply led to disaster. The Peasants' Revolt disappointed and disillusioned Luther because it made nonsense of his fundamental contention.

The Lutheran movement looks very like a case in which an idea led directly to dramatic social changes. But the printing press had been invented nearly a century earlier, and without the prospect of mass circulation of the *Bible* which this invention made possible, Luther's thesis would have lacked feasibility.

Some twenty years after Luther there appeared a maniacal reformer of a different kind. This was John Calvin (1509–1564), whose I-confidence was such that he had little hesitation in interpreting the will of God to men, and whose authoritarian intellect produced an influential psychological doctrine. According to Calvin: (1) I am by nature depraved, and no amount of I-cultivation will make me any more acceptable to God; so also is the world depraved, but changing this is possible. (2) Unceasing effort and moral rigour are necessary to change the world and this cannot wait until a rational plan is worked out to reach ultimate ends. Indeed such ultimate ends, while they are within God's purview, are certainly not within mine. Therefore lack of knowledge of what might characterise an ideal world in God's eyes is no excuse for idleness. I must act. Those actions which contribute to the realisation of God's plan will be successful, all others will fail. Success is simply an indication that I am working along lines approved by God. (3) I am predestined – elect or not-elect – from the moment of birth. This is God's choice and nothing I can do will change it. (4) Human choice is an illusion. Everything works according to laws instituted by God and no choices made by me will affect the spiritual outcome for me, nor will they have any effect on these laws. The choices I believe I make could not possibly affect God's plan.

Armed with this malignant doctrine, Calvin had an interesting career as a reformer. When he first developed his heretical ideas and his opposition to the authority of the Pope, he was a law student in Paris. He took himself off to Geneva, then the sin city of Europe, as offering a safer habitat, but his reforming zeal soon proved too much for the city fathers and he was invited to leave, which he did. A few years later, however, he was invited back and promptly set about cleaning the city up. He established the notorious Council of Geneva, with himself at its head, and through it became a dictator. During his rule he suppressed all frivolous activities like sport, dancing and gambling, everything in fact which took time from labour or religious worship, instituted domestic policies to ensure that private homes were kept free of such abominations as Catholic icons, tortured and murdered anyone who expressed any form of respect for the Pope, established the principle of universal education so that everyone might be able to read the *Bible*, and set modern democracy in motion – although it doesn't look in the least like what we think of democracy now. Martin Sevetus, who made some of the first discoveries about the circulation of the blood was one of the victims who was hanged, drawn and quartered for entertaining ideas not satisfactorily anti-Catholic.

Calvin's primary support came from the wealthier stratum of society – the merchants and guild-masters, for whom a population devoted to labour was preferable to one devoted to carefree enjoyment of life. There was also the question of money-lending, a matter of concern to wealthy goldsmiths. Its condemnation by the Catholic Church as usury made it a monopoly of Jews – except for the inevitable black market – and it was this that enabled them to survive and flourish better in Europe than elsewhere, despite being defined as moral outcasts. Calvinism removed the embargo on money-lending for its followers and so enabled them to compete with the Jews in a very lucrative occupation.

Not all the strains of thought in Puritanism as it spread over Europe emanated directly from Luther and Calvin, both of whom pre-date the major scientific discoveries of their time. Copernicus's hypothesis of the heliocentric universe appeared in 1543, but it was published post-humously, so he was certainly working on it at the same time as the reformers were busy. Then came Galileo, Kepler and others, who step by step demonstrated the consequences of abandoning the anthropocentric view of the world and substituting a deterministic view based on the notion that every observable effect had a cause; that nature, because it worked on this underlying principle was above all orderly and its order could be discovered.

The scientific temperament and the Puritan outlook agreed closely on the question of order. Order in nature and the denial of free-will to man led many Puritan divines to preach that the whole of God's creation worked on absolute determinism. The world was to be seen as wholly controlled by laws whose author was God. It was man's proper aspiration to discover these laws, for knowledge of them would not only be knowledge of God but would enable men to understand more clearly how they might work in accord with him. This intimate connection between God and order became so completely accepted that system, rationality, accountability, orderliness, logicality, became Puritan criteria against which anything could be judged for its worthiness.

What the Puritan apologists had in mind was not reason or rationality as these terms are applied to action, for in that context they imply free-will and human choice. Their attention was fixed upon certain kinds of order which present a compelling appearance of being beyond human intervention. Systems such as logic and mathematics and, later, Newtonian mechanics assume an absolute quality because they are independent of human values, purposes and emotions and seem to exist on a plane which places them beyond the influence of the human act. In this light it is not difficult to understand that the Puritans should regard them as partaking of a divine certainty against which the more subjective grounds on which ordinary human judgements were made could be seen as at best flimsy and at worst frivolous. It is an attitude consistent with the solemn search for a general order underlying the flux of experience. The deep concern with order was no passing phase. As late as the 19th Century the belief was widespread that the world was governed by unbreakable Laws of Nature. This idea is not entirely done with even in our day.

Modern psychology has inherited from the emphasis on order and science over these centuries a commitment to the belief that the real nature of the person is to be described only in terms compatible with science – in mathematical or mechanical terms which detour around the problem of free-will and choice. All personality theories testify to this. It is significant that many of the foundations of scientific psychology are compatible with a number of the trends of Puritan thought – notably absence of free-will – which leads to the derogation of subjective experience in favour of using standards of measurement derived from physics, investigation of public behaviour rather than private worlds, an attitude which treats people as reactive rather than active. Scientific psychology is predominantly a product of Protestant cultures, so the connection is doubtless not imaginary.

Max Weber's essay *The Protestant Ethic and the Spirit of Capitalism*, first published in 1904–5, maintains that Calvinism and the other Puritan sects set up the psychological conditions which account for the appearance in the West of a unique form of capitalism, and also for the accumulation of a uniquely successful body of scientific knowledge. Both capitalism and science have existed elsewhere and at other times, but never with the emphasis on the rational which is the legacy of extreme Puritan asceticism.

The influential creeds contained in Puritanism were those which defined the ideal of the *calling*. Of this Weber says that the Protestant literature is saturated with the idea that faithful labour on the part of those for whom life offers no other opportunities is highly pleasing to God. Also it legalised the exploitation of this willingness to work, in that it also interpreted the employer's business activity as a *calling*.

Asceticism as preached by the Puritans was a reforming doctrine. It was a continuation of the struggle within a monasticism against the secularising influence of wealth, which was seen as the root-cause of corruption in the Church. So it was directed at the salvation of souls and rested on the principle that anything which diverted men from the ordered life of the saint was anathema. Sport was obnoxious and could be tolerated only if shown to be necessary for physical recreation – certainly never on Sundays. So was the theatre, nudity, eroticism, much literature and art, idle talk, conspicuous consumption and all activities which implied lack of rational purpose. Simple enjoyment of what life had to offer was debilitating and destructive, and enjoyment of wealth was condemned.

These attitudes were at the time anti-authoritarian since they brought the Puritan sects into conflict with traditional authority residing in aristocratic elites. But they gave an ethical foundation not previously known to the rational uses of wealth, i.e. for the needs of the individual and the community over the 'glitter and ostentation of feudal magnificence'. Since feudalism rested on an unsound economic base, the Puritans set the solid comfort of the middle-class home as an ideal. They also gave an ethical basis for the acquisition of wealth so long as this was acquired and used for purposes other than one's own enjoyment.

Wealth itself was nevertheless a temptation and pursuit of riches for their own sake was not approved. Neither were dishonesty and avarice. Restless, continuous systematic work in a *calling* was defined as the highest means to asceticism and the most undeniable proof of genuine faith.

The psychological restraints which previously existed against the acquisition of wealth were removed, but new restraints on its consumption imposed. The latter made it available (as savings) for productive reinvestment. Weber notes that in Holland, dominated by strict Calvinism for only seven years, the tendency to accumulation remained extremely high thereafter. No doubt the fact that Calvinism provided an ethical basis for charging interest on loans helped to foster this continuing enthusiasm.

The contradiction in a life devoted to acquiring what cannot be enjoyed is not easily resolved and all the Puritan divines have been troubled by it. Weber sees the secularising influence of wealth as the process to which all forms of asceticism are opposed, and notes John Wesley's foreboding about the self-defeating possibilities of ascetic religion. Wesley's recommendation was that the Methodists should give away their wealth so as to grow in grace and lay up treasure in heaven, but the solution is not only contrary to the Protestant Ethic, it is impossible since major capital installations cannot be divided.

It seems evident that if the ascetic attitude to life is to stand the test of this otherwise pointless exercise of effort, there must exist a profound belief in one's religious destiny. The Reformation was therefore very much the individualism of its time, levering against the psychological sway of the traditional authorities of society, church, state and aristocracy, using as its lever the very concern with one's 'I' that had been inculcated by the Catholic tradition over the long period of its ascendancy. In their place, however, arose the legal-rational authority of capitalism and its associated bureaucracy.

Weber's 'new capitalism' includes the rational organisation of formally free labour under regular discipline, attunement of work and production to a regular market, the separation of business from the household (including legal separation of corporate from personal property) and a rational system of book-keeping. All these are supported by the development of a rational structure of law and administration. Capitalism is then a form of social organisation based on the allocation of fixed duties to hierarchically arranged positions. The duties are fixed through the introduction of general rules, often written regulations. Since this applies not only to the separate institutions of the State but to the State itself (in which the general rules take the form of laws), a high degree of concord can be developed between the State and its constituent institutions, although the extent to which every institution is forced to conform to the requirements of the centralised authority vary. The latitude for such variation is great – as between, say, the extreme of a fascist or communist system on the one hand and the high degree of local autonomy practised in English democracy on the other.

The formal authority to give orders includes rules delimiting the coercive means at the disposal of officials. Only persons who have appropriate qualifications are employed. The hierarchy generates an ordered system of super- and subordination in which there is a supervisor for every office (except the highest). Ideally the governed have the right of appealing against the decision of any office-holder to a higher authority.

Weber is quite explicit that bureaucracy is a machine and that it is an instrument in which people are merely functionaries. This impersonal character means that the mechanism will readily work for anyone who knows how to gain control over it. A rationally ordered system of officials continues to function smoothly after the enemy has occupied the citadel, this being clearly exemplified every time a political party is turned out of office and one with different aims takes over control of the same public bureaucracy.

This system distributes authority by specifying the powers to be exercised by the person occupying each organisational position. This authority is attached to the position rather than to persons. When such an organisation is fully developed and operating correctly there is little to suggest a distinction between power and authority, for it is difficult for any person to exercise forms of power which are not authorised or to fail to exercise those powers which the rules require him to. The ordered system of super- and subordination together with record-keeping and a scientifically-based new technology, give the 'new capitalism' its distinctive bureaucratic character – all developing through the impulse towards a rationalisation of action originally set in motion by religious propaganda but later becoming self-supportive through its material success.

The form of authority that operates in this system differs from earlier types because it is attached to a position, not a person, so it is the position which claims the greater stability and importance. It gains this character because its functions are considered essential to the production of some material or service. There could, of course, be much argument about the desirability of producing this or that item, but the Protestant Ethic prevented any debate on the matter by asserting that the value of anything was not to be ascertained by men and so no argument about the desirability of anything can be conclusive. Consequently, everyone is relieved of any obligation to show that the organisation serves such abstract purposes as contributing to human welfare. If there is something rather odd in a conscience which acknowledges the positional rather than the personal, it is nevertheless effective.

Material goods, however, are forms of socially generated labour power, as Marx would say. A host of separate organisations engaged in producing different kinds of such power was a result of this transformation, and it was upon these institutions that the power of the modern state was built. The legal systems were therefore modified to protect and promote the power-generating institutions, and this endorsement meant that a large part of the moral responsibility for what they did devolved on the State. The State took on the mantle of moral authority which had once been the exclusive province of the Church; in the modern nation state which developed from the Puritan principles, the State not only adopted the modern form of democracy but retained its authority over the major instruments of power.

Weber reduced authority to three 'ideal-types', the *Charismatic*, the *Traditional* and the *Legal-Rational*. Charismatic authority is directed wholly at a person, usually one who offers a solution to some recalcitrant problem, and the solution offered is usually of a kind which both defines the problem more clearly and gives the impression that the person offering it holds the key to understanding the central problems of existence. Charismatics are almost always assassinated. Traditional authority is well represented in the feudal system where position and person were usually connected by birth and there was a certain element of paternalism expected, so that the welfare of the inferior depended on the personal favour of the superior. Here the inferior's estimate of the superior as a person could intrude on what was due to his position. Legal-rational authority, in contrast, eliminates the personal and much of the uncertainty that goes with it and concentrates directly on whether a certain task gets fulfilled.

The great social change set in motion by the Reformation was a rise to prominence of legal-rational authority over the traditional type which characterised the feudal system. In terms of my earlier comparison between the Augustinian theory and Aquinas's amendment, the Reformation sees the transfer, not only of secular authority to the temporal rulers, but of spiritual authority as well, for monarchs and constitutional governments become 'spiritual leaders' of their nations. Since this spiritual authority focuses the national interest it is not surprising to note that wars between nations appear as one of its concomitants.

Weber's thesis has been attacked on several grounds, the least effective being that capitalism pre-existed the Reformation in various times and in many places. Weber never denied this, simply maintaining that the way it developed after the Reformation was quite different from anything that went before. It has also been attacked on the grounds that the Protestant Ethic was itself merely a by-product of the changes in modes of production which had already commenced before the Ethic appeared – a criticism inspired by Marxist thought. And it has also been criticised on the grounds that both economic changes and the new ideas were intertwined and mutually reinforcing in bringing about the changes in organisation. I need not defend Weber against these charges for they can be admitted without disturbing the core of his thesis.

Weber's argument claims that Puritan propaganda, directed at people's moral susceptibilities, was able to spread the conviction that the capitalist was steward for profit, not its consumer, and that the worker could and should work hard and produce as much profit as possible with confidence that it would not be wasted but would go to enrich everybody. This doctrine was effective because: (1) people were already anxious about their spiritual destiny owing to the long development of individualism under Catholicism; (2) it was already seen to be possible to create new forms of capital. This meant that capital could be acquired without robbing anyone who already possessed it. Had this not been the case, the only way of acquiring capital would have been through theft, and it would not have been feasible to claim that one could get rich without immorality; and (3) the call for faith in the stewardship of the capitalist has some rational grounds in that real capital is of a kind which does not lend itself to personal consumption by its owner. Its usefulness depends on its function in increasing the production of consumable goods, and these consumables must find their way into the possession of consumers.

Weber's thesis does not claim that modern European capitalism was caused by the Protestant Ethic, but that its particular form was promoted by it. Weber saw individual action as directed by conscious decisions and if this perspective is accepted it is impossible that capitalism could have developed so strongly without the willing support of those concerned. Yet it was clearly not a planned invention. It was what Weber calls an 'unintended event' arising from the combined effect of the activities of a large number of people whose actions were actually planned to save their souls.

6

Living Politically

*'We are much beholden to Machiavelli and others, that
write what men do, and not what they ought to do.'*

(Francis Bacon)

Shakespeare called him 'the murderous Machiavel' and
Edmund Burke claimed to discern 'the odious maxims
of a Machiavellian policy' underlying the tyranny of the
French Revolution. The Catholic Church banned his
books and his name is still associated with murder, deceit
and vicious cunning in political affairs. His name is
Niccolo Machiavelli and he lived from 1469 to 1527 –
through the period known as the high Renaissance.
Indeed the year of his death is also the year the Renaissance ends with the sacking of Rome by the Lutherans
under the command of Charles V.

The Renaissance was a time of revival of art, letters and
learning in Europe and marks the beginning of the transition from the medieval to the modern world. The era
of Leonardo da Vinci, Michelangelo and Raphael was
characterised by a willingness to entertain the great pagan
virtues and contrast them with Christian virtues. From
Paul to Augustine the history of Christianity is the history

of the widening gap between two worlds – Church and State; this world and the next; Pope and Emperor; city of God and earthly city. The *Sermon on the Mount* makes it clear that it is the meek and the mild who shall inherit the earth – the powerful are ignoble. Christian virtue emphasises humility, compassion and brotherly love. Pagan virtue, on the other hand, emphasises courage, vigour, manliness, strength, fortitude in adversity, discipline and power. Can these moralities be harmonised in the world of politics? Are Christian values compatible with political leadership?

Never one to follow the dictates of convention, Bertrand Russell in his *History of Western Philosophy* noted that many people are shocked by Machiavelli, and he certainly is shocking. But many others would be equally so if they were equally free from hypocrisy. Machiavelli's political philosophy is scientific, based upon his own experience of affairs and his close reading of the pagan classics, concerned to calculate the means to political ends, regardless of the question whether the ends are to be considered good or bad. Much of the evil that attaches to him is due to the indignation of hypocrites who hate the frank admission of evil-doing. Whilst agreeing with Russell that Machiavelli is free from hypocrisy, I believe that Russell's view of Machiavelli as a scientist is mistaken. Maurizio Viroli is closer to the mark when he argues that Machiavelli was not a founder of political science but the restorer of the Roman conception of politics as civil wisdom. Machiavelli retrieved and refined the conception of political theory as a rhetorical practice. He was a narrator and, above all, an orator. He wrote as a noble rhetorician to persuade others of the importance of the ancient political principles they had forgotten. He regarded political life as an exercise in the power of eloquence to be set alongside the power of arms. He was an avid republican and was committed to the rule of law. To be free a person must not be dependent on the will of others. It is the rule of law that underpins political liberty.

Machiavelli was the son of a lawyer and was educated in the *studia humanitatis* – the humanistic studies – which meant that he had to prepare for a career in public service by studying the (pagan) classics, Latin, rhetoric, diplomacy, ancient history and moral philosophy. In 1498 he was catapulted from relative obscurity to the post of Second Chancellor of the Florentine Republic, reporting to the Council of War. After a disastrous diplomatic mission to France he wrote of the folly of procrastinating and the danger of appearing irresolute. He called for bold and rapid actions on the part of rulers. He cites as examples the Holy Roman Emperor, Maximilian, who was 'weak, too lax and credulous and too influenced by every different opinion put to him.' On the other hand, he observed and admired Cesare Borgia: 'The Duke is superhuman in courage who thinks himself capable of attaining anything he wants. He controls everything himself, governs with extreme secrecy and is therefore able to execute his plans with devastating suddenness'. Borgia taught Machiavelli that men must be won over or destroyed.

In 1512 Machiavelli was dismissed from office by the Medicis, falsely implicated in a plot against the new rulers, tortured and effectively exiled to his farm on the outskirts of Florence. He decided to spend his enforced leisure writing. He completed *The Prince* in 1513 although it was not published in his lifetime. He also wrote *The Discourses on Livy*, *The Art of War*, two plays (*La Mandragola* and *Clizia*) and a *History of Florence*.

The Discourses contains a theory for the conditions for Republican rule based on the Roman model. Machiavelli follows Aristotle in the belief that the three forms of government – monarchy, aristocracy and democracy – have irresistible tendencies to become, respectively, tyranny, oligarchy and anarchy. Prudent legislators, he thinks, refrain from adopting any one of these forms and choose one that shares in them all. He acknowledges, however, that in times of crisis republics need a prince – an almost superhuman figure who flies in the face of 'necessity' and 'fortune'. I shall not follow him further in his republican sentiments but consider his famous discussion of princes.

All discussions of society involve assumptions about human nature, so it is important to start with Machiavelli's attitude to his fellow man. Men are 'ungrateful, fickle, liars and deceivers, they shun danger and are greedy for profit, while you treat them well they are yours. They would shed their blood for you, risk their property, their lives so long as danger is remote; but when you are in danger they turn against you. Any prince who depends entirely upon promises and has taken no other precautions ensures his own ruin; friendship which is bought with money and not with nobility is paid for, but it does not last and it yields nothing. Men worry less about doing an injury to one who makes himself loved than to one who makes himself feared. The bond of love is one which men, wretched creatures that they are, break when it is to their advantage to do so'.

He combines this starkly pessimistic view of human nature with a definite political attitude to Christianity which has: 'glorified humble and contemplative men and set up as the greatest good humility, abjectness and contempt for human things'. Machiavelli believes that Christianity has placed no value in strength of body or in any of the pagan virtues and by imposing an other-worldly image of human excellence, it has not merely failed to promote civil glory but has helped to bring about the decline and fall of great nations. He is one of a long line of historians who attribute the fall of the Roman Empire to its adoption of Christianity as the official religion. Christianity is, for Machiavelli, a slave morality which is inconsistent with the noble pagan virtues that secured for Rome its pre-eminent position in world affairs. He thinks that the price we have paid for Christian truth is too great – it has made the world weak and turned it over as prey to wicked men. If princes insist on making it their business to be good among so many who are not, they will not only fail to achieve great things but will surely be destroyed.

Machiavelli believed that the most important concept in political life is power. According to the classical heritage that Machiavelli admired, one achieves power by *virtu* and *fortuna*. Fortune is a Goddess and since she is a woman she is most attracted by the *vir* – true manliness and courage. As Machiavelli says: 'being a woman, she favours young men because they are more ardent and because they command her with great audacity'. Christianity rejected this idea of a Goddess and made 'fortune' a blind power – fate. With the recovery of the classical values in the Renaissance, however, 'fortune' was combined with 'will' and contrasted with 'fate' (which is beyond human will). Thus Shakespeare's Cassius to Brutus: 'if we fail in our efforts to attain greatness, the fault must lie not in our stars but in ourselves'. Machiavelli was convinced that the new maxim for the prince should be: 'when in doubt, attack' or, following Livy, 'fortune favours the bold'. Those with sufficient *vir* are those who, when uncertainty reigns, seize the day.

In referring to *vir* as manliness it is important to remember the difference between sex and gender (I am constantly asked in questionnaires to declare my gender!) Sex is male or female; gender is masculine or feminine. There is no inconsistency, therefore, in talking of masculine and feminine males; masculine and feminine females. Machiavelli has quite a lot to say, indirectly, about matters of sex and gender. It has to be admitted that he has no positive role for women in a republic. He says the French when resisted 'became cowards like women'. He repeats Livy on the Franks who 'slacken off worse than women'. In *La Mandragola*, Callimaco says: 'Do not get yourself down, like a woman'. Yet he quotes approvingly a 14th Century poet: 'Keep quiet, O males, women know how to wield the sword, they know how to rule empires'. He believed, in other words, that special men and women could be princes, but they had to be people of *vir* – masculine. He cites as examples Joanna of Naples (1326–1382) who killed her husband and daughter and fought and won many battles. He also admired Madonna Caterina Sforza

(1463–1509), Countess of Forli, wife of Girolamo Riario, who held power after her husband was assassinated in 1488 until Forli was overthrown by Cesare Borgia in 1500. After she and her children had been taken prisoners by conspirators in 1476 she tricked them into allowing her to enter a heavily guarded fortress so as to persuade the guards to open the gates. Her captors laughed at the suggestion until she reminded them that they had her children as hostages. They seem never to have read *Medea* because they let her go whereupon she warned the guards to prepare for battle, appeared on the walls of the fortress, spat on the assassins, threatened them with fearful revenge and telling them that she was still able to bear children, raised her skirt and showed them her genitals screaming 'this is a real woman'. The conspirators fled and, unbelievably, the children survived. This beautiful, remarkable woman clearly influenced Machiavelli's thinking about women of *vir*, as did Rosamander, the sixth century queen who was captured by King Alboin who killed her father, fashioned a drinking bowl of his skull, married his daughter and made her drink out of her father's skull. Incensed with a passion for revenge, she exchanged places with her maid, slept with the girl's lover, and threatened to expose him unless he killed her husband. He meekly obeyed after which they fled the country and she tried to kill him with a cup of poisoned wine. As the poison began to work he forced some of the wine down her throat and they died together, if not in each other's loving arms.

Machiavelli admires these powerful women but admits that their sex can create military if not political difficulties for them. Being women, weapons do not suit them, but neither do they suit priests and business men. In Act 3 of his play *Clizia*, Machiavelli writes thus of women:

'The one who offends woman
Wrongly or rightly is mad if he believes
Through prayers and weeping to find mercy in her.
As she descends in this mortal life,
With her soul she brings along
Pride, haughtiness, and of pardon, none;
Trickery and cruelty accompany her
And give her such help
That each enterprise increases her desire;
And if contempt bitter and ugly
Moves her or jealousy, she acts and handles it:
And her strength exceeds mortal strength.'

Machiavelli admits, with delight, that some women would do much better than men in politics. Of Lucrezia he writes: 'she is beautiful, virtuous, courteous, and fit to rule a kingdom.' But women are also objects of love and thus have the ability to turn a man's body and mind upside down. Callimaio in *La Mandragola* says about loving a woman: 'I feel as though my whole body from the soles of my feet to my head has gone wrong: my legs tremble, my vitals are shaken, my heart is torn out of my breast, my arms lose their strength, my tongue falls silent, my eyes are dazzled, my brain whirls.' Love can turn a sad life into a beautiful dream. Machiavelli knows from personal experience that loving women can perform the miracle of changing one's life because of their beauty, elegance and nobility. Just as it can enrich life, love can give endless pain: 'the soldier dies in a ditch and the lover dies in despair.' The hot breath of romance grows cold.

Machiavelli knows that love will bring him pain but being in the presence of a woman's beauty is too overwhelming: 'I nevertheless feel so great a sweetness in it, both because of the delight that rare and gentle countenance brings me and because I have laid aside all memory of my sorrow, that for anything in the world, would I desire my freedom – even if I could have it.' So says the man of *machismo*. But if *machismo* means a manly display of strength, and if manliness entails autonomy, Machiavelli's philosophy of life has little to do with *machismo*.

Machiavelli tells me that if I want to be a prince I should be wise, just, courageous, strong, sober, respected and feared, severe, shrewd. I should avoid being hated, win friends, create obligations, destroy those who can injure me, confer benefits gradually, use cruelty sparingly, honour those who are dependent and protect myself from those who are independent. I should not be too generous, give my word lightly, use trickery and deceit when necessity commands. In short, I must combine in myself the qualities of the lion and the fox. I should under no circumstances appear fickle, irresolute, frivolous, effeminate, cowardly or indecisive. With respect to my staff I must insist on competence and loyalty, demand self-sacrifice, get others to do my dirty work, shun flatterers, seek advice on my terms (and only from a trusted few), and adhere to my decisions rigidly.

In the 1960s psychologists became interested in the teachings of Machiavelli and constructed attitude scales composed of items adapted from *The Prince*. Those who endorse Machiavelli's views are characterised by their emotional detachment, whereas those opposed are emotionally involved with people around them. Research studies show that scores on Mach scales are unrelated to measures of intelligence (so one can be a bright or dull Machiavellian), political preference (right- or left-wing Machiavellian) or psychopathology (sane or insane Machiavellian). Mach scores are, however, related to measures of aggressiveness, assertiveness, achievement-orientation, manipulativeness, sensation-seeking, dogmatism and masculinity. If I were a Machiavellian I will, according to research studies, cheat more, confess less and be able to hold another's eyes while telling plausible lies. I am better than non-Machiavellians at bargaining because I control the bargaining relationship and act decisively. I like ambiguity and privately ignore others who appeal to justice and fair play. I am unresponsive to ethical or personal concerns and de-personalise social interactions. Whilst I personalise relationships for tactical purposes, I am unresponsive to personal attacks. More accurate than the sentimental types in interpersonal perception, I am good at discovering personal weaknesses in my opponents and can present myself as the very opposite of the tough-minded person I am.

When I ask such questions as: how may the strength of any rule, law, myth, strategy be assayed? my answer is: attack it! So when I am faced with an unstructured social situation I move to control the structure and exploit the resources. Faced with a structured situation I engage in half-hearted performance and use my spare capacity to undermine the relationship to my advantage. I have come to realise that people who lack Machiavellian characteristics become emotionally involved in relationships and frequently accept the structure imposed on them by others. However, when they become emotionally involved with Machiavellians, like me, they generally lose out in the social encounter because of my ability to detach myself emotionally from the relationship while vigorously pursuing my personal goals.

But am I really a Machiavellian? If I was I would not admit it.

Machiavelli has been accused of promoting a philosophy of masculinity, manipulation, *machismo* and mendacity. But he is also a considerable philosopher of liberty. Above all, he emphasises the importance to princes of ingenuity, of using one's intelligence for the benefit of the State, of striving for political power with glory. He lived in an age of despotism which fostered the utmost individuality in tyrants and men of *vir* alike. These people were obliged to mobilise all their inward resources because they were determined to obtain the greatest satisfaction from a period of power that might be very brief. Machiavelli was not a Machiavellian – he was an adviser to Machiavellians. He watched with awe princes of courage and determination who would stop at nothing in their desire to achieve civic glory.

Above all, Machiavelli emphasises political intelligence – or ingenuity. No better example of Renaissance ingenuity can be found than in the actions of the citizens of Siena who, to show their gratitude to a courageous general who saved their town, met to vote him a handsome reward. Unable to decide on a truly grand reward they remembered their *Iliad* and the glory that attaches to the bravest warriors when they become Gods. No greater reward could be given to a conquering general than to be worshipped as a God. But to be worshipped as a God, he had to be dead. So they killed him and worshipped him as a God.

Machiavelli's realistic analysis of political power set the agenda for the political philosophies of Thomas Hobbes, John Locke and Edmund Burke. Of the three, Locke is the most important and his influence is at its most obvious in the foundation of the political system of the United States of America.

The bridge from Machiavelli to Locke is Thomas Hobbes (1588–1679) who was born prematurely when his mother panicked after hearing of the approach of the Spanish Armada: 'fear and I were born twins.' He went to Oxford at age 15 where he rejected Aristotle in favour of Galileo who he met in 1636. He had a strong empirical bent but, unlike most empiricists, he was strongly influenced by mathematics. He even claimed to have squared the circle. Inevitably, the professors of mathematics made him look silly, although he was taken seriously enough to be allowed to teach mathematics to the future Charles II. His obsession with mathematics meant that, although he insists on the scientific function of philosophy, he places less emphasis on experiment and induction and more emphasis on deduction from first principles.

He solved the dualistic problems of mind and body by dissolving them in favour of a mechanistic materialism. The task of philosophy is to study reality, which is represented by causal relations between bodies in motion.

Freedom is unimpeded movement. The existence of God is not a philosophical topic and theology is irrational. As a materialist and nominalist Hobbes is committed to the view that we can have no idea of the infinite or of the immaterial. Words such as 'immaterial' or 'eternal' are gibberish. 'Words whereby we conceive nothing but the sound are those we call absurd, insignificant and nonsense. And if a man should talk to me of immaterial substances or of a free subject I should not say he were in error, but that his words were without meaning, that is, absurd.'

Hobbes places great emphasis on language arguing that reason gives no conclusions about the nature of things, but only about their names, which depend on the imagination, and imagination on the bodily organs. In short, reason establishes the connection between words only. He has been called a 'sceptical nominalist' because he promotes the view that universals have no existence independently of being thought and are therefore mere names representing nothing that really exists. Nominalists deny anything like Plato's *Forms* and are critical of those who turn verbs (to think) into abstract nouns (thought) and then treat the abstract nouns as if they are concrete nouns. Concrete nouns refer to 'things'; abstract nouns do not refer. So when a concrete noun is removed, the thing to which it refers remains; when an abstract noun is removed, nothing remains. The habit of treating abstract nouns as concrete nouns is called 'reification' and it is, for nominalists, a philosophical sin. Obvious examples of reification include feeling, belief, value, creativity, need, memory and, significantly, mind, which has the convenient ability to house the other abstract nouns. So we speak carelessly about feelings, thoughts and values 'in the mind' as if the mind is a thing whereas it is merely an abstraction. As a nominalist and a materialist, Hobbes tried to develop a philosophy that synthesised physics, psychology and politics.

Hobbes' psychology assumes that human passions are nothing more than motions. External objects stimulate the sense organs and a motion arises in the brain which travels to the heart and is called passion. Humans are driven by their passions and pleasure and pain determine what is good and what is evil. Madness is to have stronger and more vehement passions than normal, and where these passions tend to evil we are inclined to call their hosts 'mad'.

Hobbes accepts that humans deliberate on and will actions, although he defines deliberation in terms of passions. Consistent with his materialism is his view that animals also deliberate and will. The consequence is that humans have no more freedom of the will than do beasts. 'Such a liberty as is free from necessity is not to be found in the will either of men or beasts.'

All humans are motivated by self-interest and the desire for power; altruism is impossible. Egoism is therefore virtuous. 'Of the voluntary acts of every man, the object is some good for himself.' I am a nucleus of hedonism, acting blindly on the 'prompting of the passions' – I react to situations that arouse fear and behave in such a way as to attempt to eliminate the source of fear. My essential egoism ensures that life in a 'state of nature' is certain to be 'solitary, nasty, brutish and short'. Hobbes' assumption about human nature forms the basic premise for an argument that leads by inexorable logic to the conclusion that the order and civility that characterise me are imposed by society and enforced by it. To protect myself from the destructive effects of my own ferocity, my only recourse is to submit myself to a sovereign.

The working out of details of the sovereign's power Hobbes attempted in *Leviathan*, where it is held that the sovereign with whom I must make my contract is not a collectivity but another person. As a citizen, I am a unit who has ceded virtually complete power to the sovereign and so allow my relationships with other citizens to be governed through this. This makes society a highly centralised organisation in which I have very restricted bargaining power vis-à-vis my sovereign, and none with my fellows except through the sovereign. The free use of my personal ability to harm others is renounced by the agreement to abide by rules emanating from the sovereign. Thus agreement generates the sovereign's authority that extends to the use of power to maintain the civil order where it is threatened by deviants. This mechanism for the moderation of potential conflict is the first necessity for social life. Upon it as a basis can be built the constructive forms of cooperation that generate the powerful society, *Leviathan*.

Hobbes' thought was a response to the current events in which he participated. He was personally involved on both the royalist and commonwealth sides during the wars that wracked England during the 17th Century and he was dismayed by the destructive consequences of civil war. No doubt his language is often chosen so as to pander to the pride of kings. For example, the sovereign is a person, not a mob and it is his power rather than authority that is emphasised. But that power arises because it is conceded by the citizens, not as a divine right, and that point must have conciliated the parliamentarians to a degree.

Hobbes' analysis is an influential one, partly because the basic premise about human nature is supported by the frequency of violent conflict among human beings. It also has aspects in common with Judaism, with Freud, with the early social Darwinists and with various forms of totalitarianism, but is less vulnerable to logical objections than most of these. Emergent from it is the recognition that development of social power depends on accepting the necessity for centralisation, a thesis that can scarcely be denied on the historical evidence.

The anti-individualistic aspect of the Hobbesian picture lies in the right of the sovereign to exert forcible control over me in the interests of social solidarity. Insofar as this might be exercised to prevent me intruding on the rights of others, few would be unwilling to concede its necessity. But Hobbes requires the cession of all power to the sovereign and that would seem to set no limits on the extent to which I am to be subjected to coercion. Although the theoretical deduction that my complete subjection to the group will generate the most powerful society is logical, its universal acceptability cannot be assumed.

After living in ill health for more than 30 years, Hobbes died in 1679. At the end he remarked that 'he was 91 years finding a hole to go out of this world, and at length found it.' He died as he lived – a witty and sceptical humanist.

Less witty but equally humanistic was John Locke (1632–1704) – doctor, diplomat, civil servant, philosopher, economist. He was a true contract theorist, in that he took the independent existence of both society and the person for granted; but unlike Hobbes he accorded the person the primary place. He argued that people enter into political association for the sake of some gain and in order to achieve this gain they subject themselves to many limitations. But they expect and usually receive a net gain. The gain takes such forms as security, protection and a legal system for weighing up conflicts between the interest of individuals, the protection of property and the like.

Thus for Locke I am a rightful unit – an end in myself. My rights must be respected and infringements on my autonomy call for justification. Any sacrifice of autonomy on my part should be voluntary and should be subject to recall if the State does not provide the gains that constitute the reasons for its existence. Belonging to a society is rather like being a shareholder in a public company. If I do not approve of the way the company is being run, I can use my voice and vote in an attempt to change it, and if this is ineffective it is rational for me to sell out and re-invest in some other company that does provide a net gain. At the very least, negotiation with the sovereign powers must be possible; the balance between the limitations on my personal autonomy and the gains made possible by co-operation must be under constant examination; the moral imperative always lies in preserving my personal autonomy, and the justification of the State depends on what it does about this. And for Locke the State is a collective of all the individuals who comprise society.

Locke places me and other individuals in a powerful moral position vis-a-vis the State. I have bargaining power and room for manoeuvre. Society exists to emancipate me from pressures arising from the conditions of human existence and ensure for me as much autonomy as is practicable. The key to the nature of the Lockean contract lies in the way he conceives of 'original human nature'. In his *Two Treatises on Government* Locke lays it down that all men are naturally in a state of equality wherein all the power and jurisdiction is reciprocal, no one having more than another. The equality of which he speaks is that equal right that every man has to his natural freedom without being subject to the power of any other man.

Locke is dealing with an abstract man, so that when he speaks of men being 'originally' free and equal he does not mean that men had equal intelligence, strength, etc., at some remote period of history nor that equality and autonomy are guaranteed by life in the wild. He means that society is a contract in which every person is joined with all others; and what every person brings to the contract is himself, a commodity which he obtained for nothing; and that since the aim of the company is gain, it would be unjust to set the price of the gain higher to one person than another.

The person is, for Locke, a moral concept and if this concept did not exist there would no longer be a basis for claiming that persons have any reality. Society is simply a contractual arrangement and what concerns everybody is whether it is an equitable one. Locke is a strong protagonist of democratic government and a believer in the notion that restraints on the person should be held to the minimum necessary for the maintenance of a stable and just society, or 'civil government'. But more than that he is concerned that they should operate equitably. He was aware of and agreed with Plato's opinion that democracy leads to tyranny, and he proposed the celebrated remedy – the placing of legislative and executive powers in different hands, so that the people who form the government are not able to exempt themselves from the laws they make for others. This suggestion has had enormous influence on political constitutions the world over, especially in England, France and the United States.

Many of Locke's principles are now so deeply embedded in out thinking that they seem to reflect moral ideals that have been with humanity since time immemorial. Equality before the law seems to be inseparable from justice. But the practical problems that stand in the way of it have not been solved. I become indignant if governors exempt themselves from the laws that they make for my regulation – but they often find ways of doing so. I like to believe that all people should get what they deserve from society but find it impossible to get as far as ensuring that all have an equal opportunity. Equality of gain is a principle of the free use of personal powers and becomes blurred by individual differences in what is to be regarded as gain.

Locke did not deny individual differences in enterprise and ability. On this point he took the extreme environmentalist position, so that such differences are attributed to the kind of education given to the person and not to the prior nature of man. Before socialisation human nature is, in his view, a *tabula rasa*, a blank tablet. Like Hobbes, he rejects the theory of innate ideas in favour of the view that material objects impinge on our senses and we learn from experience that these stimuli come in regular combinations that we associate one with the other, e.g. apple with colour. From these experiences we generalise to form concepts so that we can think about objects when they are not present. Our knowledge derives originally from experience and that is its guarantee of validity. This experience is sensation and reflection, and by reflecting on the former we acquire such concepts as thinking, reasoning, doubting.

Like all empiricists Locke has to explain how we can have direct knowledge of external objects. And the answer is that we cannot. External objects impress themselves upon us and thereby create an idea of the object in our mind. But it is the idea of the object that we know, not the object itself. What we see is not what we get. The view that the mind duplicates the external world is called 'naïve realism'; Locke's view has come to be known as 'representative realism' because the mind represents the external world but does not duplicate it. So the question of what things are *really* like has no meaning.

Locke's common sense stands out in high relief against the modern concept of a scientific psychology. By asserting that the notion of the person rests on a moral assertion he implies that there is really no other basis for it. Modern scientific psychologists would not accept this as relevant. They would take the position that the concept either rests on some discoverable empirical basis or is not admissible in scientific discourse.

In a famous exchange between two great philosophers, Gilbert Ryle said to Bertrand Russell: 'Locke invented common sense.' Russell replied: 'By God, Ryle, you are right. No one had common sense before Locke – and no one but Englishmen have ever had it since.'

Like Locke, Edmund Burke (1729–1797) attempted to give to the relationship between the person and the State a relatively balanced character. But his work is so coloured by his negative reaction to the excesses of the French Revolution and the Terror which followed it that he emphasises the dependence of the person on society. After all, Burke had only recently heard of the executions of king and queen, the September massacres, the organisation of the Terror, and the rule of barbarism which destroyed the glittering empire of monarchical France. This emphasis was reinforced by his equally negative reaction to the strongly individualistic propaganda of such people as Rousseau which tended to overshadow any significant place for the individual in society. What Burke was particularly worried about was the tendency of revolutions to end in centralised and irresponsible power. He writes in his *Reflections of the Revolution in France*:

'If the present project of a Republic should fail, all securities to a moderate freedom fail with it. All the indirect restraints which mitigate despotism are removed; insomuch that, if monarchy should ever again obtain an entire ascendancy in France under this or any other dynasty, it will probably be, if not voluntarily tempered at setting out by the wise and virtuous counsels of the prince, the most completely arbitrary power that ever appeared on earth.'

He was right. The French Revolution produced Napoleon and the Russian Revolution produced Stalin. Yet Burke was a defender of the American Revolution so that he did not, in principle, oppose all revolutions. To understand the difference between the various forms of political change was Burke's primary project. And a crucial difference is between sweeping changes (which he thought stupid) and piecemeal changes (which he thought intelligent).

Burke adopts Aristotle's view that man is a political animal at its full value and so regards talk about contracts or the possibility of life outside the State as idle nonsense. Practical politics was, in his opinion, not something one could, or should, base on abstract notions of human nature, or for that matter the psychology of the individual. To approach human nature at all one must first take account of the actualities of social life. The state is best regarded on the model of the organism, with the indivi-dual fitting into the body politic as an organ fits into the living body. This analogy exalts the State and places the individual in a position where he must accept that he has certain functions to perform and sacrifices to make in order that society may survive and prosper. Burke does not advocate any specific form of society – he leaves his discussion at a general level. We might envisage society as a tree, and the individual as a leaf. The latter are wholly supported by the tree and are inconceivable without it: the tree is not merely incomplete, but would wither away in proportion to the failure of leaves to perform their essential functions. The dependence is mutual, but this principle does not enable us to be precise about all the functions each is to perform.

Burke is willing to specify some of these functions, however, and so we find him agreeing with Hobbes on at least one fundamental point, as is clear from the following quotation from his *Reflections*:

'Government is a contrivance of human wisdom to provide for human wants. Among these is to be reckoned the want, out of civil society, of a sufficient restraint upon their passions. Society requires not only that the passions of individuals should be subjected, but that even in mass and body, as well as in the individuals, the inclinations of men should frequently be thwarted, their will controlled and their passions brought into subjection. This can only be done by a power out of themselves; and not in the exercise of its function, subject to that will and to those passions which it is its office to bridle and subdue. In this sense the restraints of men, as well as their liberties, are to be reckoned among their rights.'

But in addition society has its positive side:

'It is to be looked upon with . . . reverence; because it is not a partnership in things subservient only to the gross animal existence of a temporary and perishable nature. It is a partnership in all science; a partnership in all art; a partnership in every virtue, in all perfection. As the ends of such a partnership cannot be obtained in many generations, it becomes a partnership not only between those who are living, but between those who are living, those who are dead, and those who are to be born'.

Like Hobbes, Burke accepted the essentially conservative attitude that men without proper restraint will be evil and are not to be trusted. He held that the form of a living society expressed a large part of the wisdom distilled by generations of experience, and maintained that this was not to be wantonly jeopardised. He was opposed to radical destruction of the old systems (such as the activities of the French revolutionaries) and recommended gradual, piece-meal changes governed by expediency and arbitration. To base the reconstruction of society on theoretical notions of the essential goodness of man – such as propped up the French adventure – was to Burke sheer folly. He agreed with Plato and Locke that the tendency of democracy is towards tyranny, especially the tyranny of the mob, main-taining that: 'Those who are subjected to wrong under multitudes are deprived of all external consolation. They seem deserted by mankind, overpowered by a conspiracy of their whole species.'

There are times when Burke's organic analogy seems to lead him back to the Judaic position where men were uncomprehending parts of a revered system. Yet the fact that he could discuss the social system as if he were not part of it shows that he did see the individual, or a few of them, as having a degree of independence. He was simply trying to recommend a conscious and discriminating respect for society, implying that he believed that humans could choose what features were worth preserving and what should be changed – and could give effect to their choices. Underlying this attitude, unfortunately, is the ever-popular but substantially false assumption that social change is under control. This belief is always insidious, and nowhere more so than in a cultural climate where there is a class or persons thought of as rulers, or the ruling class. It is part of a politician's stock in trade, of course, to persuade his electors that he and his friends are capable of controlling change. And as with Marxists and other radicals in recent times it is always possible to convince large numbers of people that some section of society to which they do not belong is doing the ruling. We might, therefore, forgive Burke this assumption while noting that it is certainly fallacious. If it were true, history would be much more predictable than it is.

Burke's views are clearly a product of the milieu in which he found himself, but for all that they do not entirely lack general applicability. Living at a point in European history when the old aristocractic order of society was openly threatened, he feared the kind of confusion which was to become reality in 19th Century industrial England, when the 'partnership in every virtue, in all perfection' became a state of economic tyranny for large sections of the population. They became factory operatives with little bargaining power and few effective champions among the wielders of power. It is easy now to argue that the worst features of the Industrial Revolution might have been avoided if the franchise had been extended earlier than it was; but on the other side, it could also be argued that these evils were the result of a revolution (in this case in manufacturing techniques) which, by Burke's concept of government, should have been introduced gradually and with due care taken to preserve the stability and vitality of the society at each step. Burke argues for controlling change so that the best of the past is preserved: 'One advantage is as little as possible is sacrificed for another. We compensate, we reconcile, we balance.'

Burke's political philosophy has probably suffered some neglect because he has been regarded as primarily a Tory politician. He might claim to be more than this, for he had a scholarly knowledge of the important philosophical issues of the day and published on many of them, including that persistent modern topic, the psychology of sense. Aside from this, his political outlook, while not yielding a well articulated model for either the person or society, nevertheless does two things. It distils what is best in the conservative perspective on social policy, and it leads by default as it were, to the question which has more and more come to be regarded as central to modern social science: how is change to be controlled? It leads in this direction because without the power to control social change there can be no power to preserve the advantages accruing from the past. The conservative program then becomes an impossible dream.

7

Living Mindedly

*'Mind, n. Its chief activity consists in the endeavour
to ascertain its own nature, the futility of the attempt
being due to the fact that it has nothing but itself
to know itself with.'*

(Ambrose Bierce)

While receiving educational instruction from his grandmother, Bertrand Russell asked her about the difference between mind and matter. Her legendary reply was: 'What is mind? It doesn't matter; What is matter? Never mind.' One scientist/philosopher who did mind was René Descartes (1596–1650).

Descartes was one of the very important thinkers who emerged after the Renaissance and is rightly called the father of modern philosophy because he wrestled with the question: where in a mechanical, Galilean, scientific world is there a place for freedom and faith? His importance rests on the fact that he faced the dilemma introduced to European philosophy by the conflict of scientific thought with the religious worldview. He was himself a devout Catholic and was unwilling to relinquish belief in the soul, while being an incisive scientific thinker. A modern psychologist might say that he was motivated to reduce the 'cognitive dissonance' produced by the apparent conflict between two sets of propositions which appeared to be true but mutually incompatible. He certainly was one of those people who find thinking to be an activity which produces the most intense delight, and I suspect that ferreting out a dilemma to think about was a cultivated habit. In any case, the story is that from childhood on he spent each morning in bed where he could think undisturbed. When friends were admitted to his bedroom, found him still in bed and asked what he was doing, he would reply: 'I'm thinking'. And so he became a philosopher.

Descartes was an independent gentleman, at times a mercenary soldier, and at all times an intellectual. There is a story which says that during one of his military campaigns he had a dream which gave him the principle for using algebra to represent geometry – what is called analytic geometry – and that he carried this principle around in his head through sixteen years of war and adventure before publishing it.

His place as a forerunner of biology depends on his argument that mechanical or causal events should be sought as the explanation of bodily functions, that is, bodies can be explained on the same lines as machines. At the time this could be regarded as a reasonable suggestion only if bodies could be separated from souls, and in the context of Christian beliefs this posed something of an intellectual problem where humans were concerned. No difficulty arose with animals, for Christianity already taught that these had no souls. They could therefore be regarded as automata and subjected to a search for mechanical laws. Man's body, if it could be treated as distinct from his soul – and everybody agreed that soul and body were at least different – must also be amenable to investigation as a machine. It was then necessary only to define the soul as something incapable of interfering with the way the physical body operates to open the way for the direct, scientific investigation of the latter.

His belief in the existence of an immaterial soul was not based on respect for the authority of the Catholic Church nor on respect for the wisdom of the ancients. He was not impressed with these as sources of reliable knowledge. But he did accept the existence of innate ideas such as those of God, 'I', time, space, motion, substance and the fundamental geometrical axioms, holding that these are not implanted by experience but held with a certainty and strength that must be accounted for. On this basis he was prepared to seek proofs for the existence of the soul. On the other side, he accepted without reservation the scientific viewpoint and its leanings towards materialism. In other words, he held the central tenets of both the religious and scientific worldviews to be substantially true, and devoted his life to reconciling them.

He proposed that the body is a machine and that its physiology can be studied and explained according to the principles of physics. It is composed of matter, which is extended substance. This doctrine opened the way for the scientific approach to physiology, especially through the study of animals by vivisection – because animals had no souls according to the theology of his day. The soul, on the other hand, is unextended and free, and as such it is not in space. It consists of all that is in me and which I cannot conceive as a bodily organ or function. It knows the perceptions and emotions which arise within the body. It wills actions but once having done so, the body runs them off mechanically. In some cases, as in reflexes, even the willing is not in evidence. The soul therefore interacts with the body and Descartes proposed the pineal gland as the point of this interaction, no doubt because it is the only part of the brain which is not one of an opposed pair of organs. This imaginative bit of fiction actually served very well to separate the soul from the rest of the body, leaving the matter to be viewed as a perfectly mechanical contrivance on which freedom of the soul did not intrude. Obviously, if the soul is not in space but is connected to the body in time only, it is difficult to see how it could 'enter' or interact with a gland in the brain.

This doctrine that soul and body are two quite different kinds of entity which interact only in certain special ways is know as Cartesian Dualism. In proposing his doctrine Descartes was not a religious heretic. He was not abolishing the soul although he did think it prudent to live in Holland where he was less likely to incur the wrath of the Church. What he did with this doctrine was to present the philosophical world with a problem which has been with it ever since. On the one hand there is the material world in which we live and the physical body which we must maintain by physical means; on the other hand is the conviction held by many people that they are something more than flesh, bone and nerves. The Cartesian approach to this dualism shows how such a dilemma can be clarified. For Descartes the soul must be what is left after the body has been abstracted. This clarifies what is meant by the soul, but does not abolish it.

The type of mechanistic thinking of the body which was envisaged by the Cartesian doctrine is beautifully illustrated by Harvey's discovery in 1615 of the circulation of the blood and the pumping action of the heart. An informative analogy can be drawn between a lifeless hydraulic system – say the circular system of a refrigerator – and the circulation of the blood in the body, and the analogy carries over into the practical management of the two systems. Leaks must be stopped, pipes must be kept clear, the pump must be kept working, and so on. The search for this kind of understanding of events is in the same tradition as the earlier use of a mechanistic outlook (by Copernicus and Galileo) in examining the phenomena of astronomy, except that in physiology science seems to be coming closer to uncovering knowledge crucial to our understanding of life. After all, cosmology is only a cosmology; changes in the way we describe the movements of the heavenly bodies, even the movements of the earth, seem unlikely to affect us too closely. Successful enquiry into the workings of our own bodies seems to promise some possibility of reaching an understanding of life itself.

There is, however, more to the matter than this. Scientific knowledge of the kind discovered by Harvey extends man's powers to intervene to his own advantage in the natural course of events. Knowledge of cause and effect relationships in medicine has enabled us to interfere very effectively with diseases, and in many cases to take important steps towards promoting repair of physiological damage. It is little wonder then that that part of Cartesian doctrine which recommends bodies be regarded as machines and understood through the principle of cause and effect has stimulated a long-sustained and partly successful enterprise aimed at increasing our power of protecting the body. The Cartesian doctrine of the soul has had a much less exciting career – for it is not clear how we should go about studying something so impalpable as a soul.

So far as the existence of the soul is concerned, Descartes' proofs are usually summed up in the famous saying: *Cogito ergo sum* – 'I am thinking therefore I exist'. He arrived at this conclusion after resolving, in the *Discourse on Method*, to accept nothing as true which he did not clearly recognise to be so: that is to say, to accept nothing in his judgements beyond what presented itself clearly and distinctly to him, so that he should have no occasion to doubt it. Applying this method of Cartesian doubt – to seek for an internal truth after he has systematically doubted everything, including his own body – he concluded that he could not doubt that he is doubting, and since doubting is a form of thinking, he must exist because he is thinking. So in his *Second Meditations* he tells us that while he wanted to think everything false, it must necessarily be that I who thinks exists and this intuition is so certain that all the extravagant arguments of the critics are incapable of upsetting it. He therefore concluded that it would be the first principle of his philosophy – 'I think therefore I exist'.

Descartes' method of doubt is a consequence of his rejecting the authority of ancient texts and the views of learned men. He therefore rejected arguments claiming validation of knowledge from external sources. Since he was firmly committed to a belief in the truths of science and the truths of religion, and since these truths are clearly incompatible because the former are mechanical and the latter are spiritual, he strove for the truth that underlies both. So a consequence of his thinking was that if objective sources of knowledge cannot pass the test of systematic doubt, then the sole certainty or ultimate truth is to be found in subjective experience. But this does not mean that subjective ideas are based on impressions received from the external world, as the British empiricists were later to maintain, because it is difficult to believe that doubt is a function which arises from simple impressions received from outside the body. Thoughts based on impressions received from external sources may be doubted, so there must be some process independent of the impress of the environment.

Expressed logically Descartes' axiom is: 'I exist because I think'. This entails that when I am not thinking I do not exist. So Descartes wonders whether he exists only when he is conscious, for it might be the case that if he ceased to think he should cease to exist. At first blush it sounds absurd to claim that I go in and out of existence. What he is saying makes sense if we make an obvious distinction (popular with Catholics) between human beings who exist (when they are conscious) and all the other objects of the world, including animals, which simply are. A rock is (ist); a conscious human being (ex)ists, in the sense that he stands out from, is different from and superior to, a rock. So human beings exist because and when they are conscious and consciousness is the defining characteristic of all that is human. The crucial question then is: what is this thing called consciousness?

Before considering Descartes' answer, it is necessary to make a further distinction between 'I' and 'Me', as in the proposition 'I am conscious of me.' Here the 'Me' is the object of consciousness and so can be studied objectively, in the manner of psychological investigation. The 'Me' is therefore what psychologists, friends and I myself study. It includes my body, and past and present behaviours. Clearly, this is not the case with 'I' since 'it' is not an object of consciousness; 'it' is the subject of consciousness. Some philosophers will later say it *is* consciousness, but Descartes is committed to the notion – *ego cogito ergo sum* – there is an 'I' behind consciousness as it were. 'I' – we cannot even write 'the' 'I' unless, like Descartes we allow the possibility of an immaterial 'thing' which thinks – cannot be studied according to the methods of science, nor can it be located in physical space. Yet it is what stands behind consciousness and thinking and so we should add to Descartes' famous slogan an 'I', or in Latin, *ego*. *Ego cogito ergo sum* better expresses Descartes' view because it emphasises an 'I' which is the subject of consciousness and which defines what it means to be human. Since matter is defined as extension in space, and since 'I' is not material because if it was it would be an object for itself, 'I' cannot 'be' anywhere. To ask: where is 'I'? is to pose an incoherent question which can receive no coherent answer according to the objectifying methods of science. So Descartes is forced to conclude that 'I' is an immaterial thing that thinks. But what is an immaterial thing that thinks? It is the soul.

Descartes believes that he is a soul (a thinking thing that is conscious, doubts, understands, asserts, denies, is willing, is unwilling, which also feels and imagines), and he has a body contingently attached to the soul. But how does he get the soul into the body? By assigning it the function of thinking. In *The Passions of the Soul* he lays it down that the soul exercises its functions in a small part of the brain. Now when the body dies, the brain obviously perishes also but, Descartes maintains, the soul as a substance closely joined to the brain is immortal and survives the death of the body.

In *The Concept of Mind* British philosopher, Gilbert Ryle, writes that Descartes left as one of his philosophical legacies a myth which continues to distort clear thinking. He does not mean to imply that a myth is a fairy-story. Rather it is the presentation of facts belonging to one category in the idioms appropriate to another. To explode a myth is not to deny the facts but to re-allocate them. And this is what he tries to do in his justly famous book when he says with typical forcefulness that he shall speak of Descartes' Myth with deliberate abusiveness, as the dogma of the 'ghost in the machine'. His aim is to prove that it is entirely false, that it is one big mistake – a category mistake. Ryle argues that it represents the facts of mental life as if they belonged to one logical category when they actually belong to another. Ryle has, in his turn, been criticised for his inability to deal with the elusive notion of 'I' which, whilst not amenable to scientific investigation, haunts our waking lives.

We owe to Descartes a philosophy which is still productive of serious scholarship today, as different aspects of the central dilemma are brought into focus by philosophers. If philosophy teaches me how to talk to myself, Descartes offers me a language with which to understand what it means to exist as a human being. His philosophical journey has had a dramatic influence on Western consciousness. He is rightly called a rationalist because he defended the view that knowledge is derived primarily from 'reason' which is conceived as the working of the mind on innate ideas contained within. *A priori* knowledge (knowledge which is prior to experience) is, for Descartes, the most important path to the truth.

There are, of course, more fruitful ways to understand consciousness than by relying on spiritual concepts, such as Descartes'. An example can be found in the work of George Herbert Mead who believed that consciousness (or 'mind') is socially constructed. He emphasises the importance of language in the growth of I-consciousness, the development of the person(ality) into 'I' and 'Me' through play, role-taking and games, the way in which we develop conscience by 'taking the role of the generalised other', and the emergence of creativity. His theory of 'I' stresses the existence of an element in human nature which is prior to socialisation and inaccessible to it. This element is related to the power of choice, the power of language and the power to transcend social rules and conventions.

George Herbert Mead (1863–1931) was associated with the American pragmatist movement of thought which commenced with Charles Sanders Peirce, William James and John Dewey. In *Mind, Self & Society* Mead argued that consciousness is not some entity within me but a process that comes into existence through my inter-action with others: consciousness develops and exists only in the social process of experience and activity, which it presupposes.

My primary adjustment to an environment lies in the act that determines the relation between 'I' and the envi-ronment. An act is an ongoing event that consists of stimulation and response and the results of the response. Behind these lie my attitudes and impulses that are responsible for my responsiveness to a stimulus and for the adequacy of the response. So when I read a book this is an act which is different from other acts and relates me to something external to myself. 'Reading a book' is not a statement about me as a separate entity, nor about the nature of the something external. Since such acts as 'reading a book' are labelled symbolically, language is of crucial importance.

The important step in the Meadian approach to language involves the action of 'significant gesture' and it is therefore important to understand what is meant by 'significant'. When I indicate by gesture to another person what that person is to do, I am conscious of the meaning of my gesture insofar as I take the attitude of the latter towards that gesture, and tend to respond to it implicitly in the way the other person responds to it explicitly. Thus if a policeman holds up his hand to indicate the traffic to stop, this gesture has meaning in that the consciousness of the policeman and the consciousness of the drivers agree that it is to be responded to by stopping. This shared awareness of a relationship between the symbol and the act it signifies is the necessary condition for consciousness.

Unlike animals, however, I have the additional capacity to think the symbol to myself rather than utter it and thus to call up the expected response in thinking. So I may maintain a conversation with myself or rehearse the possible consequences of real speech or action. 'If I say X, he will do A. Do I want that? No, I don't. So I will say Y, in which case, he will do B, which accords well with what I want because it enables me to do C, which I desire.' By this point I have definitely entered an area where I-consciousness must be called on as a general term for the kind of ability implied. There is a significant difference between the conditioning of reflexes in animals and the human process of thinking by means of symbols because these symbols are the means of selecting stimuli so that the various responses can organise themselves into action.

Mead then considered the importance of childhood play in learning. He believed that what children were doing in play was a trial and error version of 'taking the attitude of the other'. A child can be observed adopting, say, the role of teacher, and expecting another to play the role of student. He can be seen to correct the other person who does not respond to his communications and actions in the proper way, and this process of trial and correction is reciprocal, so that a viable relationship emerges within some framework of play. In this way the capacity to generate a range of personal relationships is learned.

Having learned to control one's activity so as to call forth certain responses on the part of others, there is still the problem of what responses it is appropriate to promote in this way. Social activity is not just a series of interchanges in which each summons from the other any response which lies within his capacity and suits his whim. It is organised. Here Mead appealed to the notion of a game. In organised games there is the necessity for understanding the general framework, which includes the object of the game, the relations of all players with each other, and that of the opposition to one's own side. All this Mead clustered into the concept of 'taking the attitude of the generalised other'. The organised community which gives the person unity may be called the 'generalised other' – and the person is constituted not only by an organisation of individual attitudes, but also by an organisation of the generalised other.

In the internal conversation, the rehearsal of possible lines of action, the generalised other responds to my proposal by calling to consciousness the response of others. It provides, not the anticipated response of some single person, but a response shaped by the way my proposal affects the social group. It has the functions of umpire and critic rolled into one; but there is no umpire, only my fellow-players abstracted into something like a group consciousness.

But if the person is composed of the 'attitudes of individual others' plus this version of group consciousness, what is it that puts forward proposals to be judged for their possible effects? The answer is that the person is internally divided into 'Me', the object which is the anchor point for the relationship with outside objects, and 'I'. 'I' is the proposer. If performance ensues, 'I' instantly becomes 'Me' because performance expresses a relationship with others. But 'I' is not socialised, it is never an object. It is in principle unpredictable, it is in fact the principle of unpredictability.

Mead's thinking is grounded on the following: I-consciousness, on which the distinction between human and other animals is based, language being an important concomitant; consciousness and meaning; the dual perspective of the person as both 'I' and 'Me'; the introduction of social rules making for an internal structure not unlike what we call 'conscience'. And he introduces 'I' to explain I-consciousness, novelty and creativity. 'I' is, of course, utterly mysterious. It is spontaneous but seeks self-expression. At the same time it has an evaluative capacity implying rational sensitivity whose source Mead does not explain. And if one looks at Mead's version of society (the 'generalised other') this replies to the proposals of 'I' in terms of social judgement based on rules and conventions, which echoes the way the Protestant Ethic subjected individuals to the judgement of their peer group.

Mead's person is not a conditioned robot but is engaged in meaningful action. He found consciousness, not in a mysterious 'mind', but in social interaction – and he tried to understand consciousness so as to accord with the facts of society on the one hand and the notion of the autonomous person on the other. He suggests that the 'I-Me' dialectic comes into play when we deliberate on choice. He consolidates the larger society into the 'generalised other', a kind of group consciousness which has rules for conduct against which behaviour is judged for morality and effectiveness. 'I' is introduced to argue for the existence of an element in human nature which is inaccessible to socialisation and is related to my power of choice and my power of symbolic communication.

'I' represents the introduction of a free and unaccountable element in a system which otherwise attempts to remain within a scientifically, deterministic framework. Mead's attempted to push such an account of human behaviour as far as it could possibly go; after doing so he found himself unable to encompass those kinds of actions which require that the person should be both subject (private) and object (public) and it was at this point that he introduced the paradoxical window of freedom.

There are two unsolved problems in Mead's account. One is the central question of how we get from the 'gesture' – which is originally the initial move in an action – to the symbol, which has no such empirical relationship with what can be manipulated 'in the head.' Part of Mead's explanation is that symbols gain their meaning, initially, from occurrence in close contiguity with the response, object or activity which they come to mean. Mead suggests conditioning as a possible explanatory mechanism but never commits himself in any detail. Conditioning may be used to describe what happens on occasions when two events are more or less regularly linked but it will not account for the symbolic relationship, for the most obvious feature of this is that the symbol and referent are not linked by any necessity. The sight of a chair does not call forth in me the response 'chair' even sub-vocally, and if I ask someone to pass the salt, the sound of my own request does not stimulate in me a tendency to pass the salt, which is what Mead claims. While I *can* rehearse the response I expect from the other and thus anticipate it, the point is that I am in no way compelled to do so. It is the nature of symbols that the same symbol does not always call forth the same thought and the same thought may be expressed in various symbols. I might express my request for the salt by saying: 'Please facilitate my access to the sodium chloride' and this is not the same stimulus as 'Pass the salt.' It is symbolically equivalent.

The second problem I see in the Meadian theory is the reliance on the social structure to generate the unity of the 'I'. What is difficult to agree with here is the implication that living in a social context will necessarily produce this unity. There seems very little to prevent any person from perceiving social affairs as relatively chaotic, in which case the stabilising influence from which Mead's 'I' takes its unity would be unavailable. Still, I do not think Mead is wholly wrong here; we do find rules and conventions in social life which are stable, and some of us do go through periods of high conformity, as in adolescence, when the greatest sign of failure is to be out of step with the conventions of peers. Probably we are then developing a unified social identity based on taking the attitude of the other. Nor do I think we should overlook the evidence from highly ordered sub-cultures, such as can be found in religious orders, where changes in the rules and routines can be shown to have disastrous effects on the stability of susceptible individuals.

Nevertheless, I contend that the creation of the unified 'I' is a process which begins very early in life when 'I' begins to emerge as the author of our actions, and is only confirmed by the social process of learning how actions fit into social roles. I would therefore argue that the 'generalised other', having its origin in the social structure, confirms an already existing stability in the 'I' by presenting an established set of patterns from among which one might select.

In *On Our Own Now*, American writer Gore Vidal presents his view of the difference between the public self ('Me') and the private self ('I'): 'Each of us contains a private self and a public self. When the two have not met, their host ends to be an average American, amicable, self-deluding and given to sudden attacks of melancholy whose origin he does not suspect. When the two selves openly disdain each other, the host is apt to be a strong-minded opportunist, equally at home in politics or advertising. When the selves wrangle and neither is for long dominant, the host is more a man of conscience than of action. When the two are in total conflict, the host is a lunatic – or a saint.'

American libertarian psychiatrist, Thomas Szasz, has built on the Meadian thesis that consciousness develops through the shuttling back and forth of demonstrations of meaning between people. His central thesis is that consciousness is mediated through language which enables us to engage in self-conversation. The 'mind' is not a thing but is identified with the dialogue within. As a psychiatrist he is interested in the logical implications of Mead's thesis for the phenomenon known as 'mental illness'. Clearly, if there is no such thing as 'mind', there can be no such thing as illness of the mind or 'mental' illness. And if there is no such thing as 'mental illness', there can be no such thing as 'mental health' either.

The practical and legal implications of this argument are outlined in Jeffrey Schaler's book, *Szasz Under Fire*, where Szasz can be seen in action. In 1980 he testified for the prosecution at the trial of Darlin Cromer, a 34 year-old white woman who was charged with murdering a 5 year-old black boy, Reginald Williams. Cromer, who often talked of 'killing niggers', virtually told police that she abducted the boy, strangled him and buried his body near her home. She told a court psychologist that it is the duty of every white woman to 'kill a nigger child', adding that she hoped to start a race war. Cromer's attorney argued that she killed because she was a paranoid schizophrenic – she did not hate blacks, she was suffering from a mental illness. To undermine this argument the prosecutor called upon the experience of Thomas Szasz who, in 1961, had published *The Myth of Mental Illness*.

Szasz began his testimony by pointing out that there is a significant difference between a medical diagnosis and a psychiatric diagnosis. Medical diagnoses deal with objective lesions of the body, broken bones, diseased livers, and so on. Psychiatric diagnoses deal with behaviours that human beings display, and they have to be interpreted in cultural terms and, therefore, people will arrive at different interpretations. Homosexuality was, for example, recognised as a mental illness in the 1960s. It is no longer a mental illness in the 1980s, but smoking and gambling are.

The Prosecutor asked: 'How do you treat gambling, do you take away the money?' whereupon laughter erupted in the court. The judge was so amused by the absurd humour involved in what psychiatrists call a mental illness, that he answered the question himself. 'You win.' That is Szasz's recommendation also.

When asked what disease, if any, Cromer was suffering from, Szasz said that she was suffering from the consequences of having lived a life very badly, very stupidly, very evilly. She was a bad student, a bad wife, a bad mother. She used illegal drugs, then she escalated to illegal assault, and finally she committed murder. Life is a task. You either cope with it or it defeats you. If you do not know how to build a productive life, you can always destroy.

Szasz did not base his testimony on the results of a 'psychiatric examination'. Indeed, he refused to examine Cromer. 'I regard the practice of (psychiatric examination) as the epitome of junk science and refuse to participate in it'. Since there is no objective test for mental illness, as there is for melanoma or pneumonia, what psychiatrists pretentiously call an 'examination' is a conversation with a person and observation of his behaviour. The psychiatrist's conclusion is his opinion about the person's so-called mental state, at the time of the examination. Since there is no objective test for mental illness Szasz believes that the practice of examining a defendant months after the alleged crime is prima facie absurd. 'However, our legal-psychiatric system accepts this fiction as truth. Few people – and hardly any psychiatrists – are interested in questioning, much less rejecting this charade. Thus, for the prosecutor determined to prevail against the insanity defence, the best tactic is to confront and unmask the defence psychiatrists as quacks, hired guns masquerading as 'medical experts'.

During the trial Szasz was asked to elaborate on his view that the question of whether or not an individual was suffering from schizophrenia is not relevant to the question of whether or not they are responsible for their acts. In his reply he pointed out that schizophrenics are responsible, and since it is not now general practice to lock them up, they have all the freedom and rights that the rest of us have, and therefore, all the responsibilities that accompany those rights and freedoms. In short, they are responsible for what they do.

The jurors convicted Cromer of murder.

Thomas Szasz has demonstrated a life-long commitment to a libertarian philosophy of freedom and his championing of the values of autonomy and responsibility. The distinguishing feature of a libertarian philosophy of responsible freedom is the belief that self-ownership is a basic right and initiating violence is a fundamental wrong. As a psychiatrist he is in a position to know that psychiatric practice is based on the belief that self-ownership – epitomised by suicide – is a medical wrong, and that initiating violence against people labelled 'mental patients' is a medical right. Psychiatry is, therefore, a major threat to freedom and dignity. To realise the libertarian project, it is essential to understand and unmask the pretensions and base rhetoric of psychiatry. The first step involves treating people as persons – as moral agents – which means we have to stop trying to unravel the riddle of a mythical entity called the 'mind'. His argument that the 'mind' is not a thing has enabled Szasz to undermine the pernicious view that the 'mind' can be ill, and so the mentally ill are not responsible for their 'condition'. But without responsibility there can be no freedom either since responsibility is anterior to freedom. The second step involves treating people as persons and not victims of their environmental conditioning or brain chemistry. In short, libertarians, if they act according to their values, will attack the medicalisation of moral behaviour.

Szasz began his crusade against the medicalisation of moral behaviour in *The Myth of Mental Illness* which contains a disarmingly simple thesis. Since illness can affect only the body, and since the 'mind' is not a bodily organ, the 'mind' cannot be ill, and so mental illness is a metaphorical illness – a myth. And if mental illness is really brain illness as is widely believed today – chemical imbalances and so forth – then it is not mental illness, and mental illness is still a myth.

The modern concept of 'mind' as an immaterial 'thing' – separate from the body yet in communication with it – is attributed to Descartes. Although this view is widely accepted today Szasz claims it is false, the product of a mistranslation. There is no French (or German) noun corresponding to the English 'mind'. Yet translators have employed 'mind' when Descartes used the French word for 'soul'. In *The Meaning of Mind* Szasz argues, rightly in my view, that it is a mistake to blame Descartes for the division of the human body into body and mind and to name this dichotomy 'Cartesian'. Instead, it would be more accurate to view him as a pioneer neuromythologist, in that he claimed to have discovered evidence for locating the soul inside the cranium.

Szasz points out that today 'mind' functions as both

verb and noun. Yet it was not always so. Before the 16th Century people had souls, not minds. 'Mind' meant only minding (as in 'mind the step'). As a noun, the (scientific) mind resembles the (religious) soul, although it is less likely to be granted the ability to survive bodily death. Mind – from the Latin *mens* which meant will or intention – is not a thing (material or immaterial) but an activity which is reflected in its status as a verb. Much confusion has resulted from the unfortunate tendency to turn verbs into abstract nouns, and then treat the abstractions as if they are concrete nouns, or things. If mind is not an entity 'it' cannot be in the brain or in any part of the body. And there can be nothing 'in the mind'. Thoughts, feelings, wishes, memories are abstractions – I think but I have no thoughts, I feel but I have no feelings, I remember but I have no memories. Thoughts, feelings, memories are not in the mind because there is no mind for them to be in, and they are not things in any case. So, we have no minds even though we mind; how and what we mind is who we are.

Because there is no observable entity called the 'mind' Szasz identifies the concept in terms of activities which we attribute to it, notably, thinking. The ancients believed that thinking is talking to oneself. So Socrates says: 'I describe thinking as discourse – as a statement pronounced not aloud but silently to oneself.' Petrarch (1304–1374): 'The written, spoken, contemplative word is the true medicine for self-healing. Montaigne (1533–1592) noted: 'We have a mind capable of turning in on itself; it can keep itself company. It talks to itself.' And Vico (1668–1744): 'The mind is the total of what a person does and says.'

According to these philosophers, mind(edness) is a moral and psychological concept and not a 'thing' to be studied by biologists, neuroscientists and psychiatrists. So 'mind' is not brain, personality or psyche, but a person's ability to have a conversation with himself. The person is both speaker ('I') and listener ('Me').

Minding is, therefore, the ability to attend and adapt to one's surroundings by using language to communicate with others and with oneself. Because we attribute this ability only to intelligent beings, minding implies moral agency which we attribute to some, but not all, persons. We do not attribute the ability to mind to infants because they cannot communicate effectively by language. To be recognised as minded is to be acknowledged as a moral agent, an individual who is willing and able to function as a responsible member of society. And this assumes a capacity to mind which we identify with the capacity to think, which is the ability to talk and listen to oneself. There is an obvious connection, then, between minded-ness and language and since reason is a function of both, so too is unreason.

If there is no such thing as a mind, there can be no illness of the mind. The notions of 'mental health' and 'mental illness' are, therefore, profoundly problematic. The problematic nature of mental illness has been revealed in two ways: (a) by critical analysis of its logical status; and (b) by critical analysis of its empirical status. The logical status of mental illness is problematic because illness affects only the body and since the mind is not a bodily organ, it follows that the mind cannot be ill. Mental illness is, therefore, an oxymoron. Since logical impossibility entails empirical impossibility the debate should end here. But a feature of the mental illness industry is its startling insensitivity to language and logic. The most obvious example is the popular view that illnesses of the 'mind' are, in fact, illnesses of the brain. If so, they are bodily illnesses and not mental illnesses and the category 'mental illness' is self-contradictory and redundant. Either way, mental illness is a myth.

The empirical status of mental illness is problematic because the authors of the *Diagnostic and Statistical Manual of Mental Disorders* (DSM IV-TR) admit that 'no definition adequately specifies precise boundaries for the concept of 'mental disorder'. They add: '. . . the term "mental disorder" unfortunately implies a distinction between "mental" and "physical" disorders that is a reductionistic anachronism of mind/body dualism.' And so it does. But the authors then embrace this dualism when they assert: 'A compelling literature documents that there is much "physical" in "mental" disorders and much "mental" in "physical" disorders.' Had they been logical they would have concluded that there are bodily illnesses and there are (mis)behaviours (misleadingly called 'mental disorders'). They could then have dispensed with 'mind' and 'mental' entirely. But this would raise embarrassing questions about why we call misbehaviours illnesses or mental disorders.

Misbehaviours are called 'mental disorders' even though there are no objective, medical tests by which they can be diagnosed. Diagnoses of 'mental disorder' are, putative, that is, they are not real diagnoses. And so we encounter in DSM IV – one of the great works of fiction

– such 'mental disorders' as: academic disorder (failure), binge-eating disorder (gluttony), disruptive behaviour disorder (argumentativeness), expressive language disorder (swearing), mathematics disorder (difficulty with symbols), phase of life disorder (desire to be younger or older), rumination disorder (thinking), written disorder (illiteracy).

Psychiatrists tell us that mental health is about balance in our thoughts, feelings and behaviour. But who determines 'balance' and on what criteria? It should be obvious to clear-thinking people that 'thoughts' and 'feelings' cannot be studied objectively – they are inferences from behaviour, generally in the form of communications, and often complaints. 'Thoughts' and 'feelings' are abstract nouns which are reified as concrete nouns. We do not have 'thoughts' and 'feelings' like we have colds; we communicate our thinking and feeling to others. Diagnoses are based on these communications and since their evaluation is based on some moral code, diagnoses of mental illness are based also on that moral code. In short, bodily illnesses are diagnosed on objective medical criteria; mental illnesses are diagnosed on subjective moral criteria.

The standard scientific measure of illness is bodily lesion, objectively identifiable by anatomical, histological or other physico-chemical observation or measurement. Yet I am told by mental health practitioners and government bureaucrats that mental illnesses 'are just like any other: heart disease, diabetes, asthma.' This is patently false since they are not, and cannot be, diagnosed on the basis of signs. If they were diagnosed objectively, they would be bodily illnesses. People do not catch a mental illness, they do not pass a mental illness to another, they do not have inoculations against a mental illness, autopsies do not reveal a mental illness, and mental illnesses run in families in the way that speaking English runs in families.

Since Szasz's position is frequently misunderstood and misrepresented, it should be emphasised that when he says that mental illness is not an illness he does not deny the reality of the behaviours to which the term refers, or the suffering the 'mentally ill' may experience, or the problems they create for their families and friends. He merely classifies what people call 'mental illness' differently than those who think they are diseases. When a lesion can be demonstrated physicians speak of bodily illnesses; when none can be demonstrated but when physicians want to treat the problem as a disease, they speak of mental illnesses. The term 'mental illness' is, therefore, a semantic strategy for medicalising socio-economic, moral and political problems. Furthermore, Szasz concedes the possibility that some persons now diagnosed as mentally ill might suffer from a genuine disease. In that event, it would be possible to ascertain by means of objective tests, whether a person suffers from a real illness.

Critics argue that Szasz's view ignores the experiences of the 'mentally ill' and so it is difficult, if not impossible, to question the suffering and disability associated with most mental illnesses. Szasz disagrees. In *Szasz Under Fire* he says that it is easy to question it. It is self-evident that many people whom psychiatrists characterise as 'severely mentally ill' do not suffer; they make others suffer. After all, how do we know that people suffer? We know it because they say so and because they ask for help. The 'paranoid schizophrenics' beloved by the writers of fiction do neither. If such persons were suffering it would not be necessary to incarcerate them and treat them against their will.

Mental illness is, then, metaphorical illness which we literalise at our peril. If moral problems are re-defined as mental illnesses, notions of right and wrong, freedom and responsibility are replaced by notions of healthy and sick, unfreedom and non-responsibility. The progressive medicalisation of moral behaviour produces a society in which individuals are labelled, not as moral agents, but as victims of their mental abnormalities or body chemistry, to be treated medically for their wayward behaviour. According to this view, modern neuroscience is a misdirected effort to explain 'mind' in terms of brain functions, and psychiatry a misdirected effort to explain mental illness as brain disease. A consequence of these efforts is the undermining of the notions of moral agency and personal responsibility. The view that the mind is the brain is not an empirical finding but a rhetorical ruse concealing humanity's struggle to control individuals by controlling their language. 'Illness of the mind' is a logical impossibility.

Szasz is particularly critical of those neuroscientists who argue that the 'mind' is the brain. In arguing his case against such mind-brain identity theorists as Dennett and Searle, he points to the covert political-economic agenda of neuroscience and its biological reductionism. The present state of neuroscience reflects a long-standing alliance between science and state. The ostensible agenda of neuroscience is the quest for scientific understanding of the brain, but its real agenda is to elevate to the level of scientific fact the doctrine that (mis)behaviour is biologically determined and that holding individuals responsible for their (mis)behaviour is unscientific. Moral agency is thereby explained as chemical sufficiency; misbehaviour as chemical deficiency. Neuroscience or neuromythology?

Szasz also attacks the popular view that memory is a noun which names an entity located in the brain. He argues that whilst memory depends on the brain, it is not in it. Memory is a matter of producing rather than reproducing. It is a communication and not a transfer of an engram from neurochemical processes into 'factual information'. Viewing memory as a function of the brain, many neuroscientists accept the existence of an entity called 'false memory' and thus a newly invented mental illness – False Memory Syndrome. The crucial element here is, however, not false memory but false accusation. 'Why do young women search for their "lost memories" (of sexual abuse)? To make themselves feel better which was Freud's aim? Or to make others (men) feel worse (which is the aim of radical feminists)?' In either case, the finder of the 'lost memory' must take responsibility – and must be held responsible – for what she does with what she finds.

Szasz accepts George Herbert Mead's view that 'mind' is mediated through language which enables us to engage in self-conversation. Since thinking, talking to others and talking to oneself are voluntary acts, responsibility can be seen as the paradigmatic self-conversation, since conscience is a particular kind of self-conversation where the person's inner dialogue concerns the goodness or badness of his own conduct. Szasz suggests that we treat the concepts 'right' and 'wrong', 'responsibility' and 'mind' as a single entity. Conversely, the view that 'mind' is brain is a rhetorical flourish, not a scientific hypothesis, let alone a fact. Its purpose is to enable individuals to evade their responsibilities for their actions. The language of minding implies responsibility; the language of mind/brain protects us from the difficulties of facing up to our responsibilities. A mind/brain cannot be held responsible for murder.

On Szasz's view minds can be 'sick' only in the ways jokes can be 'sick'. Mental illness is not something people have, but is something they do or say. Madness is a form of mutiny, insanity a kind of insubordination. The metaphors of mental illness function as euphemisms for problems in living, as excuses for crime and misbehaviour, as stigmata for invalidating adversaries and as medico-legal fictions. When obesity, gambling, self-starvation, murder and drug-taking are called illnesses alongside diabetes, tuberculosis and syphilis, the category 'illness' becomes perfectly elastic, accommodating virtually anything one wants to place in it, including metaphorical illnesses. To logically minded folk this is merely amusing but it becomes especially serious when children are drawn into this net of semantic confusions and base rhetoric. An unamusing example is the invention of 'Attention Deficit Hyperactivity Disorder' (ADHD) which was voted into existence by a show of hands at a 1987 meeting of the American Psychiatric Association. More than eight million children worldwide are being forced to take Ritalin – cocaine with a PG rating – for this 'mental disorder'.

Szasz's conclusion is that if there is no mental illness, there can be no 'treatment' or 'cure' for it. The introduction of psychiatric considerations into the criminal law – the insanity plea and verdict, diagnoses of mental incompetence to stand trial – corrupt the law and victimise the subject on whose behalf they are ostensibly employed. Involuntary psychiatric interventions, such as 'diagnosis', 'hospitalisation' or 'treatment' cannot be justified medically, legally or morally – they are crimes against humanity.

8

Living Sceptically

'Sceptical doubt both with respect to reason and the senses, is a malady, which can never be radically cured, but must return upon us every moment, however we may chase it away.'

(David Hume)

During his last days on earth Socrates proudly announced that after a life of philosophising, he knew that he knew nothing, which was more than others knew. According to the ancient sceptics, however, he could not even know that and Socrates, of all people, was criticised for being dogmatic on this point. What, then, does it mean to live sceptically?

Ancient scepticism is associated with Pyrrho (360–270 B.C.) who served with Alexander in India, where he was not quite so sceptical as he was later to become. His travels impressed upon him the fact of cultural diversity and the inability of men to agree with each other over anything, which he saw as confirmation of the views of the Sophists. Like them, he added moral and logical scepticism to scepticism about the data of the senses. After all, sticks look bent in water, the earth looks flat, and railway lines appear to meet on the horizon. If we relied on the evidence of the senses we would believe many things which are clearly false. Or are they? Common sense and the evidence of the senses are not, it seems, good guides to the facts of the natural world. So Pyrrho promoted the view that there can never be any rational ground for preferring one course of action to another.

Diogenes Laertius tells us that Pyrrho denied that anything was honourable or dishonourable, just or unjust: custom and convention govern human action. He led a life consistent with this philosophy, going out of his way for nothing, taking few precautions and facing all risks as they came. That he lived to the age of ninety seems to be due to his friends who kept him out of harm's way, although there is a story which casts doubt on this and demonstrates how philosophy was lived by some of his students.

While out walking Pyrrho fell into a ditch and was unable to get out. After a while some of his students appeared on the scene, but since they could see no reason to believe it was Pyrrho in the ditch, or that if it was he would be any better off by being rescued, they walked on and left him to his pain and solitude. Some time later, he was rescued by people not imbued with the sceptical philosophy.

He began life as a poor and reclusive painter. He was of even temper so that when a friend left the room while he was speaking he would finish what he wanted to say to no audience but himself. His indifference to personal suffering and the suffering of others was part of his philosophy so that when a friend fainted he walked on, and whilst some criticised him for his callousness, his disciples praised him for his philosophical consistency. When asked why he was talking to himself, he said that he was training to be good. And when his fellow passengers were unnerved by a storm at sea, he remained calm and confident and, pointing to a pig that was happily eating, told them to emulate the animal's disposition.

Pyrrho was constantly engaged in overthrowing the dogmas of all philosophical schools, but promoted none himself, or so he argued (dogmatically?) 'We determine nothing', was his motto, and 'every saying has its corresponding opposite'. We should therefore suspend dogmatic belief and judgement and systematically doubt everything. When faced with the criticism that he is himself a dogmatist in his everyday living and that he could not survive if he suspended all belief and judgement, Pyrrho confessed to human weaknesses and recognised that it is day and he is alive, and many other apparent facts of life; but with regard to the philosophical beliefs of his opponents, he always suspended judgement because they are not, and can never become, certain. Pyrrho was prepared, on practical grounds, tentatively to accept the evidence of his senses and was prepared to admit to seeing or recognising this or that, but was not prepared to be dogmatic about how we see and how we recognise this or that.

The Pyrrhonian sceptic lives his life undogmatically, following the dicates of his body, the evidence of his senses, the laws and customs of his community, without committing himself to any judgement about them. The Pyrrhonists flourished until around 200 A.D. and were especially influential in the medical communities of Alexandria where they combated the dogmas of diverse medical groups. Pyrrhonists claim that scepticism is a purge that eliminates everything including itself, so that the sceptic is able to live unconcerned about matters beyond the evidence of the five senses.

Pyrrho's pupil, Timon (320–230 B.C.), was another philosopher whose scepticism helped him live to the age of ninety. He was a great lover of wine and I like to think this is the reason he lived to such a grand age. He wrote plays, poetry and pornography and never tired of attacking the 'dogmatic' philosophers who claimed that, through reason, they could arrive at the truth. He had only one eye, often referred to himself as Cyclops, had a wonderful sense of humour, although he was not averse to the use of scorn so that when a man marvelled at everything Timon replied: 'Why do you not marvel that we three have but four eyes between us?' pointing to his disciple Dioscurides who also had only one eye. Asked why he had come from Thebes, he said: 'Why, to laugh when I have you all in full view!'

Plato and Aristotle believed there were certain, self-evident starting-points, or axioms, for deductive arguments that led to true conclusions. Timon, on the other hand, showed that every argument proceeds from premises that it did not establish and so there can be no foundation of certainty. There are, therefore, no self-evident starting points and deductive arguments are mere exercises in clever reasoning from dubious beginnings. The search for truth is thus futile. Philosophy is concerned with inventing imaginative premises for deductive consequences to be developed therefrom. Since the premises can never be true, the conclusions can never be true, although they may be interesting or useful.

It is ironic that Plato's Academy – the home of philosophical truth – was, from 230 B.C., in the hands of the Sceptics for 200 years. No doubt the stage was set for the Sceptics by Socrates's famous acknowledgement of his earthly ignorance, although I suspect it was meant ironically. It probably meant: 'I don't know, but I hope to.' The Sceptics prefer: 'nobody knows and nobody can ever know.' But it is this dogmatic element in the Sceptics' thinking that exposes them to criticism. How can they know what they claim to know? Can they claim that they do not know anything without falling into contradiction, since they know that?

Critics of ancient scepticism, such as Bertrand Russell, have argued that this philosophy appeals to the lazy and the mentally indolent, although it has to be admitted that it has the power to help people stop worrying. Why worry about the future if it is uncertain and unknowable? But if it is unknowable how do we know it is uncertain?

The Sceptics' slogan is: 'I am certain of nothing - not even of the fact that I am certain of nothing.' So, for the Sceptics, there is no criterion of truth and knowledge is therefore impossible. Later Sceptics relied on two arguments to prosecute their case.

(a) Nothing can be rendered certain through itself. Witness the variety of opinions between which no choice can be made with certainty.
(b) Nothing can be rendered certain through anything

else, since the attempt to do so involves either an infinite regress or a vicious circle, that is, assumes in the proof of anything the conclusion that has to be proved.

Sextus Empiricus (160–210 A.D.) is the only Greek Pyrrhonian sceptic whose works have survived. They were rediscovered in Europe in the 16th Century and, so seriously was he taken, that by the end of the 17th Century he was known briefly as the 'father of modern philosophy'. It was largely due to his sceptical challenges to dogmatic thinking that stimulated Descartes to establish a philosophy grounded on certainty. Sextus argued against the possibility of proving any conclusion syllogistically. For example, 'all men are mortal' can be proved only by induction that involves the conclusion 'Socrates is mortal'. We cannot know the former without knowledge of the latter – thus a vicious circle. Descartes, scientists and scientifically-minded philosophers accepted the sceptical challenge.

The period of the high Renaissance (1450s–1527) witnessed the beginnings of the scientific movement which was destined radically to transform Western consciousness. In the natural sciences the figure of Leonardo da Vinci is prominent even though his empirical method of collecting facts (often from corpses) and developing theories from facts brought him into conflict with the Christian rationalists of his day. Leonardo wanted to know everything but basing his work on facts, which seems to us an obvious thing to do, was by no means pleasing to the religious authorities who began their speculations with theories. Thus, Leonardo contributed unwittingly to the great debate that was to transform Western consciousness in the modern era – the debate about starting points in scientific investigation. Should the scientist or scholar begin with theories or should they begin by collecting facts derived from the data of the five senses? And if they do rely on sense data, how do they meet the sceptics' challenge?

One Renaissance man – Niccolo Machiavelli – philosopher, diplomat, social scientist, took up the challenge. Science is concerned with what is the case rather than with what should be the case and Machiavelli's reputation as a social scientist, whether deserved or undeserved, is based on his realistic concern with what is the case. Thus Francis Bacon said that we are much beholden to Machiavelli who wrote about what men do and not what they ought to do. But clearly, Machiavelli went beyond the facts of human nature and political leadership when he claimed, for example, that the nature of man is everywhere and always the same. And is it always the case that fortune favour the bold? Even a hard-headed realist like Machiavelli has a strong tendency to combine facts with *a priori* assumptions about human nature. His assumptions concerning the basically evil nature of human beings conflicted with his commitment to facts. In philosophical language we might say that his rationalism (use of assumptions not derived from experience) conflicts with his empiricism (use of assumptions derived from experience).

The idea that theories are the result of innate ideas is characteristic of rationalists, whereas empiricists believe that theories are inductively inferred from facts. Aristotle was an early proponent of the use of induction in science and whilst he praised Socrates for raising important questions, he criticised him for giving no answers. For Aristotle the deductive reasoning of Socrates and Plato should be combined with the patient accumulation of facts, and inductive inferences from facts to theories.

Francis Bacon (1561–1626), in his *Novum Organum* published in 1620, develops this position with considerable vigour. He warns us about the dangers of the 'idols of the mind' - of our tendency to commit grievous errors of reasoning. We must, if we are to think scientifically, be careful to avoid errors – hasty generalisations and vain attachments to theories. The cure for these errors is: (a) purge the mind of all preconceived theories; (b) collect facts by observation and experiment; (c) make reasonable inferences from the facts. The theories thus created are universal generalisations from facts, and from these theories testable predictions can be deduced. So the scientific method, according to Bacon, involves inductive reasoning from facts to theories, and deductive reasoning from theories to predictions, which are tested by the accumulation of new facts.

The debate between Bacon's empiricism and Descartes' rationalism dominates the 17th Century and marks the transition from the medieval era to the modern. For if theories are inferred from facts alone then Descartes' philosophy of innate ideas is false.

The official opposition to Cartesian rationalism came from an Englishman, John Locke and a Scot, David Hume (1711–1776) who argued that knowledge is derived primarily from experience. All significant knowledge is *a posteriori* (based on experience) and *a priori* knowledge is either non-existent or tautological.

Locke argues, against Plato and Descartes, that there are no innate ideas. In his *Essay Concerning Human Understanding* Locke lays it down that we are born *tabula rasa*: Let us suppose the mind to be an empty bucket, without any ideas; how does it come to be filled? How does it come to contain all the materials of reason and knowledge? To this Locke answers in one word – experience – from which all our knowledge is derived.

But empiricists have to face the problem of how we have knowledge of external objects. What we appear to know are only ideas of external objects. Since the mind, has no other immediate object but its own ideas, which it alone can contemplate, it is evident that our knowledge is only concerned with them. Empiricists appear to be saying that the world we know is really the idea of the world in the mind. How then can we know that there is a 'real' world?

Empiricists who follow Locke are forced to conclude that a world independent of experience of it is impossible to know – we can never know what the world is 'really' like. And so human knowledge presents us with a permanently insoluble problem. We are, it seems, forever cut off from the world of matter – all we know are ideas of the world and never the world itself. Locke started, as common sense dictates, with objects experienced by subjects. But he leaves us with experiences and experiencing subjects – knowledge of material objects is impossible.

Hume took Locke's arguments further by demonstrating that the existence of experiencing subjects is as unwarrantable an inference from experience as is experience of the world of objects. He argued that 'I' (mind, psyche, self, soul, personality - the same argument applies to all) cannot be found in experience and so cannot be known directly. As he famously says in his *Treatise of Human Nature*: 'pain and pleasure, grief and joy, passions and sensations succeed each other and never all exist at the same time. It cannot therefore be from any of these impressions that the idea of 'I' is derived and so there is no such idea.' To assert the existence of anything else (such as mind and matter) is to make an inference which cannot be proved.

Hume arrived at this position by distinguishing impressions from ideas. An impression is said to be vivid and compelling, as when a nurse inserts a hypodermic needle. An idea is a faint image of this experience as when one thinks about it later. Feeling is associated with impressions, not with ideas. The impressions must occur before the idea can be generated: both are simple and unitary. Complex ideas are built up from simple ones by the process of association. Association follows three laws: contiguity in space and time, resemblance and cause-effect. Ideas which are aroused close together, which bear similarities to one another, or which fit the cause-effect pattern, become attached to one another and form complex ideas.

When Hume examined himself he came only upon impressions of something else. If there were an 'I', he argued, it must be something which persists through pain and pleasure; but he could catch himself only in the act of having some particular perception, never without and never with anything which was common to all particular perceptions. Sleep or death removed the particular contents of awareness, but then nothing remained. Hence there is no 'I'. Given the premises the argument is irrefutable. It almost seems tautological for the premises exclude 'I' as an object of scientific study.

But if there is no such thing as 'I', how is it that many people are convinced that there is? Hume's answer is that 'I' is a bundle of disparate ideas which are brought into contiguity when we mull over our experiences. Contiguity is like magnetism, so that all the ideas cohere. But they are not linked by any necessary relationship – merely by the historical accident that the original impressions all occurred to the same set of senses. From a scientific viewpoint 'I' is a fiction.

Hume's commitment to the empiricist mode of thinking and his willingness to push his premises to their logical conclusion seem to leave us little choice. If science is to be empiricist it is not going to deal with 'I'. In fact Hume's philosophy established the point that what we are doing when we describe objects is to describe our ideas and these may not correspond with the real world at all.

Hume then turned his sceptical 'I' to two important issues: causation and induction. Concerning causation: we think we know that fire causes heat but we do not know that because causation is not something perceived. We can perceive that A is bigger than B, or that A is on top of B, but we cannot perceive that A causes B. Hume concludes that causation is an expectation that what has been conjoined in the past will always be conjoined in the future. But we cannot know that the future resembles the past because what does not yet exist cannot be perceived. We suppose it will but that is merely a matter of habit - intellectual laziness.

Hume is now led to the 'problem of induction'. He asks: what logical justification can there be for the belief that the future will be like the past? Answer: there is no justification in logic. He then asks a psychological question: why do reasonable people have beliefs (that the future will be like the past) in which they have great confidence? Answer: because of the repeated association of ideas, or habit. If Hume is correct his conclusion follows – reason plays a minor role in human affairs. Knowledge is based on beliefs which are irrational, and so there can be no such thing as a rational belief or action.

Hume argues (1) inference from experience is not deductive, (2) it is therefore an irrational process (due to the association of ideas). In other words, when I generalise from facts to produce theories, I move beyond the facts. When I reason from theories to predictions, my reasoning is deductive because the predictions are contained within the theories. Since deduction is logic(al) and induction is not deduction, induction is not logic(al). Here Hume is arguing as a deductivist because he believes that if inference from experience is not deductive, it cannot be rational because all rational inference is deductive. Nor can I escape from this view by arguing that since induction has worked in the past, it can be relied upon in the future. That is to argue inductively for induction, which begs the question.

By the end of the *Treatise* Hume adopts a sceptical attitude towards metaphysics, God, mind, matter, 'I', causation, induction. What then is left for philosophers to do? They can hand over to scientists the task of searching for empirical truths by observation and experiment, and help them by cleaning up language – weeding the garden, so to speak. To accomplish this a tool is needed – Hume's Fork – with which nonsense can be identified and eradicated allowing the linguistic garden to flower in the form of the two types of propositions – analytic and synthetic – which can deliver truth.

Analytic propositions (including tautologies) are expressed by sentences whose negation leads to self-contradiction; which are independent of observation; which are true by definition; which are necessarily true. Example: all tall men are tall; charismatic leaders have special personal qualities; all bachelors are unmarried. Analytic truths are redundant, verbal truths which provide no new information about the physical world.

Synthetic propositions are expressed by sentences whose negation does not lead to self-contradiction; which are based on experience; which are not true by definition; when they are true they are not necessarily true (they can be false). Example: all tall men are blondes; charismatic leaders are intelligent; all bachelors are happy. These are the empirical propositions of science.

Propositions which are neither analytic nor synthetic are nonsensical and these include statements of value. Hume makes a clear distinction between statements of fact (what is the case) and statements of value (what ought to be the case). He notes in the *Treatise* that in every system of morality which he has studied authors move from statements about God or human nature to moral judgements - from 'is' to 'ought'. And he wants to know why he should accept an 'ought' when it cannot be deduced from an 'is' - a matter of fact.

In *An Enquiry Concerning Human Understanding* Hume gives us his famous manifesto: 'when we visit libraries, persuaded of these principles, what havoc we may make. If we take into our hand any volume; of divinity or metaphysics, for instance; let us ask: does it contain any analytic truths? If not, does it contain any synthetic truths? If not, commit it then to the flames for it can contain nothing but sophistry and illusion.'

Bertrand Russell (1872–1970) was an admirer of Hume and towards the end of a long life wrote in his *History of Western Philosophy* what amounts to a cri-de-coeur. Russell believes that Hume is one of the most important philosophers because he developed to its logical conclusion empirical philosophy and by making it self-consistent made it sceptical. Hume represents a philosophical dead end. To refute him has been a favourite pastime among philosophers but Russell finds none of their refutations convincing. Nevertheless he hopes fervently that something less sceptical than Hume's system may be discoverable. He devoted his intellectual life to attempting to discover whether there is any answer to Hume within the framework of an empirical philosophy. If there is no answer to Hume's scepticism, there is no intellectual difference between sanity and insanity. The lunatic who believes he is poached egg is to be condemned solely on the ground that he is in a minority or that the government does not agree with him. This is a desperate point of view for Russell and he hopes that there is some way of escaping from it. If there is, Russell did not find the escape route.

Hume's philosophy is out of fashion in our postmodern world. He was a member of the great Scottish enlightenment which flourished in the 18th Century and included his friends, Adam Smith and James Boswell. In *The Life of David Hume, Esq. Written by Himself* which was published posthumously in 1777, Hume describes himself as being naturally of a sanguine and cheerful temper which enabled him to recover quickly from the sad fact that his *Treatise of Human Nature* fell 'dead-born from the press', without even exciting a murmur among the zealots. The same fate befell his favourite book *Principles of Morals* (1752). Nor was he unduly disappointed by his two unsuccessful applications for a professorship in philosophy which were awarded to two justly forgotten plodders. In 1775 he was struck with incurable bowel cancer. 'I now (April, 1776) reckon on a speedy dissolution. I have suffered very little pain from my disorder; and what is more strange, have, notwithstanding the great decline of my person, never suffered a moment's abatement of my spirits; insomuch that were I to name the period of my life which I should most choose to pass over again, I might be tempted to point to this later period. I possess the ardour as ever in study; and the same gaiety in company. I consider, besides, that a man of 65, by dying, cuts off only a few years of infirmities; and though I see many symptoms of my literary reputation's breaking out at last with additional lustre, I knew that I could have but few years to enjoy it.' He was sociable, good-tempered, cheerful and moderate in his passions. His equaniminity was only threatened by the consequences of his sceptical thinking when, with over-heated brain, he would leave the solitude of his study, seek his friends, dine well and play billiards. Like so many philosophers he was a confirmed, and thus happy, bachelor who took a particular pleasure in the company of 'modest women'. He freely exposed himself to the wrath of political and religious fanatics and remained unper-turbed when they hurled their abuse at him. His friends never had occasion to reprimand him for his character or conduct although the fanatics 'would have been glad to invent and propagate any story to my disadvantage; but they could never find any which they thought would wear the face of probability.'

Hume is widely regarded by those who value lucidity and intellectual honesty as the greatest philosopher to have written in the English language. And he was, according to all reports, one of the nicest men who ever lived – the French called him 'le bon David'. He even befriended Jean-Jacques Rousseau who was, as we should nowadays say, paranoid. Inevitably, Rousseau claimed Hume was plotting against him. A thorough-going atheist, Hume was a firm believer in the power of science to overcome super-stition and ignorance and so achieve a humanity we are capable of but have never fully realised. But his intellectual honesty and rigour led him to a radical form of scepticism and away from philosophy.

Karl Popper (1902–1994) took up Russell's challenge and devoted his philosophical life to attempting to save the scientific method from Hume's corrosive scepticism.

He agreed with Hume that there can be no logical justification for inductive inferences. But he disagreed with Hume's psychology which assumes that we engage in inductive inferences because of the repeated association of ideas, or habit. In recent times Hume's psychology has been transformed into behaviourism and Hume's 'repeated association of ideas' is known as 'conditioning'. Popper disagrees with Hume's psychology because he believes that both induction and conditioning are myths. If he is right then we are forced to the conclusion that (a) induction is not a logical process; (b) induction is not a psychological process; therefore (c) induction is a myth.

Popper bases his critique of conditioning on the argument that combining two empiricist assumptions produces a logical error. Combining the assumption of *tabula rasa* (the mind is originally empty of ideas) with the assumption that we learn inductively (by the repeated association of ideas) leads to a logical inconsistency. This is because repetition presupposes similarity and similarity presupposes a point of view – a way of judging what is or is not similar. Popper argues that repetition presupposes an expectation (or primitive theory) by which similarity is assessed. Since the assumption of *tabula rasa* prohibits innate capacities, which would include the ability to assess similarity, expectations must be innate otherwise the process of conditioning cannot begin. Popper concludes that, contrary to the empiricists' assumption of *tabula rasa*, expectations are *a priori* (prior to experience), a conclusion which drives him into the rationalists' camp. So knowledge does not develop by the mere accumulation of sense data but proceeds by the modification of innate expectations (or primitive theories). We are born theorists!

Popper develops an activist theory of learning (rather than the passive form of learning based on conditioning) in which humans literally impose their theories upon the world and evaluate the results. Knowledge proceeds by trial and error elimination. In order to grow and mature humans need to engage in trials (take risks) and eliminate the errors which inevitably result therefrom. People who are reluctant to take risks are what psychologists call 'neurotic'. But so are people who, having taken appropriate risks, do not eliminate errors from their lives. Popper's philosophy contains, therefore, the germ of an as yet undeveloped theory of abnormal psychology and psychotherapy. Humans have an innate need for regularity – that is, for a world that conforms to their expectations. Often they are wrong in their expectations and so there is a need constantly to modify their theories. In this way mature humans pass from a dogmatic to a critical stage of thinking. A degree of dogmatism is necessary in order properly to test theories. But the willingness to expose theories to test, and thus to falsification, is the hallmark of the mature person.

Popper is thus squarely in the Socratic tradition of Western thought in which the importance of argument is emphasised and the delight in running errors to ground is obvious. Argument is the basis of critical thought and both are essential for growth. Life is concerned with encountering and solving problems and this calls for the bold propounding of trial solutions which are subjected to criticism and error elimination. Thus Popper's emphasis on the falsification, rather than the confirmation, of theories.

Theories which open themselves to falsification (such as Einstein's theory of relativity) are scientific. Theories which cannot in principle be falsified are not scientific. Popper includes in the category of non-scientific theories those of Sigmund Freud and Alfred Adler. Marx's theory, on Popper's view, is scientific in that it yielded testable predictions. In *The Open Society and its Enemies* Popper launched a devastating attack on Marxism, arguing that, since a scientific theory must yield falsifiable predictions, and Marxism did yield such predictions, Marxism is a scientific theory. The problem is that the predictions have been falsified. As such, Marxism is not a theory worth pursuing further, at least from a scientific viewpoint.

Popper does acknowledge that attempts to immunise Marxism from falsification, such as combining it with Freudism, have succeeded. For example, Marxism predicts that in capitalist societies the proletariat will be the most revolutionary class. Yet scientific research shows that the working class is not a revolutionary class. But this apparent failure of Marxist theory can be defended by mixing Marx with Freud and arguing that 'consciously' the proletarians are conservative, but 'unconsciously' they are revolutionary. This 'vulgar Marxism' cannot be falsified and so does not constitute a scientific theory. Those who believe it do so for 'religious' reasons.

In his later work Popper developed his (Socratic) rationalism in a (Platonic) idealist direction. He argued for the existence of 'three worlds' (material objects, mental processes and a world of theories). Popper's 'World 3' is a 'world' of objective theories, problems, possible solutions, error elimination, unintended consequences, more problems, and so on. It is a world of objective knowledge and it is separate from a world of subjective knowledge which is separate from a material world without knowledge. Popper vigorously defends his model of 'World 3' because he wants to rid science and philosophy of subjectivism and relativism. Knowledge is objective – it does not depend on any one person or group of people, even though people have to interpret it. One is reminded here of Plato's Theory of Forms to which Popper's World 3 has been compared.

Popper's philosophy has attracted widespread criticism because, despite his intentions, it leads to a radical scepticism. On Popper's view, theories are guesses to be weeded out by criticism. This approach includes the world of natural selection in which sense organs are to be seen as embryonic scientific theories, a social world in which society is composed of scientist-like individuals engaged in falsifying theories, and an abstract world of objective knowledge. These 'worlds' are governed by rationality which is the critical approach to life. Those who embrace Popper's 'critical rationalism' are imaginative masters of deduction (since induction is a myth). Deductivism, in Popper's hands, leads to the conclusion that we should prefer the best-tested theories – theories which have survived repeated attempts to falsify them. These theories are not true, but they are to be preferred to theories which have been progressively falsified or theories which have not been subjected to attempts to prove them wrong.

But critics are bothered by the deep scepticism that infects Popper's philosophy. Theories are bold guesses riddled with uncertainty and science is a game. As a man of practical action I ask: 'Upon which theory should I rely for practical action (from a rational point of view)'? Popper's answer: 'You should not rely on any theory for no theory can be shown to be true.' 'Well then, which theory should I prefer for practical action'? Popper's answer: 'The best-tested theory'. But why should I prefer any theory at all? Indeed, why should I even accept falsified experiments, for such an acceptance would seem to involve me in an inductive inference (an experiment falsified today will achieve the same result tomorrow)? Popper's tautological answer: 'the same test produces the same result'. But is this not a Pyrrhic victory when a trivial truth has to be used to save a philosophy from refutation? Consequently, many of Popper's critics claim he has failed to develop a fully non-inductive philosophy of science: he underestimates the importance of induction and an irrational element in science, and overestimates the logic of science and the objectivity of scientists.

Theories can be immunised against falsification. Furthermore, the observation statements on which falsification depends are fallible as Popper admits in *The Logic of Scientific Discovery*: the empirical basis of objective science has nothing 'absolute' about it. Science does not rest upon bedrock; it rises above a swamp. And Popper does not seem too distressed to admit that the acceptance or rejection of observation statements ultimately rests on a decision reached through a process much like trial by jury. This admission brings critics to the conclusion that Popper's philosophy is irrationalist. How, for example, am I to resist this conclusion when Popper tells me that science is not a system of well-established statements; nor is it a system which steadily advances towards the truth? Science, he says, is not knowledge and it can never claim to have attained truth, or even a substitute for it, such as probability. I pause here to ask: what then is the point of scientific investigation? If I admit, as he insists I should, that there is no possibility of ever finding the truth, how can scientific tests assist me in searching for the truth? Why should scientists bother to test their theories at all? Would it not be the case that any theory would be as 'conjectural' after testing as it was before?

It is little wonder that some of Popper's lapsed disciples, such as Paul Feyerabend (1924–1994), should announce that, as far as scientific method is concerned, anything goes. In his best-selling cult book *Against Method* he writes that science is much closer to myth than scientifically-minded philosophers are prepared to admit. Science is just one of the many forms of thought developed by human beings and it is by no means the best. It is conspicuous and impudent but is superior only for those who have decided in favour of a particular ideology or who are ignorant of its assumptions and practices. Feyerabend argues that the separation of state and church should be supplemented by the separation of state and science because science is just another dogmatic religious institution. Science, he claims, has no greater authority than any other form of life and its aims are not more important than are the aims that guide the lives in a religious community.

Feyerabend's aim is to remove obstacles that specialists create for traditions different from their own and to prepare the removal of the specialists from the centres of society. Traditions are neither intrinsically good nor bad; they become good or bad by applying some tradition. So infanticide or the torture of children is only to be regarded as 'bad' from the perspective of those who find it distasteful. He claims, for instance, that there is 'objectively' not much between anti-Semitism and humanitarianism. A free society should allow all traditions equal rights and equal access to centres of power. This can only be achieved if the present domination of society by science is altered. So Feyerabend advocates the removal of science from the centres of power together with the intellectuals who support it. We need not, he thinks, fear that the separation of state and science will lead to the breakdown of technology because there will always be people who prefer being scientists to being masters of their fate and who gladly submit to the meanest kind of intellectual and institutional slavery provided they are well paid and appropriately praised for their work. He is incensed at the idea that these well-paid scientific slaves should be allowed to impose their ideology on children in the guise of 'progressive' theories of education. If he had the power he would not allow them to teach the fancies of science as if they were the only factual statements in existence.

Feyerabend, writing in Berkeley, California (where else?) in the 1970s and 1980s became something of a cult figure and replaced Popper as the most influential philosopher of science in America where Popper was not as popular as he was in Britain. Feyerabend was a child of his times who appealed to those who had become disenchanted with science and who favoured relativistic thinking about everything, except relativism. If Hume's scepticism produced Popper, Popper's scepticism produced Feyerabend who, incidentally, was once one of Popper's favourite disciples. Then Feyerabend turned on the father, Popper (and Mrs. Popper too). The vehemence of his writing contrasts with his self-confessed 'would not hurt a fly' attitude to life. But Feyerabend delights in paradoxes. He claims, for example, that when it comes to scientific method 'anything goes'. But when it comes to criticising Feyerabend's work, anything does not go. The second half of his book *Science in a Free Society* is titled *Conversations with Illiterates* and the poor folk so named are the critics of his first book. In his replies to his critics Feyerabend is constantly pointing out how they misunderstand him, fail to follow his reasoning, refuse to accept that X 'discovered' Y, and so on. Anything goes?

In *The Plato Cult* Australian philosopher, David Stove (1927–1994) argues that Popper's philosophy of science represents a Jazz Age reaction to the breakdown of established order and the overturning of various forms of authority: political, moral, religious and scientific. As the old structures dissolved after 1918, Marxism, anarchism, Freudism, Dadaism and numerous other isms that promised a Great Reversal competed for the minds of intellectuals and politicians. A bewildered bohemian, might one day find himself a political leader of equally bewildered folk. Popper was a perfect example of a philosopher determined to practise the Great Reversal. Traditionally, the distinguishing mark of scientific propositions is that they are verifiable: Popper says they are falsifiable. The method of science has been essentially inductive: Popper says it is deductive. Caution is a virtue in science: Popper claims audacity is a virtue. Scientific conclusions are supposed to be certain: Popper says they are never more than guesswork. Scientists claim that scientific conclusions have a high degree of probability in their favour: Popper says that no theory ever becomes more probable when favourable evidence is discovered. In short, Popper stood traditional science on its head.

Stove argues that Popper, Feyerabend and legions of their fans embrace irrationalism about science because of an extreme belief about what is required for one proposition to be a reason to believe another. They believe that absolute certainty is forever out of reach; but they assume that only absolute certainty allows us to talk of rational belief. They exhibit what Stove calls a 'disappointed perfectionism', which is associated with an irresponsible, frivolous levity (for example, Feyerabend's suggestion that scientific laws should be decided by popular vote). Disappointed perfectionism has led to the frivolous elevation of the 'critical attitude' into a categorical imperative the result of which has been to convince millions of university students and their teachers that intellectual life consists in directionless quibble which leads to widespread relativism and nihilism.

Stove argues, against Hume, that there are good reasons to believe inductively-derived propositions. Hume's scepticism about induction (i.e. it is illogical and hence irrational and unreasonable) is the basis for his radical scepticism about science. His two main propositions are:

(a) inference from experience is not deductive;
(b) it is therefore a purely irrational process (based on the association of ideas).

Now (a) is irrefutable. 'Some observed ravens are black, therefore all ravens are black' is an invalid argument; this is the 'fallibility of induction'.

But (b) is untenable since it assumes that all rational inference is deductive. Since 'rational' means 'agreeable to reason', it is the case that our use of reason often ignores deduction and emphasises the facts of experience and inferences therefrom.

Stove attempts to defend induction from Hume's scepticism by arguing that scepticism about induction is the result of the 'fallibility of induction' and the assumption that deduction is the only form of rational argument. The result is inductive scepticism, which is that no proposition about the observed is a reason to believe a contingent proposition about the unobserved. The fallibility of induction, on its own, does not produce inductive scepticism because from the fact that inductive arguments are invalid it does not follow that something we observe gives us no reason to believe something we have not yet observed. If all our experiences of flames is that they burn, this does give us a reason for assuming that we will get burned if we put our hand into some as yet unobserved flame. This might not be a logically deducible reason but it is still a good reason. But once the fallibility of induction is joined with the deductivist assumption that the only acceptable reasons are deductive ones, then inductive scepticism does indeed follow.

Hume's scepticism about science is the result of his general inductive scepticism combined with his commitment to empiricism, which holds that any reason to believe a contingent proposition about the unobserved is a proposition about the observed. So the general proposition about empiricism needs to be joined with inductive scepticism to produce Hume's conclusion because some people believe that one can know the unobserved by non-empirical means, such as faith or revelation. As an empiricist Hume rules these means out as proper grounds for belief.

So to assert the deductivist viewpoint is to assert a necessary truth, that is, something that is trivially true not because of any way the world is organised but because of nothing more than the meanings of the terms used in it. When the sceptic claims that a flame found tomorrow might not be hot like those of the past, he has no genuine reason for this doubt, only a trivial necessary truth.

But postmodern sceptics are not interested in truths, trivial or otherwise. They are influenced by Wittgenstein's idea that language is indefinitely extendable and so there is no essence that binds all uses of language. Words have a 'family resemblance' among their various uses and no more can be said about their essential meanings. The meaning of a word (like I) is its role in a language game. When the rules of a language-game are violated language goes on holiday and this results in metaphysics or madness as Lewis Carroll demonstrates when the King tells Alice to look down the road and asks her if she sees anybody. 'I see nobody on the road,' she replies. 'I only wish I had such eyes,' says the King. 'To be able to see Nobody! And at that distance too!'

Ludwig Wittgenstein (1889–1951) saw himself as a kind of linguistic therapist whose task is to help people understand the different language games in which they are immersed. 'My aim in philosophy is to show the fly the way out of the fly bottle.' When we take words out of one language game and insert them in another, confusion results. In the hands of people without I's this can lead to anarchy. It also gives comfort to those lost souls who embrace cultural relativism and who long for a sense of community while emphasising the important differences between communities. There can, for Wittgensteinians, be no hidden I – nothing to which psychological terms refer since all are soaked in culturally- and rule-bound language. A private language is impossible, and so we cannot speak of I. Wittgenstein wrote shortly before his death: 'God may say to me: 'I am judging you out of your own mouth. Your own actions have made you shudder with disgust when you have seen other people do them.' Which sounds as though he was an I.

Postmodernists follow Wittgenstein's assertion that since all human experience is linguistically-bound, and languages are community-bound, the world is created by language and community practices. So if my language and community tell me I have no I, well bad luck for me! Using Wittgenstein's idea of language-games, postmodernists assert that objectivity is unattainable because language-games make it impossible for anyone to grasp reality. There is simply no fixed point from which it is possible to judge the truth of I. Truth is a word which forms part of a discredited language-game which once dominated Western thought. Those days have passed and postmodernists have embraced a rampant relativism in which there are no facts (it is a fact that there are no facts!). Experiences are not of facts but are 'narratives' and thus fairy-tales. The objects of our experiences are not things but 'texts' and, as Derrida said, there is nothing outside the text. The challenge for (anti)philosophers is, therefore, to deconstruct the meanings of 'texts'. This means that there can be no single or definitive meaning so that texts will be forever open to interpretation. Even the authors of texts cannot make claims about the objectivity (nasty word) of their work, nor can they claim to have priviliged access thereto. Authors are themselves caught up in the world of sliding discourses and changing meanings. So authors must join the queue and interpret their works along with their readers.

Before succumbing to the fact of death, Michel Foucault (1926–1984) asserted that discourses are attempts by their users to overpower others. Texts should therefore be constructed to expose this heinous human motive. Indeed our Me's (there are no I's for postmodernists) can be revealed by the process of deconstruction. I will not belabour the affinity with the Freudian technique of unmasking lies and prejudices by analysing one's unconscious motives. It is unsurprising, therefore, to find that postmodernists are deconstructing Freud's lies and prejudices by analysing his unconscious motives, ad infinitum, ad absurdum.

But the more important influence on postmodern thinking is the Nietzsche of *The Will to Power* who believes that the true world is a mere fiction and the life world a mere construction moulded by the workings of the will-to-power in human beings. Human psychology and sociology are grounded on a war of all against all.

Foucault follows Nietzsche in his belief that the appropriate model for understanding human beings is war. All social encounters are dominated by the desire for domination and the need to resist. Discourses or 'regimes of knowledge' are the product of power and serve the interests of a particular class. Foucault wants to liberate me from regimes under which I (unconsciously) suffer. I can achieve this worthy project by genealogical analysis of a discourse – unmasking its history and power. In this way I can liberate myself from coercive discourses, that is from 'regimes of knowledge and truth.' With luck I can then turn myself into a work of art. What type of art I create is up to me. I should try to live a beautiful life without concerning myself with the meaning of 'beauty'. Whilst I should prize self-mastery through personal choice, there is no 'I' to do the choosing. But Foucault faces a problem: if there is no possible ground for personal choice, ethical commitment is problematical. If social encounters are dominated by the will-to-power, it is difficult to see what Foucault would count as rational authority. If there is no rational authority, but only self-assertion, there is no difference between choosing to be a clergyman or a criminal.

What am I to make of the postmodern attack on objectivity and truth? Does a sceptical claim about objectivity and truth apply to itself? It is one thing to acknowledge the importance of social, historical and cultural factors and how they influence human practices. It is quite another to claim that all is I-less interpretation. If postmodernists insist on analysing themselves in relativistic terms, their suggestions must be understood as non-relativistic accounts of the facts of themselves. Furthermore, postmodern criticism of the imperialism of the Eurocentric perspective uses a language of morality which is derived from that perspective.

I do not advise any sane reader to read the postmodern literature, if such it can be called. What am I to make of Barthes' assertion that the author is dead? Or Derrida's hysterical outbursts, such as: 'Reason is a tyranny - I am outraged (who cares?) by the totalitarian arrogance implicit in the claims of reason.' Does this totalitarianism extend to Derrida's assertions? Foucault is equally shrill and inconsistent when he announces grandly that knowledge depends on power and 'the reason of rationalism requires – creates – sexism, racism, imperialism.' Kristeva (a woman) declared that 'woman as such does not exist' and Dworkin claimed, seriously, that 'all men are rapists'. Feyerabend asserted that when it comes to science, anything goes. And Irigaray took this seriously when she asked: 'Is $e=mc^2$ a sexed equation? Let us make the hypothesis that it is insofar as it privileges the speed of light over other speeds that are vitally necessary to us. What seems to me to indicate the possibly sexed nature of the equation is not directly its uses in nuclear weapons, rather it is having privileged what goes the fastest.' In short, superiority in any form is bad! And Harding, another woman, wrote: 'Science is not only sexist but also racist, classist and culturally coercive . . . Physics and chemistry, mathematics and logic, bear the fingerprints of their distinctive cultural creators no less than anthropology and history' (a tautology and so trivially true).

David Stove, held a competition to find the worst philosophical argument in the world. In *Cricket and Republicanism* he presents the judge's report. Ten candidate-arguments were submitted. Three dimensions entered into overall degree-of-badness: the intrinsic awfulness of the argument; its degree of acceptance among philosophers; the degree to which it has escaped criticism. The winner was the following:

'We can know things only: as they are related to us; under our forms of perception and understanding; in so far as they fall under our conceptual schemes etc.

So, we cannot know things as they are in themselves.

If there is a worse argument than this, the judge is still to learn of it. This argument has been accepted and used by countless philosophers, from Kant to postmodernism, yet it is difficult to beat for sheer awfulness. Stove admits that the 'warmest' entry was submited by Michael Devitt:

'People speaking different natural/scientific languages have different theories of the world (or perceive the world differently).

So, people speaking different natural/scientific languages live in different worlds.'

Stove concedes that this argument has been virtually exempt from criticism so that the two arguments are about equal on the degree to which they have escaped criticism. It may even slightly exceed the winner on awfulness. But it falls much below the winner on its degree of philosophical acceptance.

Postmodernists, Stove claims, have learned to lisp in

arguments like these. 'Their intellectual temper is (as everyone remarks) the reverse of dogmatic, in fact pleasingly modest. They are quick to acknowledge that their own opinion, on any matter whatever, is only their opinion; and they will candidly tell you, too, the reason why it is only their opinion. The reason is that it is their opinion.'

9

Living Romantically

*'By giving the common a noble meaning, the ordinary
a mysterious aspect, the known the dignity of the
unknown, the finite the appearance of the
infinite – I romanticise.'*

(Novalis)

In *The Roots of Romanticism*, Isaiah Berlin argues that the Romantic Movement was not invented by Parisian ladies who wore corsets that were too tight and covered their faces in poisonous cosmetics causing them to suffer attacks of the vapours. The Romantic Movement was invented by Germans of the male sex in the third quarter of the 18th Century and, contrary to the widespread belief that its main theme is sentimentalism, it was from the beginning to its demise in the early 20th Century a movement based on the power of the will. Its motto was not *cogito ergo* sum but *volo ergo* sum – I will therefore I exist.

The eighteenth century was the age of Enlightenment dominated by neo-classicism in architecture, music, painting, poetry and science. The intellectuals and artists who attended the famous salons of Paris in, say 1750, believed that: all proper questions can be answered; there is a method by which intelligent people can arrive at true answers; all true answers are compatible with one another (otherwise harmony and progress would be impossible); all subjects (including ethics and aesthetics) will ultimately yield their secrets to scientific investigation. This new classical age emphasised: system, symmetry, rationality, form and structure.

The influential thinkers of the Enlightenment – the French 'philosophes' (Montesquieu, Condillac, Condorcet, D'Alembert, Helvetius, Voltaire) dominated the intellectual world of Europe as their country dominated it politically. Wealthy, aristocratic, they promoted a confident worldview which, they believed, would secure for humanity undreamed-of glories. But their world was attacked and seriously wounded by humbly-born Germans (Lessing, Kant, Schiller, Herder, Fichte, Schelling, Hegel) – the sons of clergymen and teachers, unworldly and uncomfortable in the presence of the rich and famous. They could be, like Ludwig van Beethoven (1770–1827) and Caspar David Friedrich (1774–1840), boorish, insolent and unsociable. Yet they created the third and last great transformation in Western consciousness.

German Romanticism was, in part, a philosophical attack by Germans on the French. France, it should be remembered, had crushed Germany during the Thirty Years' War and had left the country broken in spirit. Germany was without a centre – it was governed by 300 princes – and without any sense of national confidence. The Germans looked to themselves for salvation and to the French with unbounded hatred. And so the intellectuals and artists determined to rid the German lands of French tyranny. If French art is neo-classical, German art will dispense with classical form. If French psychology is rational, German psychology will be irrational. If the French are realists, the Germans will be idealists – they will 'romanticise'.

The architects of the German attack on the Enlightenment attacked the view that the mind is a receptacle for ideas. Perceiving, reasoning, feeling are not separate faculties of the mind. Reasoning, for instance, cannot be separated from language and different languages produce different forms of reasoning. The early Romantics argued against universalism in ethics and aesthetics, holding that historical and psychosocial factors condition ethical and artistic concepts at different times. They emphasised expressionism (everything we do and create is an expression of our personal or collective character), belongingness (we all have roots which condition our existence), and value pluralism (values are relative to a particular time, place, group, state). Against Hume who believed that values were merely feelings, they argued that values are what one commits to – values are willed. Life is more than an association of ideas passively received from the environment. The world has no fundamental structure, purpose or meaning, as Newton and other members of the Enlightenment believed – the world is chaos. Whatever structure, purpose or meaning the world has is the result of our imposing those forms upon it. Life is a striving to create meaning out of chaos.

The Romantics argued that the 'world' has to be

constructed by humans. But since humans have different languages they will construct the world differently – what are facts to one group may not be facts to another. And if this is true of facts it will also be true of values. Values are often incompatible with one another and can never be reconciled. 'Reality' is constructed out of chaos by humans through perception and language. And since there is a kind of mythology in every language, the dominant myths of a society reflect the language used to construct and communicate them. There is, therefore, no possibility of a true language or set of myths – language or myths become dominant when one group dominates another and forces its will upon them. The Enlightenment dream of a rational universalism in ethics, politics and aesthetics cannot be realised.

The true, if reluctant, father of Romanticism is Immanuel Kant (1724–1804), in which there is a certain irony. Kant hated Romanticism and thought the Romantics were third-rate poets who were unable to engage in serious intellectual work and sought through art alternative means of expression. He was born, lived and died in Konigsberg, East Prussia. An academic for most of his long life, he was much admired for his brilliant lectures in various branches of science. Then, in his fifties, this conservative bachelor read David Hume's *Enquiry Concerning Human Understanding* (a re-write of his *Treatise of Human Nature* with the best bits left out), and it awakened him from his dogmatic (Newtonian) slumber. He saw immediately that Hume's arguments undermined his entire philosophy of science and of life and he determined to provide an answer to Hume's corrosive scepticism. Hume had shown, convincingly in Kant's view, that empiricism had failed because our everyday belief in an independent world of material objects that impinge on our sense organs can neither be validated by experience nor by logic, nor by a combination of the two. So our commonsense belief in such a world is a metaphysical belief, and is thus undemonstrable.

It was natural that the philosophers who read Hume would ask: is a philosophy of metaphysics possible after Hume? And Hume's fellow-travellers answered: No – it is not possible, metaphysics is sophistry and illusion. Kant, however, was to provide a different answer – exciting for some but unconvincing for others who claimed that Kant, having been awakened from his dogmatic slumbers, soon went back to sleep. Kant's answer was: Yes, metaphysics is possible. Philosophy's task is to investigate the form of the world by recognising that the so-called real world is unknowable – only the perceived world is knowable. And the perceived world is a world constructed by my perceiving apparatus. In short, I can only understand the world by studying the way I construct it through the categories of time, space, causality and so forth. Time, space and causality are not features of external reality; they are not to be found in the world because they are structures that my mind imposes on the world.

This theory of Kant's is similar to the Platonic-Cartesian doctrine of innate ideas. But whereas Plato and Descartes claimed that I am born with certain ideas in the mind, Kant argued that my mind is structured so that it analyses its data in terms of rules that resemble a machine which produces ideas when fed information

254

from the senses. So, for example, the mind creates 'thing-ness' although there is nothing out there called a 'thing'. Hume had, therefore, looked in the wrong place. He had, for example, looked for causality out in the world whereas it is a structuring process of the mind.

The empiricists' view that the world of independent objects causes experiences in my mind is rejected. In its place Kant claims that the perceived world is the way it is because the mind imposes form on it. My experiences are constructions that can be investigated by philosophical methods. It follows that there must also be a world-as-it-is-in-itself. That world is, however, not amenable to human understanding. If I believe in it, it is because it is a necessary presupposition of human knowledge. And so he concludes that there are two worlds, one which I can know (the phenomenal world), and one which is forever beyond the bounds of human knowledge (the noumenal world). The phenomenal world can be studied by scientists and philosophers; the noumenal world is where Kant makes room for freedom, spirituality and his God.

Kant's philosophy was an immediate success in Germany. But not everyone fell under the little master's spell. Nietzsche, writing about a hundred years later, argued that Kant's appearance was greeted with jubilation among German scholars because they believed he had found a path by which philosophers could sneak back to the divine. The idea of a 'true world' and the idea of morality as the essence of that world are, according to Nietzsche, two of the most malignant errors of all time which were, thanks to a wily and shrewd scepticism, to be embraced by philosophers throughout Europe. Nietzsche believed that Kant had reduced reality to mere 'appearance' and a mendaciously created world (the world of being) was enshrined as reality. Kant's success is, therefore, a theological success. In *The Anti-Christ* Nietzsche calls Kant, of all people, a nihilist with Christian entrails who considers pleasure an objection and duty an obligation, which is the very recipe for decadence, even for idiocy. This 'catastrophic spider' was considered *the* German philosopher, and for many, he still is.

Kant aimed to transform ordinary people so as to create a better moral world. As a man of the Enlightenment he believed that, despite empirical evidence to the contrary, humans are intrinsically good. In this belief he was following in the footsteps of his intellectual hero, Rousseau. That I sometimes behave poorly is due to my inability to exercise my rational choices. It is therefore of crucial importance that I (and all human beings) be regarded as potentially rational and that my right to exercise my rational choices be defended. If I am a mature individual I am capable of arriving at rational answers to moral questions so long as I am not prevented from doing so by malevolent authority.

The most important human attribute is the human will – the ultimate principle of freedom. Freedom is self-consciousness which takes me out of the domain of natural causation. Freedom is transcendental because it belongs to individuals everywhere and is made known to me by the fact of reason. Because my moral capacities are grounded in transcendental freedom I cannot lose these capacities, no matter how corrupt I become. If I am morally self-governed I am autonomous and so have the power to impose lawfulness on the world to create order, and to impose a moral law on society.

Kant was convinced that, whilst the will that grounds my autonomy cannot be understood scientifically, all individuals are aware of the difference between their passions and their obligation to do what is right. Although passions often come into conflict with obligation, the confusion of the two was, for Kant, an odious fallacy. I am free because I possess the power of choice. I am different from and superior to the rest of animate nature because I am free to choose what I wish. So it is the will, the power to choose responsibly, which distinguishes me from the animals. To be civilised is to be self-determined and not controlled by external or internal forces. If, for example, values are imposed on me by people in power, then I cannot be regarded as responsible and if I am not responsible I am not a moral being. And if I am not a moral being then distinctions between autonomy and heteronomy, right and wrong, are delusions. Kant firmly rejected this conclusion.

With his emphasis on autonomy and freedom of the will, Kant struck a blow against the mechanistic worldview of Newton and the Enlightenment. By exploring the limits of human knowledge he showed that scientific truths and moral truths are in different domains. When science has found all there is to find, it will not have had any impact on the moral life of human beings. Kant remained, however, a man of conservative temper and viewed with suspicion the radical changes that were occurring around him. In particular, he thought ill of the German Romantics, and predicted that their influence on the social world would be catastrophic. The Romantics, on the other hand, regarded him as a fellow-traveller in their journey towards the elucidation and realisation of human freedom. 'God, protect me from my friends', Kant said when told that one of his students, Fichte, claimed that he had 'improved' the master's philosophy. This temperamental disciple was to lead the Germans to an unrestrained form of romanticism which Kant had unwittingly given birth to.

Johann Fichte (1762–1814) was a volatile, radical German nationalist, quite unlike Kant in every respect, who believed it was his life's task to complete Kant's moral philosophy. Fichte believed that philosophy is consciousness of 'I', that is a consciousness constructed not from external sources but from consciousness itself. And the primary datum of consciousness is freedom. But if freedom is a primary datum why do so many people reject it? The philosophy I hold, he says, depends on the kind of person I am. And I have a choice between freedom and determinism.

For Fichte there are two kinds of philosophy and what is fundamental is my freedom to choose between them. There is the scientific, 'dogmatic' perspective and there is the 'idealistic' view of oneself as an active being, a free and responsible agent. Fichte rejected the mechanical, Newtonian image of the world in favour of freedom. His whole philosophy can be seen as an attack on the deterministic materialism of the 18th Century and an attempt to liberate human beings from the treadmill of a mechanically determined existence. Even so, many people surrender themselves to this very determinism and reject freedom. Fichte admitted that the 'dogmatic' deterministic perspective has great mass appeal because not all people are capable of freedom and hence will not choose freedom when it is offered to them. Where people believe themselves to be conditioned beings and victims of their base desires, they need to be liberated from the tyranny of determinism.

Fichte qualified Kant's view that we are morally obligated to treat all people as ends in themselves rather than as means to ends. We are morally obligated to treat people as ends in themselves who are in fact ends in themselves – free beings. For the remainder, coercion may be employed to force people to be free.

Throughout his work Fichte emphasises the primacy of human action over reflection. Life for Fichte, as for Goethe and later for Nietzsche and Sartre, begins with action. He follows Goethe's dictum: 'In the beginning was the act. I am not here to know but to do'. In *The Vocation of Man*, his most accessible work, Fichte maintains that I do not act because I know (as the French believe); I know because I am called upon to act. Experiences are not passively registered in my mind (as Locke and Hume believed); experience is something I create through action.

But what is the source of my power of human action? Obviously not my body since it is conditioned by external forces. Nor sensual drives since they are conditioned by bodily forces. Fichte argued that the source of power to act freely upon the world is willing. I will with freedom according to a freely conceived purpose, and this will, as the most fundamental cause, moves and shapes my body and by means of it the surrounding world. To put it another way, I do not accept what nature offers because

I must, I believe it because I will. If I embrace Fichte's radical philosophy of personal power I must admit that I want to be the master of nature, I want to have an influence on nature proportional to my power.

Fichte sets the stage for such 19th Century writers as Max Stirner, Soren Kierkegaard, Friedrich Nietzsche and 20th Century existentialists, Jean-Paul Sartre and Simone de Beauvoir, who glorify the active, dynamic willing individual. Agreeing with Hume that will cannot emerge in cognition, Fichte argued that awareness of will is a product of some form of collision. When I confront the world in action, when the external world resists my actions, then I become aware of the power of my will. In this sense, will or 'I' is not the same as 'Me'. There is, for Fichte, a primal will that I become aware of by being acted upon. This impact is the fundamental fact of my experience.

Descartes' philosophy leads me to wonder how I could validate my knowledge of the external world. Fichte answered decisively: when there is a clash between 'I' and 'not-I', between what I will and what the world imposes upon me, then I am made aware of the will because without the 'not-will' there can be no sense of will. And will expresses itself in action, effort, striving, overcoming resistance. My character can only be understood through effort – my willingness to confront and the determination to overcome the obstacles of the world.

Fichte emphasises the importance of my power freely to impose my will upon an unstructured chaotic world that is, in effect, a world of my creation. Since I am will and since I am free to impose my will on an unstructured world in order to create structure and meaning for myself, non-freedom is simply not an option for me. I must come to full consciousness of a freedom which I can use to the fullest possible degree. Just as Michelangelo imposed his will upon the marble and created the *David*, so I am condemned to create meaning for myself by imposing my will on the world. The world is a battleground of wills colliding with wills. And will is not to be subordinated to classical form. So where I find truth, structure, pattern, harmony, equilibrium, I should attack, mock, laugh (as in the tales of Hoffmann, the 'romantic irony' of Schlegel, and later Dadaism, surrealism, the theatre of the absurd). Since that leaves nothing I should act artistically to create my world. But other people have the same idea and so human relationships are fraught with conflict. In order to keep my head above water, I may need to remove myself from society. Again I think of Beethoven: 'You think I hate you. I do not. But I can't stand you'. And Caspar David Friedrich, arguably the greatest German Romantic painter: 'You call me an enemy of mankind because I avoid company. You are wrong. I love you. But in order not to hate men, I must abstain from their society'.

Friedrich studied at the progressive Copenhagen Art Academy and in 1798 settled in Dresden as a landscape painter. Many of his paintings bear the imagery of his homeland on the Baltic Sea and the white cliffs of Rugen. His romantic art went beyond the formalism of neo-classicism and the strict rules of the academic painting of his time. He always painted people from behind as if he wants me to climb within the body of his figures to share their view. Arguably he is the first painter to place a sub-jective perspective in the centre of his view of the world. His human figures form the centrepiece of nature which reveals itself to them through pure experience. Individual and nature are expressions of forms which collide with each other. And humans are at the mercy of this colliding form. Only my inner voice and the power of my imagi-nation allows me to reconstruct the world to my ends. So we see in Friedrich's painting of a graveyard a man and a woman standing over their child's grave. I can share their feeling because my imagination completes what the romantic artist merely hints at. Great romantic art, unlike classical art, is ambiguous so that artist and others can all participate in a powerful act of creation.

There is at the heart of Romanticism a tendency towards anarchistic individualism and so it is not surpris-ing that someone would sooner or later publish a book of philosophy based on himself. That man was Max Stirner (1806–1856) who, in 1844, published a book which was so revolutionary that the censors allowed it to proceed to publication thinking it too absurd to find readers, and Karl Marx and Friedrich Engels devoted 380 pages of *The German Ideology* to the task of refuting its central argu-ments. The book is *The Unique One and his Property* mistranslated as *The Ego and its Own*, and its thesis is simple: 'I have founded my philosophy on nothing (except myself)'.

Stirner believed that we are easily seduced by language, especially by abstractions. As the *Bible* says: 'In the begin-ning was the word.' And the word is misleading when it is abstract. Since all religions, political systems and philosophies are built on abstractions they must be criticised because they mislead fools and uncritical readers. Abstractions, or what Stirner calls 'spooks', devalue the uniqueness of the individual. Moreover, they are frequently used by unscrupulous people to control others. People who are infatuated with such abstractions as mankind, humanity, society, state, liberty, equality, fraternity, love, leave individuals out of account. In the name of abstractions homicidal maniacs justify their appalling behaviour, and are often forgiven for their grotesque acts.

The greatest spook of all is God – a dangerous abstraction which ruthless lunatics have used to control and murder millions of people. Before Nietzsche was born Stirner announced the death of God and the need to move beyond the Christian ideas of good and evil, which are abstractions used to avoid the difficult choices of life. Being part of a religious group may give me access to social power and believing in an everlasting happiness after death may give me a way to cope with the rigours of life. But the price I pay is that I become a slave to a morality which deprives me of my individuality. Religious belief is slave morality and Christianity is a slave religion invented by slaves for slaves. The only meaningful and coherent unit is not the Church, or the State, but 'I'. Echoing Machiavelli, Stirner says that the habit of the religious way of thinking has biased our thinking so grievously that we are terrified at the sight of our bodies in their natural state; it has degraded us so that we dream ourselves depraved by nature. The Christian is nothing but a sensual man who sees in himself a poor sinner; sensuality is recognised by

Christians as 'sinfulness', and this is what we mean by Christian consciousness.

Like all religions, Christianity substitutes ideals for sensual experience, over-values the mind and under-values the poor body. But the body makes its presence felt, often in the most acute ways, so that Christians experience feelings of guilt and inadequacy when, for example, they experience the thrill of sexuality. Such self-lacerating feelings intensify the remoteness of the ideal and lead to a downward spiral in which the individual becomes doubly dependent on religion. Stirner rejects the tyranny of religious systems and embraces himself as his own God. Like Fichte, his starting point is 'I' am 'I'. Or in the words of Ibsen: the strongest man in the world is he who stands alone.

Stirner's egoistic philosophy appeals to many anarchists because of his uncompromising rejection of all authority beyond the reach of the individual. He mounts a savage attack on liberal-democracy when he admits that he does not want the liberty or equality of men, he wants only his power over them, he wants to make them his property, material for his enjoyment. Against John Stuart Mill he sees freedom as a positive movement towards taking possession and realising one's own power. Freedom awakens my rage against everything that is not me; freedom is a longing, a romantic cry, a Christian hope. He prefers personal power to freedom because it is not a rage against the obstacles of the world but a joy over ourselves. The man who is set free is like a dog dragging a piece of chain with him, and the more freedom he receives, the more anxious he becomes and soon bleats like sheep. For

Stirner all freedom is essentially self-liberation. Egoism is self-enjoyment, self-mastery, self-overcoming and it depends on freeing myself from all ideologies by developing and exploiting my own resources.

Stirner's critique of the State is equally vehement. The State is repressive, superfluous, a despotism which freezes the will of the individual. For the State might is right and violence the means to legitimating this right because the State has always the sole purpose to limit, tame and subordinate the individual. So Stirner says he is free in no State, he is the deadly enemy of the State and he has nothing to say to the State except 'get out of my sunshine'. Rather than State worship Stirner advocates a ruthless realisation of the power of the individual.

For human beings 'existence precedes essence' – I am free to create an essence for myself. If I am compassionate or cruel it is because I choose to be so. There is no universal human nature; I am human because I am conscious and so I have the power to create myself out of nothing – I am a *creative nothing*. I can choose to become a Christian or an atheist, a hero or a coward. There is a strong temptation, however, to be a half-hearted egoist which allows me to claim that I am sometimes free and sometimes unfree. When I succeed in some task I claim I am free and deserve to be rewarded for my success; when I fail I claim I am not free and should not be penalised for my behaviour. The half-hearted egoist, who holds himself back and refuses to acknowledge his personal power to overcome obstacles, becomes increasingly resentful at his inability to achieve his self-chosen goals. His striving becomes joyless as stress and fatigue conquer him. Stirner believes in joyful striving, hurling oneself into the abyss that is always before us. Life is to be squandered, exploited, attacked. And if others cause me difficulties I must be strong enough to take decisive action, especially with members of my family. A sensible father throws out a son who will not grow up and keeps the house to himself: 'it serves the simpleton right.'

Does this mean that Stirner's philosophy disqualifies an individual from entering into a loving relationship. Not at all. Stirner was married twice and claimed that he loved both his wives. His first one died in childbirth and his second left him after he had spent most of her inheritance. She remembered him thirty years later as a selfish man who tried to live his egoistic philosophy. His views about loving relationships did not please his wife and continue to upset sentimental folk. An egoist loves another person not to make the other happy but because he enjoys the state of loving; love is based on selfishness. If I see the loved one suffer, I try to comfort her because I cannot bear the troubled crease on the beloved forehead, and so for that reason and therefore for my sake, I kiss it away. I love because I feel good when I am loving, and when I stop feeling good about loving a certain person, I 'fall out of love'. Stirner has no time for the sentimental hypocrisy that suffocates loving relationships. He believes that we love ourselves loving, and if we don't love ourselves we can't love others.

Stirner's world is full of misfits, extremists, militants, deviates and armies of peculiar characters intent on imposing their will on other people. Argument is futile in the face of the mass stupidity which characterises human society and he concludes that the majority will pay the costs of their stupidities and it will all serve them right. Stirner will live his life on his terms, let others run their lives to suit themselves.

After the sales of his infamous book dwindled, he borrowed money from friends but could see no reason to repay them. He soon lost those friends, a fact which didn't bother him unduly. After getting into trouble with the authorities, he lived on his own terms and died after being bitten by a wasp.

Not all Romantics adopted the mythical optimism of Fichte or the radical egoism of Stirner. There developed within Romanticism a pessimistic wing which viewed the world as a place of abject misery and human beings as condemned to an existence which fluctuated between pain and boredom. In such a world, human pleasure is simply the absence of pain, and living is a search for the jewels in the shitheap of existence.

The outstanding representative of pessimistic Romanticism is the unjustly neglected German philosopher Arthur Schopenhauer (1788–1860) who, after travelling through Europe as a young man and seeing many examples of appalling human cruelty, determined that life was a miserable affair and he intended to spend his time thinking about it. And so he became a philosopher. After a brief and unhappy career in commerce, he devoted himself to philosophy and art. He spent a part of each day writing, playing the flute, reading British newspapers and attending the opera. He spoke several languages, developed an interest in Eastern religions, had many unsatisfactory love affairs and remained a misanthropic bachelor who loved his dogs more than human beings. He is regarded as the most pessimistic of the Western philosophers, but one who appreciated the subtleties of Eastern thought arriving at conclusions not unlike Buddhism, but from a Western starting point. He was a child of Romanticism and distrusted the Western emphasis on rationality, replacing it (like Fichte) with the power of the will. His philosophy is, therefore, an attempt to account for the fact of human irrationality and leads eventually to the psychology of Nietzsche, Freud and Jung.

Schopenhauer's greatest work, *The World as Will and Idea* (1818) opens with: 'The world is my idea'. Schopenhauer saw the everyday world as a world of appearances – objects for a subject. What we know of the world is our interpretation of it – there are no objects without subjects and no subjects without objects. But what is the 'I' that interprets the world? According to Schopenhauer, knowledge of 'I' is a different kind of knowledge from that which we have of the external world since knowledge of oneself is of immediate reality. We know ourselves objectively in the same way as we know other appearances. But we know ourselves subjectively as 'will'. So for Schopenhauer, my body and my will are one. My body is appearance in time and space, whereas my will is reality in time only. The world is a duality – the world as appearance is the outer, physical world conditioned by time, space and causality; the world as will is the inner, subjective world conditioned by time. The real world – without human interpretations – must be unconditioned by time, space and causality. It must therefore be more like my private experience of willing than my public experience of external projects. So he calls the real world 'Will'. And we, and everything else, are manifestations of Will.

The driving force behind man's actions is not to be found in reason but in the depths of unconscious will. The ultimate reality is, for Schopenhauer, a blindly striving, involuntary force. He took from Fichte the doctrine that the will is the basic substance of the world, but whereas Fichte saw the will as a rational principle, Schopenhauer regarded it as purposeless and insatiable. The intellect is devalued to a mere tool used in the service of the will. Try as I may to use my intellect to become master in my own house, the will dominates all and leads me where it will – not where I will. Not content to accept this fact, I spend my miserable life constructing and defending a 'Me' with which to create the illusion that I am special. The reality is that I am swept along in the organic flow of life, from which I have emerged and to which I shall return at death.

Since I am embodied will striving to overcome other wills, universal suffering is inevitable. With obvious relish, Schopenhauer writes of the evil, suffering and stupidity which characterise human existence. Humans are not *homo sapiens* but *homo homini lupus* – 'man is a wolf to man'. Yet, Schopenhauer tells us, there is a temporary escape from the treadmill of life's pain and boredom. The way out can be found by a few people in philosophy or religion. But it is through art (and especially music) that I can best escape from the world's ills. Art has the power to tame the will by turning me away from the egoistic world of desire towards a state of will-less contemplation.

Great art can deliver me, if I am capable of appreciating it, to another 'world'.

Aesthetic experience is the means by which the veil which hides the true nature of the world is partially rent. I become a pure subject of contemplation and the objects of art surrender their qualities of time and space and present themselves to me as Platonic Ideas. This is why Leonardo's *Mona Lisa* and Michelangelo's *David* are great – not because they make me 'feel good' (that is what pornography does) – but because they capture the eternally feminine and the eternally masculine respectively. Bad art – which for Schopenhauer is not art at all – has the opposite effect. It stimulates the passions and is therefore pornographic. If 'art' is neither great nor pornography, it is junk. If Schopenhauer visited our art galleries he would conclude that most of modern and postmodern art is junk. He would point out that when it comes to postmodern art, the emperor has no clothes. He provides me, therefore, with an alternative to the popular view that art should be judged by whether it stimulates me or makes me feel good. Great art tames the passions and removes me from the tedious world of desire – I surrender myself to the great mystery of life. If only he were here to write about postmodern 'art'!

Schopenhauer's theory of art (and philosophy generally) is no longer fashionable. He was, in the 1890s, the second most famous European philosopher (after Kant). But he fell into disfavour during the First World War. Yet, it is fair to say that Schopenhauer has influenced more artists than any other philosopher. The list includes Wagner, Mahler, Tolstoy, Turgenev, Mann, Zola, Proust,

Lawrence, Shaw, Hardy and Conrad. There are signs that some people, having become dissatisfied with what today passes for art and art criticism, are turning to Schopenhauer's theory of art, if not to his pessimism. His day may come again. I hope that will happen.

If Schopenhauer is known today it is because of his famous disciple – Nietzsche – who inverted his pessimism to become the optimistic philosopher of life. But Nietzsche moves us from late Romanticism to Modernism, from Schopenhauer's measured prose to pyrotechnical rhetoric. Who was this inflammatory writer who only ever wrote with his blood? Why is he so widely read and written about today? Why has he been appropriated by so many diverse groups and lost souls? How is it that this sick, lonely man, writing in the 1880s, has been credited with 'inventing the 20th Century' and the modernism which characterised its first seventy years? How do we explain the popularity of this man who has one of his characters in *Thus Spoke Zarathustra* say: 'When you go to a woman, take your whip with you', although I am inclined to agree with Bertrand Russell that the average woman would have no trouble in taking the whip from him. That he was Hitler's house-philosopher did not add to his reputation, especially after 1945, and the belief that his philosophy is so dangerous that it sent him mad produced a certain reluctance on the part of many to engage with him for fear of their sanity.

Regarded by many intellectuals as the most important philosopher of the 20th Century, Friedrich Nietzsche (1846–1900), the son of a Lutheran pastor and educated in the classics, vehemently opposed Western values and institutions – Christianity, socialism or 'secular Christianity', egalitarianism, democracy, feminism. He thought that 20th Century man would be 'bungled, blotched, sickly, cerebral, emotionally crippled, scientific, resentful, anxiously repressed', whose 'happiness will be purely passive and take the form of drugged tranquillity, stretching, yawning, emotional slackness.' He associated the averaging of public thought (in science) with the averaging of public thought (in democracy) and loathed both fearing the domination of the strong minority by the weak, resentful and cowardly majority. He thought that in his time the petty people have become masters: they all preach submission, acquiescence, prudence, diligence and consideration and other petty virtues. It sickened him that a sort of mob effeminacy wants to become master of mankind's destiny.

It has been said that modernism probes into unconscious layers of modernity to confront it with its anxieties, and thereby sets itself against modernity. If true, then Nietzsche was one of the most influential of modernists. Appropriated by the Nazis and Fascists, rediscovered by left-wing French intellectuals in the 1960s, embraced by many feminists, used and abused by anarchists and numerous 'new age' souls, mentor to Freud and Jung, proto-existentialist, Nietzsche is now widely regarded as the grandfather of postmodernism, in which there is a certain irony, since the aristocratic Nietzsche would devalue most of the apologetic, politically correct values embraced by postmodern relativists. Nietzsche is the prophet of Western nihilism and its arrival in the West in the 1970s, under the name of postmodernism, helps to explain Nietzsche's relevance today since thinking people usually try to understand the times in which they live. But Nietzsche analysed nihilism in order to over-come it, not to luxuriate in it. Whether he succeeded is a matter for Nietzsche's readers to determine for themselves. And that is precisely why he wrote his 'great books'. He wanted, above all else, to encourage his readers to 'become what they are', to discover their will-to-power, to live life to the fullest and take all that the will-to-power secures for them, in the knowledge that there is no other world and so no other life.

In his early years Nietzsche wrote under the influence of Schopenhauer and Wagner. He shared their Romantic values and devoted himself to promoting German art, especially in the form of Schopenhaurean pessimistic philosophy and Wagnerian dramatic opera. He argued that the world of the ancient Greeks had achieved a remarkable synthesis of Dionysian and Apollonian values which sublimated the former's barbaric impulses into the latter's classical form and structure. But the delicate balance between man's ferocious drives and classical harmony was destroyed by Socrates, Plato, Christianity and its bastard child, socialism. Nietzsche singles out Socrates for special criticism – he never forgave Socrates for replacing the Homeric warrior as cultural hero with a man who can argue other people into the ground. With the arrival of the Socratic element in Western life, value turned from action to language, from rhetoric to logic, from power to truth, from courage to rationality, from will to knowledge. The powerful were subordinated to the thinkers; the warrior was replaced by the logician.

Nietzsche believed that the strong had been dragged down by the masses who, acting out their resentments against the powerful, substituted a new table of values for the aristocratic code of warriors. This is explicit in Christianity where the value of humility replaced the value of power. Consequently, there developed the tyranny of herd morality characterised by subordination of the individual to the 'rational' and the emotional repression that accompanied it. But this inversion of heroic values leads to weakness and cultural decadence. Even worse, by Nietzsche's time, Western rationalism had virtually destroyed itself by its unrelenting attacks on religion, tradition, science, art and itself. Western rationalism has at its heart a self-destructive mechanism by which it turns on itself – like a snake feeding on its own tail. By the 1880s Nietzsche thought that the snake had arrived at its own head. The result: the destruction of absolute values, pessimism, relativism, scepticism, nihilism.

If God is dead because we have killed him, and science is unable to fill the void left by his death, everything is permitted. And so one action or value is as good as another. When certainty is undermined the masses will panic and search for someone to lead them, to give them guidance, work and security. They will reach out for a leader and a doctrine to live by. 'Do not follow this deadly path,' Nietzsche writes, 'go your own way, find your own path in life'. After all, a student repays a teacher badly by remaining a student.

Nietzsche's books are filled with aphorisms which point towards a new 'refined' heroism – an heroic individualism. There is no more severe judge of everything undisciplined, soft and weak than Nietzsche, who believes that the decadence of the West is due to the decline of discipline and authority and the unheroic and ignoble hedonistic values which have come to dominate society. So Nietzsche turns to heroic nobility because it is a philosophy that does not force life into a super-natural world. He offers a type of heroism which disdains to offer itself to the veneration of the masses, as his coarser Homeric brother does. Nietzsche's heroism consists in not fighting under the banner of sacrifice, compassion and devotion, but in bringing about destruc-tion through an act of self-overcoming. The modern hero says to the masses: 'This is what I want; this is what I am – you can go to hell.'

Nietzsche extols an heroic individualism in the knowl-edge that it condemns man to isolation and attack because the will to stand alone is felt to be dangerous; everything that raises the aristocratic, intelligent individual above the herd and makes his neighbour quail are today called evil. How could we have allowed this to happen? This danger-ous state of affairs must be reversed by a philosophy based not on truth but will, not knowledge but power. Life is, for Nietzsche, will-to-power and once we accept this idea and embrace it, we must also accept that the only value is life and so will-to-power replaces the will-to-truth by which Western man has attempted to live for 2400 years. The search for Truth, in its religious and scientific forms, has failed and this has given rise to a pervasive scep-ticism about the possibility of any future table of values which can command universal, or even widespread, assent.

Nietzsche's answer to the nihilism of his time is thoroughly naturalistic. Spiritual values must be rejected and life accepted on its own terms. Other worlds and those false moralisms used to explain away unsavoury aspects of natural existence are not needed anymore. Humans should be strong enough to say 'yes to life', and even go so far as to assert unconditionally their willingness to live this life again, and again, an infinite number of times. The strongest humans – the higher men – will be those who combine a Dionysian, life-affirming power with the sort of intelligence that surpasses religions, ideologies and mean-spirited feelings. Man will be on the road to the status of an *Ubermensch* – man surpasses man beyond good and evil. The *Ubermensch* is an ideal towards which natural man may aspire, and 'higher men' (like the great artists) are well on the way to that exalted status.

Nietzsche thought that 19th Century man was at a cross-roads – he was facing a choice between more old life-negating cultures or a new aristocratic culture. But he wondered whether Western man is capable or worthy of a new aristocratic culture. Is it not likely that humans will, given the opportunity, revert to their herd moralities? True to form, Nietzsche plays with another solution. Perhaps rather than work towards a new aristocratic culture, the free spirits will detach themselves from the herd by following the example of Diogenes, and adopt a mocking, light-hearted, witty and cynical approach to life. If life-negating cultures decay, and life-affirming cultures develop despite our individual efforts, why not adopt an absurdist attitude to life? Perhaps ironic laughter is the best way for the free spirits to cope with Western decadence.

This 'experimentation' or 'game-playing' is very typical of Nietzsche and helps to explain his popularity today. On the one hand he tells us that he is a writer of high seriousness who has given to the world matters of the greatest weight to ponder. On the other hand he tells us that he is a buffoon, a trickster, a man of many masks and that he should not be taken seriously. The buffoon plays with language, even going so far as to proclaim that 'there is no truth', 'there are no facts', and 'all sentences are metaphors'. Now this is great fun at postmodern dinner parties and is today all the rage. But to announce that 'there is no truth' leaves Nietzsche open to the charge that his proposition is presented as a truth and so is self-refuting. There is simply no point in talking seriously with people who say, in effect, 'it is a fact that there are no facts' because they are violating the basic rules of English. It is rather like agreeing to play chess only to find your opponent making up new rules as he goes. And when Nietzsche playfully maintains that 'all sentences are metaphors' he is in effect saying that they are not literally true, and therefore they are false. But that includes his original proposition that 'all sentences are metaphors', and so it is not literally true, and therefore it is false. Therefore, if Nietzsche is right, he is wrong. When this was pointed out to him, his reply was: 'So much the better'. Is he serious, is he a poor logician, or is he playing with us?

Truth, for Nietzsche, is 'a mobile army of metaphors, metonyms and anthropomorphisms'. And common sense is 'metaphysics made routine'. He was, however, prepared to admit that we are obliged to say that common sense is 'true' because truth is that sort of error without which some living creatures could not live. Yet common sense is false because there is no order in the world for things to correspond to. The value of truth is measured in terms of power: we cannot speak of a true perspective only a dominant one. Common sense is 'the metaphysics of the herd.' And common sense fluctuates according to time and place and is determined by those in positions of power.

Nietzsche has no time for pure beings, original data, God(s), Platonic forms, substances, things-in-themselves, World Will, mind. There is only flux and chaos upon which we impose our will-to-power (or, rather, will-to-power imposes us on chaos). If Nietzsche is right, there is no such thing as Platonic 'knowing'. Knowing is not discovering some eternal truth, it is inventing – lying even. So Nietzsche invites us to lie creatively. The master of 'truth' is not the logician, but the noble rhetorician who understands that 'every word is a preconceived judgement.' Rhetoricians understand that to have power over words is to have power over people. And Nietzsche strives to be a master rhetorician – a new type of philosopher who does not argue, but commands. Language contains a philosophical mythology and to understand this is to have the power to create new philosophies. When primitive men invented a new word they believed they had made a discovery. Rather than solving a problem they had, in fact raised an obstacle to its solution. So wedded are we to the power of words we would rather break a bone than a word. Nietzsche is the breaker of philosophical bones –

the philosopher with a hammer who describes himself as dynamite.

Nietzsche offers a serious challenge to the philosophical tradition inaugurated by Descartes. Of Descartes' *cogito ergo sum* he gives a 'smile and two question marks.' First, by what logic or right did Descartes conclude that there is an 'I' that thinks? Surely, he should have concluded from his systematic doubting of everything that 'there is thinking'. Why does he insist that there is an 'I' – 'an immaterial thing' – that thinks? If things are fictions, as Nietzsche maintains, so too are mental entities. Nietzsche eliminates distinctions between matter and mind, subject and object, cause and effect, because they lead to endless and pointless philosophical disputes. One either believes both or neither, so Nietzsche resolves the many dichotomous dilemmas of Western philosophy by smashing them with his philosophical hammer. He is a true iconoclast and so titles one of his books *Twilight of the Idols: or How to Philosophise with a Hammer*.

He applies the same reasoning to the vexed question of freedom and determinism. This dilemma was invented by the Stoics and has troubled philosophers for centuries. Not so Nietzsche for whom there is no freedom of the will and no determinism either. That which is termed freedom of the will is the feeling of superiority in relation to him who must obey. I am free, he must obey. Freedom of the will is an expression of the joy of the commander. The Romantic in Nietzsche shines through in his belief that freedom is measured according to the resistance which must be overcome. There are strong and weak wills, but there is no freedom of the will. And there is no unfreedom of the will either. Some people will not give up their 'responsibility', their belief in themselves, the personal right to their merits at any price. Others, on the contrary, do not wish to be answerable for anything, or blamed for anything, and seek to lay the blame for their actions somewhere else. The latter take the side of criminals; a sort of socialist compassion dominates their values. In short, whilst there is no freedom or unfreedom of the will, people of strong will-to-power will adopt the policy of freedom of the will, whilst those of weak will-to-power will prefer to believe in the unfreedom of the will.

Nietzsche believed that those who pursue happiness and a stress-free life are 'poor in spirit'. Freedom means becoming more indifferent to stress, hard work and deprivation. He extols energy, vitality, effort and he has little patience for those who complain of the rigours of life. It is the lack of vitality in the modern world that so worried Nietzsche (and perhaps it should worry us too). He believed that the West's hedonistic life style, combined with the collapse of absolute values and objective truth would usher in an era characterised by nihilism. Such an era would reveal in all its horror the complete collapse of standards by which rank can be established and worth appreciated. We are living in the detritus of centuries of fundamentally mistaken ideas about what it means to be courageous because the vitally courageous conception of life is not concerned with comfort and security but with struggle and challenge. 'Free spirits' can rise to the heights of the challenge of human existence in a spirit of determined exuberance. These free spirits are the 'higher men' and they will look back on our culture of complaint, as

Robert Hughes describes our postmodern age, and wonder how it came about that the 'poor in spirit' came to dominate cultural consciousness.

In his psycho-cultural critique Nietzsche reveals his neo-Romantic impulses, especially when he argues for the will as the foundation of human existence. With the will-to-power he believed he had found the means to deny nihilism and affirm life. Given that I am will-to-power and cannot escape its effects, I should embrace and direct my energies towards individual fulfilment, I should 'become who I am'. This exhortation reveals Nietzsche's naturalism – there is an underlying quality in each person. And so his references to 'become who you are' are developed from his naturalistic view that I do not will, choose or possess power; I *am* will-to-power. But where does this leave 'I'?

Nietzsche tells me not to concern myself with mind, soul, psyche, ego or consciousness, but man – a creature whose existence is animate, bodily, active, social and historical. All mentalistic notions are artificial abstractions and distract my attention from the fact that man is a sophisticated, but flawed, animal. Man has no supernatural origin or extra-natural essential nature. He is different from animals because of I-consciousness which derives from his superior cunning, but which paradoxically is the reason he is the sickliest and most bungled of all the animals. The development of I-consciousness, which derives from language, gives rise to many errors that lead to death, but also to humanity.

Nietzsche's fascinating argument is that I-consciousness does not really belong to man's individual existence, but rather to his social nature. I-consciousness is really only a net of communication between human beings and so developed hand in hand with the development of language. The purpose of I-consciousness becomes clear only when the idea of agency with respect to one's performance is added to it. In the *Genealogy of Morals*, Nietzsche argues that the fundamental distinction between human action and animal behaviour is based on the development of language. This decisive step is a matter of developing the ability to operate in terms of promises, agreements, rules, values and intentions. Man is an animal who makes promises. The establishment of this possibility required the development of a form of memory going beyond the normal capacity to absorb and retain things experienced. For promising to be possible more explicit memory had to be developed. It was the social necessity of rendering human beings responsible and of developing the power to make and keep promises which was the original impetus to its development. This is how responsibility originated. Human action is not, then, completely determined by prevailing social institutions together with general biological endowments; it is grounded in the social transformation of man's fundamental biological nature, especially through language. The more exceptional forms of action – autonomy and independence – are individual transformations of a previously established social nature.

Freedom does not mean abandoning myself to my instincts which contradict and destroy each other when not subjected to rigorous controls. Freedom is having my instincts under control. This ties the notion of freedom to that of responsibility and to my human capacity to make promises. To the extent that human freedom is a reality for Nietzsche, it is an achievement and I do not achieve it merely by acting self-consciously or by learning to think of myself as responsible for my actions. Freedom is a state I can achieve if I have the will to assume responsibility for myself and become master of myself so as to render the assumption of responsibility meaningful. My freedom is measured according to the resistance which must be overcome. The highest type of free man should be sought where the highest resistance is constantly overcome. The highest men are those who can bear the greatest responsibility and not collapse under it. Independence is for the very few – it is the privilege of the strong.

Nietzsche wonders to what extent everything conscious remains on the surface. Since the direction and care of bodily functions does not enter into consciousness, he contends that a 'higher court rules over these things, a kind of directing committee on which the various chief desires make their power felt.' For I-consciousness is only a means of communication and has evolved through social intercourse. The conscious life labours in the service of the enhancement of life. Since I-consciousness is a surplus, except when it serves as a tool of our animal functions, Nietzsche is able to avoid determinism. He rejects the notion of necessity in the relation between actions and psychophysical states and thus clearly dissociates himself from determinism in its classical (and Darwinian) sense. From the fact that I do a certain thing it by no means follows that I am compelled to do it. He also criticises the free willists according to whom causal efficacy is a sign of certain mental acts performed by a self-determining conscious subject. We should take the doer back into the deed; the notion of a subject of mental acts is untenable. Our actions are not caused by our thoughts.

Nietzsche rejects the view of a single, unified 'I' – a subject of willing. But he admits that he needs an underlying principle to account for 'I' and finds this notion of a basic will in the will-to-power. All purposes, aims, choices and meanings are only modes of expression of this fundamental disposition. This enables him to play with the idea of multiple I's as expressions of will-to-power. His hypothesis: I as multiplicity.

But is Nietzsche's dissolution of 'I' into a multiplicity of drives coherent? Must there not be a single subject of one's drives? Nietzsche says no: there is body and action, but there is no actor behind the actions – it is the body that provides the unity of one's drives. The true 'I' is the body: 'the greater thing is what you will not believe in – your body and its great wisdom – it does not say 'I', but does 'I'.' The notion of 'I' as a centre of self-conscious thought, capable of directing our body towards self-chosen goals, has disappeared. Has Nietzsche lifted us above nature with his notion of I-consciousness or has he delivered us back into the great stream of organic life?

10

Living Naturally

'War is at first the hope that one will be better off;
next, the expectation that the other fellow will be
worse off; then, the satisfaction that he isn't any
better off; and, finally, the surprise at everyone's
being worse off.'

(Karl Kraus)

Evolutionary thinking has always influenced the trend of philosophical thinking. The belief in the profit to be gained by studying the body and brain as a mechanism, which stems from Descartes' intellectual manoeuvres, underlies modern philosophy and has led to 'materialism' which requires that Descartes' dualism be abandoned in favour of monism. This is accomplished by maintaining that we study the human body on the assumption that when we know about it, then we will automatically know all there is to know about 'I'.

Theories of evolution are as old as philosophy itself, but in the 19th Century they proliferated. Charles Darwin's *The Origin of Species* (1859) stimulated immense public interest which was fanned by the activities of the biologist-publicist T.H. Huxley, and for the next forty years there was a wave of 'social Darwinism' in which the theory of evolution was ingeniously applied as a gauge of the worth of political systems, ethical principles and religious beliefs.

There was also a general movement towards eugenics, the selective breeding of humans for desirable qualities. The theory gave people a way of examining features of their nature which had long been disregarded. Some of the directions which were derived from it, such as trying to breed a super-race, were clearly dangerously simplistic.

The shipwreck of many of these attempts is attributable to the fact that they were put forward at a time when very little progress had been made in delineating the part played in evolution by behaviour because, unlike the Romantics, thinkers avoided explanations of evolution based on the animal's will, even though common sense descriptions of behaviour use this form of explanation.

Darwin was not the sole originator of the theory of evolution. The Greeks, with their flair for looking directly at natural things and making startling guesses about them, were intrigued by the kinship between the bodies of different kinds of animal, man included. Empedocles is credited with originating the idea that these similarities were due to physical transitions taking place by chance over time. The same subject had been discussed by Anaximander and by Aristotle, who rejected the notion of survival of the fittest because this meant the operation of chance rather than natural law.

In the Christian era the evolutionary idea was not only forgotten but unnecessary. It is true that Augustine put forward an evolutionary interpretation of the Creation in which God was the instigator and lawgiver governing the process, but this was not officially incorporated into orthodox Christianity. I can appreciate why. God's powers would allow him to accomplish the task in any time or no time, and so long as the job were completed there would be little point in discussing the details.

Evolution remained something of an old philosopher's yarn throughout the first eighteen centuries of the Christian era, although it was touched on by Francis Bacon, Spinoza, Kant and Schopenhauer who each did something to keep it alive. The philosophers, in keeping with the general philosophical attitude that puzzling things are important, recognised that variation among individuals might be a key question.

The Cartesian impetus to the study of the physical properties of living bodies did not yield any special knowledge about variation, heredity or the transmission of characteristics until the appearance of the works of the French scientist Maupertius (1698–1759). He put forward a theory to explain the succession of varieties from one generation to another, the establishment or destruction of the species, and introduced the idea of survival of the fittest.

In 1785 Hutton published *Theory of the Earth* which pointed out for the first time the volcanic origin of many rocks and emphasised the effects of erosion in shaping the face of the earth. He argued that the form of the earth could be laid at the door of natural forces and that these had had immense periods of time in which to work. This brought him into bitter conflict with orthodox theological views – but it also made him the founder of modern geology.

The years between 1790 and 1820 saw the emergence of two evolutionary thinkers – Erasmus Darwin and Jean-Baptiste de Lamarck – who retained a purposive interpretation of human life based on the notion of 'will'. Their proposals contain elements of both the mechanistic and voluntarist traditions, and they therefore talk across a gulf which separates these two. For this reason both were disowned by the orthodox of their time, and neither was acceptable to later scientists who regarded them as 'vitalists', because they allowed that the animal's will is involved in its evolutionary destiny.

Erasmus Darwin was a leader of intellectual thought who founded a society of new thinkers which included James Watt, Joseph Priestley, Samuel Galton, Josiah Wedgwood, and Joseph Banks. It is remarkable how the societies of progressive thinkers have consistently taken the same form as the tiny symposia of the Greek academic tradition – a point for students of education. Erasmus published *Zoonomia or Laws of Organic Life* in 1794. Being a doctor, he devoted most of the work to bodily function and disease, but included also his ideas about evolution. He proposed that the crux of the selection process lay in the power to acquire mates and that the males, being in open competition for the available females, would test one another's weapons and defences. The greatest share of mates would accrue to the most able males. This notion of sexual selection was to be brought forward again by his grandson.

Lamarck's theory of evolution was not greatly different from Erasmus's, but was put forward independently between 1809 and 1816. Lamarck argued that: the production of a new organ results from a new need; the development of organs and their power of action is always in direct relation to the employment of these organs; and all that has been acquired by individuals during their life is preserved by generation, and transmitted to new individuals.

Neither Erasmus Darwin nor Lamarck was able to convince the scientists of their day. Charles Darwin was still pondering the possibility of evolution in the 1830s and in the 1840s expressed astonishment at hearing a competent zoologist admire the views of Lamarck, which he rightly thought to resemble those his grandfather expounded.

Lamarck's theory became widely known but it did not fire the scientific world. In the eyes of scientists it was too vitalistic and in the eyes of creationists it was unnecessary. Before it had had the chance to outlive these disadvantages, Charles Darwin's own version of evolution was to supplant it. Despite this, there is no doubt that Lamarck was making an impression on the public. Both serious poetry and popular science show that the evolutionary view of man's origin had already gained a wide currency by about 1850 and the subject was one for drawing-room discussions among the educated. More than this, a figure like Tennyson, knowing with one half of himself that he belonged to that aristocracy which threw up the great lyrical poets, could feel at the same time that the aesthetic imagination was being swept away by an inexorable tide of scientific fact. Man was being revealed as a self-important speck of vanity.

Despite the many scattered writings on evolution

which were in existence, the professional biologists of the mid-19th Century were still creationists and regarded species as immutable. As happens often, popular speculative thought was ahead of the scientists and evolution was receiving more attention outside the professional ranks than within, so Darwin was following in the iconoclastic path of Hutton and others. In retrospect he seems anything but iconoclastic; when he first confessed what he suspected about evolution, he wrote to Sir John Hooker that it is like confessing a murder. Rather than publish his theory of the origin of species by natural selection, Darwin spent twenty years collecting evidence and slowly convincing himself that evolution was undeniable.

Malthus, who had published *Essay on the Principle of Population* anonymously in 1798, argued that life tended to increase in a geometrical progression. Unless there were severe checks on population or the food supply increased at the same rate as the number of organisms, any living thing would soon outstrip its food supply. Malthus's arithmetic is valid, but his assumption of a purely mechanical control over population size is not.

Darwin, who already had developed a general theory of natural selection, saw that the Malthusian doctrine fitted perfectly. The large proportion of individuals who were killed off by pestilence, starvation or enemies would be those least fitted to the natural environment. Only the strong and cunning would survive to produce the next generation. Finally, in 1844, Darwin sent his thesis to a friend who wanted him to publish immediately. But Darwin was to go on collecting more evidence for the next

17 years, and even then was forced to publish before he was satisfied. The final stimulus to publication was provided by Alfred Russell Wallace, who in 1858 was ill with fever while on one of his collecting expeditions and on his sick bed his thoughts wandered to Malthus. At once he had the feverish idea of the survival of the fittest, and Darwin's whole theory burst forth. Two days later he had written it out and sent it to Darwin.

The Wallace essay, if published, would clearly forestall Darwin. But other people knew of Darwin's essay written in 1844 – fortunately for Darwin. The question of priority was settled by reading both papers together at a meeting of the Linnaean Society in July 1858, which received both with unruffled calm. Darwin published *The Origin of Species* in November 1859 and the world received the news with anything but unruffled calm. The success of the book was extraordinary and in a few years it had revolutionised contemporary thought.

A good part of the reason for the impact of the theory of evolution on the public lay in its energetic advocacy by T.H. Huxley, who became its publicity agent. He was aided in making it a public issue by the opposition of churchmen. The idea of the emergence of man through an undirected interplay of physical conditions was contrary to the Biblical account of Creation. In taking the public rostrum in defence of the theory, Huxley found himself able to make easy headway against the literal, religious interpretation of the origin of life, and thus to establish scientific biology as a full-scale competitor with religion. The result was a great deal of public controversy as to which view was true. As an aim this was hopeless, but it had useful effects in galvanising the protagonists into examining and developing their positions, much as if the trial of Galileo had been conducted by an enlightened public rather than by religious bigots. It also led to the inclusion of the biological sciences as part of the university establishment and the great enrichment of our knowledge about living things which has flowed from that science. As so often happens, controversy about opposing interpretations of the same things led to new knowledge.

Since the onus lay on the scientists to make good their position against the vitalistic view, the publication of the *Origin* was followed by a great burst of evidence-seeking among biologists. Support for the theory of evolution kept on mounting; that is, none of the evidence found in nature was incompatible with the theory; but no direct observation of changes in the physical form of animals in response to environmental factors was made for half a century. Many influential figures in the professional biological world ranged themselves against Darwin and it was a very long time before the opposition of men such as Adam Sedgwick and Richard Owen was withdrawn.

The effect of the controversy on those who took the religious side of the argument was disastrous. The popular following of religion was quite seriously affected, and the reluctance of theologians to recognise that they were in competition with a rival truth made it difficult for them to deal with it effectively. The adjustment took time, so much time that only a century later did it begin to show positive results. All the early victories went to the materialist-mechanistic mode of thinking; but its claims to be the only way to knowledge have not yet been substantiated and religion has survived.

Ironically enough, while Huxley was conducting his noisy launching of a faith in the mechanical nature of living things, one physicist was working towards the solution of a problem which was to move science away from a mechanistic system. This was the unobtrusive, unpublicised Maxwell, whose work on the electromagnetic theory of light commenced from a mechanical model full of forces, fluids, vortices and wheels through which he aimed at explaining Faraday's 'lines of force'. These had been proposed to deal with the phenomenon of magnetism. Maxwell found no adequate mechanical model but having gone as far as mechanics could go he made certain jumps in thought and arrived at a mathematical solution. He then abandoned all the mechanical scaffolding he had erected and acknowledged that the theory could only be expressed mathematically. It was this move that set physics on the road to radio, television and quantum theory.

The Darwin and Wallace theories, which are almost indistinguishable, consist of two sets of propositions. The first is that evolution has occurred. The second concerns the way in which this has occurred and depends on three assertions:

(a) that all organisms vary by chance; that is, no two members of a species are identical, but each differs from all others in some details of physical make-up;

(b) that the state of the environment will place some of the variant members of the species at a disadvantage relative to others; and

(c) given the struggle for existence in which a proportion must perish, it will be the members which are better adapted to the environment which will live to breed the next generation. Their progeny will inherit the variations which proved advantageous to their parents; the process will repeat itself, leading to a better and better 'fit' between animal and environment.

It was the interweaving of these propositions about the survival of the fittest that won the world over to the *Origin*. The 'fact' of evolution has never been seriously challenged since that time (although it was forbidden by law to teach it in some southern states of America) but the hypothesis of natural selection has been under sporadic attack from the time of its enunciation.

One of the first to deny it was Samuel Butler (1835–1902) who satirised Huxley's tendency to raise the indifference of nature to the level of a standard by which men should be judged. There is a famous court scene in *Erewhon* (1873) where a consumptive is put on trial for 'labouring under pulmonary consumption'. He is convicted of the disease, which the judge ascribes to a 'radically vicious' constitution. The sentence is imprisonment with hard labour for the rest of his 'miserable existence'. Butler was a first-rate classical scholar who at the time the *Origin* was published was sheep-farming in New Zealand ('Erewhon' is roughly 'nowhere', New Zealand, spelled backwards). He began writing on Darwinism from there but returned to England and took to writing and painting, criticised the new Darwinian dogma and earned the personal displeasure of Darwin himself.

Butler wrote to bring about the 'exposure and discomfiture of Charles Darwin and Wallace and their followers.' His thesis was that the cell controls its destiny by an inherent cunning, and useful habits are stored in unconscious memory and inherited by subsequent generations. Although he misinterpreted the *Origin* in that he did not see that evolution and natural selection were separate propositions, he realised quite clearly that natural selection relied exclusively on a mechanical means of modification, and because he considered this to be inadequate he was prepared to oppose the whole doctrine. He raised some extremely telling points but because he was not a recognised scientist his criticisms of natural selection created little stir. Darwin himself had retreated from the purely mechanical concept of direct selection by the environment in the sixth edition of the *Origin* (1872), so that by the time Butler's books were published there was some indifference about how evolution occurred. It was widely accepted that it had occurred and that was enough.

A second critic was Friedrich Nietzsche. The relation between Darwin and Nietzsche is a curious one. Whilst Nietzsche accepted the facts of evolution, the importance of man's use of tools for attack and defence, and the development of anti-instincts in the service of power, he nonetheless mocks Darwin throughout his books. Nietzsche recognised the revolutionary implications of Darwin's theory of natural selection and realised that, if true, it delivered a death-blow to Platonic, Aristotelian and Christian worldviews based on the idea of purpose in nature. However, Nietzsche disagreed with Darwin about the universal tendency of living beings to seek preservation through adaptation. He argued that organisms are centres of power that seek ever to increase their power at the expense of others, to discharge their forces because life itself is will-to-power and self-preservation is only one of its indirect consequences. He agreed with Darwin that man is the supreme exemplar of the use of cunning, deceit, reason, language and knowledge as weapons of survival and defence, but disagreed with Darwin's emphasis on external conditions determining survival and development which grants too much importance to 'random' and 'sexual' selection. Rather, Nietzsche promoted a vitalistic theory which replaces adaptation with power and thus emphasises the aggressive and creative aspects of evolution: what Darwin calls a struggle for survival, Nietzsche characterises as a struggle of wills-to-power. The successful species do not merely survive and adapt, they exploit and plunder.

Now one might reply to Nietzsche by pointing out that many organisms appear to do little more than adapt by adopting passive behaviour, such as blending into the environment, becoming immobile, hiding, and so do not display a will-to-power. Nietzsche would no doubt reply that, on the contrary, their defensive behaviour is a form of the will-to-power which manifests itself in different organisms in different ways. The litmus test of the effectiveness of one's will-to-power is, therefore, pragmatic. Does one's will-to-power enable the species to multiply and exploit nature? We might think here of viruses which may be the ultimate victors of the earth.

Furthermore, Nietzsche does not accept that it is the fittest that survive (which is a tautology in any case): species do not grow more perfect: the weaker dominate the strong again and again because they are more numerous and more clever. Nietzsche accuses Darwin of forgetting the power of the weak (that is the English for you!): the weak have more foresight, patience, dissimulation. Nietzsche might point to a horde of ants that can kill a lion by force of numbers – the great 'blond beasts' can be brought down by the herd. This very idea nauseated Nietzsche, offending his aristocratic sensibilities.

Erasmus Darwin, Lamarck and Nietzsche represent a tradition in evolutionary thinking which has persisted, fallen into disrepute, been revived and fallen again; but throughout the 19th and 20th Centuries it has never been effectively scotched despite opposition which has sometimes been impassioned. It cannot be scotched until the scientists' promissory note about explaining all behaviour in mechanistic terms is redeemed. In this context 'all behaviour' includes that of the scientist.

The heart of this line of thinking resides in Erasmus Darwin's argument that from the beginning to the termination of their lives all animals undergo perpetual transformations which are, in part, produced by their own exertions in consequence of their motives (especially pleasure and pain) and many of these acquired propensities are transmitted to their posterity. This argument precedes Lamarck's theory by some fifteen years, but uses the same central principle. While Erasmus Darwin and

Lamarck are similar, Charles Darwin differs from both. The key to this difference lies in Lamarck's first law which says that 'life by its internal forces tends continually to increase the volume of everybody that possesses it', that is, living things are inevitably successful in enhancing themselves.

Sir Alister Hardy who has, in *The Living Stream*, re-examined Lamarck in the light of what he considers to be unjustified criticism, points out that although it is not explicitly stated in his *Laws* Lamarck repeatedly says that it is through changes in habit and not through the direct effect of environment that the heritable changes occur. Circumstances influence the form of animals, but it must not be taken literally, for the environment can effect no direct changes whatever upon the organisation of animals.

Hardy suggests that it is wrong to connect Lamarck's name with the belief in the inheritance of acquired characteristics, if that belief relies on the direct effects of the environment. Experiments such as Weissman's in 1885, in which the tails of mice were cut off at birth for many generations, arose from a naive misinterpretation of Lamarck's views. No matter how many generations of mice were subjected to this treatment the length of tails did not alter; but this procedure did not test Lamarck's hypothesis, for the latter depended on the use which the animal made of the organ. If an environment has been arranged in which tails were useless or a hindrance to survival, that would have been another matter. Hardy suggests that the Lamarckian thesis depends on changes of habit.

Hardy argues that if a population of animals should change their habits on account of changes in or curiosity about their surroundings, then variations in the gene complex will turn up in the population to produce small alterations in the animal's structure which will make them more efficient in relation to their new behaviour pattern. These more efficient individuals will tend to survive rather than the less efficient, and so the composition of the population will gradually change. This evolutionary change is one caused initially by a change in behaviour. Hardy is here, like Nietzsche, envisaging an organism that searches the environment for exploitable features, and when it finds them it adds their exploitation to its repertoire of habits. Structural changes favouring the new capabilities then follow, in such a way that profitable old habits are not seriously impaired. This makes the organism a sort of empire-grabber, and his method of conquest a process of extending his repertoire of effective action. Such a course of evolution would seem to point straight to the development of man; but it does not accord with a theory which sees the organism as being wholly at the mercy of environment.

Hardy divides the influences bringing about evolutionary change into two classes: external where (a) selection pressure is exerted by other organisms (predators, competitors) thus producing a form of selection which may be inter-specific (competition and combat between different species) or intra-specific (rivalry between members of same species); and (b) selection by the inanimate environment where influences which involve the behaviour of the animal whose instincts are governed by the gene complex and where new modes of exploitation are discovered.

In explaining the progression from amoeba to man more is required than merely showing how the organism has survived. The amoeba has done this as well as man, without becoming like him. One has to show why some organisms went in for new activities for which there was no precedent, why and how they managed to retain old alongside new habits so as to build up an extensive repertoire of possible action, how they manage to produce the effective action in a given situation, and finally why the discovery of new ways of dealing with the environment came to be valued in its own right.

So, in summary, there were two ancient evolutionary ideas: one that species were akin and could have evolved one from the other; the second that there was an order in the animal kingdom which had been placed there at Creation. In the 19th Century the former view which had for centuries dropped into obscurity, was re-instated as a competitor with the biblical view. To those who thought about the matter the two explanations were incompatible. The deadlock was broken by Darwin and Wallace who advocated a mechanistic explanation which made physical changes in species possible. But why did they so readily reject 'Lamarck's nonsense'?

The answer begins with Descartes' separation of body and soul and his belief that it was the soul that could 'know' and 'will', but could not affect the mechanical laws governing the operations of the body. The Cartesian soul had all the attributes of what is called 'mind', but it could in no way interfere with the physical realm, which belonged to science. Now Lamarck's theory used the 'felt needs' of the animal as an explanation of bodily modifications, that is, it stepped across the Cartesian division by maintaining that 'mind' affected the physical world. Therefore it did not respect that limitation to the physical realm on which Descartes had based his argument for the legitimacy of the scientific study of living things. Darwin and Wallace did respect this limitation.

The success of the scientific approach to physical phenomena rests on the uncovering of cause and effect, which rests on observing instances in which one event invariably follows another. From this arises the principle of determinism, which holds that every event (rather than 'effect' – which would be tautologous) has a cause. Some people have since attempted to extend this principle to include 'mental events' but it is obvious that this has no justification in Cartesian thought, for whether it is argued that one 'mental event' may cause another, or that a 'mental event' may affect the physical operations of the organism, one is stepping outside the legitimate materialism for which the reliability of the physical sciences arises. Neither Darwin nor Wallace would countenance any form of explanation which employed any principle other than those known in the physical sciences.

They were therefore restricted in the kind of explanation they could accept by the materialist/determinist prescription they had adopted. Given that the intellects of our two scientists were thus focused, and given that they both believed evolution had occurred, their recognition of the value of Malthus's arithmetic seems quite simple. They had only to add one small step – that bodies removed from the population were less able to survive than those that did survive – and they had the doctrine of natural selection.

But what of the systematic differences between humans and lower animals? Despite the feelings of 'new agers' it can hardly be doubted that some animals are more versatile in dealing with hostile environments than others, and might for that reason be classed as superior. The question then becomes whether a hierarchy of superior behaviours can be set up to the point where the superior animals (man) have evolved counter-evolutionary capacities. What type of capacity might be involved in acquired counter-evolutionary power?

When one animal is placed lower on the behavioural hierarchy than another, the number of environmental features which act as effective agents of natural selection on the lower will exceed the number of agents which act effectively on the higher. The higher animal will possess effective defences against a greater proportion of the potential threats contained in the universe than will the lower. In particular, the higher animal will:

(a) show less stereotypy in behaviour than the lower animal;
(b) show sensitivity to the value of a greater number of environmental features than the lower animal;
(c) show the ability to respond to a greater number of patterned relationships than the lower animal;
(d) display behaviour which implies greater emotional differentiation than the lower animal;

and will, as a species be less subject to the lower species than the lower animal is to it, as regards power to survive.

But what about the impact of culture?

Clifford Geertz has argued that human-like ancestors possessed simple but significant forms of culture, such as tool-making, weapons and strategy for hunting and defence. No animal like *homo sapiens* appeared until about 200,000 years ago. These facts suggest that the appearance of *homo sapiens* was preceded by well over a million years of evolution during which man, in his proto-human form, evolved in company with culture. Here is the crucial and inescapable fact of human evolution.

Regardless of the precise time-scale, tools and similar evidence of culture show that the relationship between organism and environment was changing long before *homo sapiens* emerged as such. Geertz's conclusion, which seems beyond question, is that each accretion of culture conferred on its possessor such survival potential as to redirect natural selection from the physical form appropriate for direct dealings with the environment to the physical forms necessary for employing culture to the same end. In other words, the human nervous system evolved under a selection impetus directed by culture. Therefore it became a vehicle for culture.

The invention of tools undoubtedly changes the relationship between animal and environment to the advantage of the tool-user. The invention of an effective weapon or strategy will place its possessor in a better position vis-a-vis the environment than genetically based changes in bodily form. Cultural artefacts would give access to more sources of food and new means of defence against threats from other species. Since the proto-human was probably a marginal animal, largely a scavenger without a secure niche of his own, tools, weapons and strategy would enable him either to exploit otherwise inaccessible sources of food or to intrude upon the food of other animals. The result to be expected would be a great increase in the numbers of proto-humans at the expense of other species. The scarcity of proto-humans suggests that this did not occur.

In all probability the main factor in holding the proto-human population down to small numbers was internecine warfare. In competition for scarce resources *Homo* had no option but to come into conflict with his own kind. Living in small groups, survival in times of emergency might well mean invasion of the territory of another group, leading to open conflict. In such a situation the safest course is to eliminate one's nearest and most dangerous competitor, and the more technically able group would undoubtedly eliminate the less able, especially its exponents of culture – weaponry, tool-use and strategy. The result would be a severe culling of those with inferior endowment in cultural capacities, and since the fate of a small group could well depend on one very able individual – usually a dominant male – such individuals might be expected to enjoy social advantages, such as access to a greater number of females.

Inevitably, genetic characters underlying cultural capacities would be favoured, and the organism would change towards the form best adapted to cultural activities, viz. the large capacity brain. The selection process would continue until *Homo* had turned his marginal position in the ecology into a dominant one and had arrived at some way of ameliorating intra-species competition. Until the latter had occurred the cultural advantage of one group might well mean the extermination of its neighbours; more likely it would mean destruction of the males of the losing group and the absorption of its females – leading to genetic redirection.

Cultural capacities in modern man are abstractions formed on the basis of certain kinds of behaviour. When we say that a man has a capacity to speak or use tools effectively we infer powers which may be expressed in speech or hunting. It is difficult to deny that these powers reside in the nervous system. A blow from a stone will crack a nut, or my rival's skull, and that is what it means to use a stone as a tool. The use of tools would seem to be closely related to the concept of cause. Similarly, the use of plans, strategies and social organisation depends on the recognition of relationships. And finally, at a superior level of sophistication, the use of language again depends on the perception of relationships.

What distinguishes the functioning of the human nervous system is that its control over behaviour operates at a general level rather than with the precision, detail and finality found in the lower organism. This generality shows up in many ways: the ability of humans to recognise in one situation the same relationships as in another; the great variety of ways of behaving which are possible within the limits set by genetic control; and in the enormous amount of learning of culture which the human infant must accomplish before it can operate as a human being. The stage of final, stereotyped responses to specific situations which is the criterion for adulthood among the lower animals is never reached by some human beings. A greater proportion of the human life-span consists of infancy than is the case for other animals.

Geertz is surely right when he says that men without culture would not be the clever savages of William Golding's *Lord of the Flies* thrown back upon the cruel wisdom of their instincts; nor would they be nature's noblemen of Enlightenment, talented apes who had failed to find themselves. Humans are incomplete animals and we complete ourselves through culture. The evolved human brain cannot, therefore, express its powers except through 'I' which is soaked in culture.

An account of the development of culture through the stages of human evolution would contain much about battles and invention. In the early stages of this history the battles provided tests of cultural adaptability between small groups of proto-humans and thus exerted a form of selection pressure favouring the culturally inventive. The superiority of one group over another would rest not only on the possession of suitable weapons but also on the detection of patterns in the behaviour of the enemy. Where the sterotyped behaviour of non-humans is concerned the observer has little difficulty in anticipating the sequence because it is fixed. But one cannot deal with other men in so simple a fashion. For humans dealing with humans, an appreciation that the other party may be following rules is essential for success in attack or defence. In ultimate life or death struggles even rule-following introduces an element of predictability into the rule-followers' behaviour which offers advantages to enemies able to detect it. In the proto-human stage of evolution, therefore, the ability to detect rule-following must have been of biological advantage and in conflict this must have reacted to raise the biological value of behaving in ways which did not permit the opponent to detect the operation of a rule. Selection would favour those capable of behaving in unpredictable ways, an ability which could not appear except in those able to detect and follow rules. This principle is still fundamental to military strategy. An enemy whom one cannot outdo in unpredictability is a very dangerous enemy indeed. Natural selection, via intra-human conflict, produced an organism capable of falsifying, by his behaviour, any prediction which he could himself make on the basis of rules about behaviour.

Once opponents are evenly matched on these abilities, however, conflict between small groups is not likely to produce a clear-cut result in the short term, and if protracted, will interfere with the actual food-getting and subsistence on account of which it was undertaken. Stalemate ensues.

In the course of history many techniques have been utilised to break this deadlock, including: enlarging one's group (empire-building) so as to outnumber one's opponents; the perfecting of social organisation so as to make it into a tool whose output of power can be focused on the opponent's weak points; and inventing 'secret' weapons to which the enemy has not devised a counter. To become large a group must establish a climate where rule-following does not expose the individual to attack and to achieve this an over-arching rule must be made for the in-group to the effect that one member shall not take advantage of other members' vulnerability. Furthermore, rule-following is used as a means of focusing the efforts of individuals so as to generate the additional power which results from cooperative effort. This power is directed at maintaining the immunity of the group from human attacks as well as overcoming physical threats to survival.

Organised groups therefore serve as a shelter against all natural selection pressures, but especially those exerted by man on man. Insofar as they are effective in the latter function they mitigate the necessity for preservation of the capacity for unpredictability which man acquired in his proto-human stage, thus blunting the leading edge of evolution. At the same time the group protects many members who would, in its absence, constitute the bio-logical 'tail'. These are the people who are not capable of the cultural inventions – the new tools, the new sciences – which raise the survival potential of their possessors above that of other men. Their preservation, which has reached its highest level in human history through the rise of medicine, means that the genetic variability of *homo sapiens* will increase, and so will the gap between the most and least able of the species.

With the appearance of a civilised ethic man has inter-fered in both the pace and direction of his own evolution. It may well be that this is the unintended consequence of action originally taken on pragmatic grounds, but there is nothing unintended about the restrictions placed on their members by human groups. Unlike herd animals for whom the full expression of their biological nature is in no way detrimental to the group, men are not well adapted to group life. Their biological nature allows that they may be dangerous to each other and to their species. What we call civilisation is almost certainly an imperfectly realised anti-evolutionary compact which is put into effect through a highly conscious social organisation. But this differs from the group life of other animals because the requisite conformity does not exhaust the potentialities of human nature.

If the existence of a group is to be maintained among humans, the anti-social potentialities of its members must be defused. If the group is to produce anything that an individual could not produce by himself some conformity and some predictable activities must be engendered in an organisation capable of highly unpredictable behaviour. Now because these things occur it might seem possible that a well organised society would secure all men against the anti-human potentialities of men by eliminating the unpredictable in human behaviour; that is by total control. If this were possible it would mean the end of unpredictability and its derivatives, invention and creativity. An end to these would mean that the group would be caught in an inflexible system of regular behaviour; man's vulnerability to other men would have been overcome, but at the sacrifice of its capacity to meet changed conditions and to deal with still-evolving competitors. In civilisation, therefore, we must expect to find some evidence of tension between the full expression of individual powers and the requirements of social regulation.

Appeal is sometimes made to the theory of evolution to support assertions that man is not what he seems. Instead, he is really a mosaic of ancient animal instincts which govern all he does without realising it; or he is a machine whose behaviour is determined by mysterious forces originating in the digestive tract or sexual organs. There is nothing in the fact of evolution to validate these allegations, nor does the mechanical operation of the natural selection process exclude the production of unique organisms – indeed the reverse is true. Certain tenets of scientific policy ('We can learn something about humans by examining their evolution as an animal: if one wishes to identify causes one must adopt the determinist approach which assumes all events are caused') cannot be converted into psychological statements without doing injustice both to the observable facts and to the scientific perspective.

Where the philosopher is concerned it is man as he is that needs explanation. The value of models which fall short of this is low and they distort the reality by overemphasising some aspects of human nature at the expense of others, and consequently misdirect the investigator. Nevertheless, a broad biological perspective does contain directions for philosophy which are worthy of attention.

(a) Among highly evolved specialists, behaviour will tend to be precisely fitted to a limited environment and hence more stereotyped.

(b) Among highly evolved generalists, such as humans, where psychological phenomena have played an essential part in evolution, the degree to which the drive to survive under existing conditions can satisfactorily explain behaviour is less and the extent to which purposiveness enters into behaviour is proportionately increased. The immediate goal of any specific behaviour may not manifest any direct connection with the biological end of survival. The connection will often be indirect, as when learning prepares the organism to meet novel contingencies.

(c) If humans have such counter-evolutionary capacity as to be at the top of the behavioural scale, part of this capacity will lie in their relative lack of stereotyped behaviour and part of their dominance over other animals in the ability to detect and take advantage of stereotypy in their behaviour. Detection of any hitherto unrecognised stereotypy in human behaviour would make it possible for the discoverer to seize a dominant position over the human race.

(d) The fact that the human nervous system has evolved in interaction with culture rules out the assumption that the workings of the human nervous system can be explained in terms of response to features of the environment which are independent of culture.

The inadequacy of mechanistic formulations in philosophy may be shown without appeal to evolution. Reasons, intentions, purposes, inclinations and meanings have no place in mechanistic explanation. Mechanistic science, it is sometimes argued, offers a way of getting at a truer explanation which will render such existential forms of explanation obsolete. This idea would mean that we have been completely mistaken about ourselves and all social relationships for millennia. If we find this inconceivable, then we must accept that mechanistic explanation will of necessity converge on existential explanation. Mechanistic explanations must therefore be enriched so as to become compatible with existential forms.

11

Living Existentially

*'Responsibility, n. A detachable burden easily shifted
to the shoulders of God, fate, fortune, luck, or
one's neighbour. In the days of astrology it was
customary to unload it upon a star.'*

(Ambrose Bierce)

Existentialism is a philosophy of human existence which developed out of German Romanticism and became popular in Western Europe during and immediately after the Second World War. Existentialism is not a unified philosophy but has survived through the highly personal writings of thinkers who are united in opposition to systematic, mechanistic models of human nature. Its central themes are choice, responsibility and authenticity which all depend on the fact of human freedom. Freedom does not have the same meaning as liberty, in the sense of being at liberty to act. Rather, it refers to the internal or personal freedom to choose to act in responsible or irresponsible ways. Choice is here contrasted with determination – the widespread belief that as individuals we have no (or few) choices since we are the victims of our biological inheritance, environmental conditioning or personality traits. In the century in which Karl Marx and Sigmund Freud achieved cult-hero status, psychological, sociological, and biological determinisms have pervasively influenced our ways of thinking about human freedom, or the lack of it. Existentialists argue that psychological determinism is dangerously false and has contributed to the undermining of our civilisation.

Many people, on the other hand, value freedom as a licence to do whatever they want to do without regard for the freedom of others. This form of anarchy is but a short step to the barbarism of those who see society as a battle of wits in which the bullies thrive, the mediocre survive (because of their large numbers), and the individualists go to the wall. Here survival of the fittest means survival of the masses and their domination by modern barbarians whose horizons rarely extend beyond their enjoyment in coercing others and the material possessions they accrue. The result is what Nietzsche called nihilism and those living in such an era will have little time for principles or standards of excellence because nihilism amounts to the belief that there are no important differences anymore – in art, literature, music, science. The dominant value is egalitarianism which disguises a frustrated and therefore dangerous need of power. For this reason Nietzsche predicted that nihilism must lead to the decline of Western civilisation either by implosion (since the absence of standards makes the recognition of achievement impossible), or by barbaric takeover (since those not contaminated by nihilism and decadent egalitarianism are willing to coerce others). Consequently, responsibility is re-defined for, without the restraint implied by responsible freedom, liberty is impossible because those with more power will soon deprive those with less of their freedom.

Existentialists did not invent the idea of responsible freedom, which goes back to the ancient Stoics, to Christian scholars, and to the German Romantics. But it was the existentialists who secularised it. Whilst existentialism is a child of Romanticism, it became a rebellious adolescent. The Romantics offered a consoling view of a chaotic world in which man is considered to be a manifestation of a 'superior reality', variously described as the World Will, Humanity, the Absolute, which leads man inexorably to some definitive triumph. The atheistic existentialists grew away from such comforting delusions and emphasised the instability and uncertainty of a human existence which cast doubt on any prospect of eternal bliss. Existentialism affirms that man is a finite reality who is thrown into a world he did not choose and abandoned to a power which may sabotage his efforts. Man's freedom is always situated and hindered by many forces which can overwhelm those who lack the heroic determination to confront the contingency of the world. Whilst Romanticism has a tendency to spirituality, existentialism is a concrete philosophy of this world and emphasises the difference between conscious human life and the non-conscious material world. Humans *exist* because they are conscious; humans are free when they are conscious.

Existentialism, then, is a philosophy which represents an attempt to reassert the existence of individuals against the social and intellectual conditions which threaten to encapsulate them. Soren Kierkegaard (1813–1855), a Danish Lutheran, is the founding father. Kierkegaard follows Fichte in his attempt to reassert the importance of free-choosing, self-creating individuals against the deterministic, authoritarian systems which threaten to subjugate them. And so he is vehemently opposed to systematic models of person and society.

Kierkegaard writes to emphasise, in his own way, the gulf between categorical descriptions of social relationships, (e.g. as specified roles) and the process of relating, between relating to another as an object (a means to an end) and authentic communication between people as subjects (relating to others as ends in themselves). He rejects the structured personality as a psychological trap which submerges individuality in biological and social structures and expresses strong suspicion about the objective-subjective distinction. Where psychology aims for an objective view of people as a scientific ideal, Kierkegaard regards it as not only a relatively easy position to adopt and exploit, but as leading away from the moral ideal of empathy. This can be seen clearly in his *Diary of the Seducer* (1843). Seduction is the process by which one is induced through trickery into willing to be possessed, while the seducer remains unpossessed. If it is possession and domination one wants, seduction (or ironic love as Kierkegaard calls it), is what is called for. And this means treating other people as objects while remaining a subject. Seduction means exploitation.

Kierkegaard points again and again to such experiences as human love and empathy in order to persuade us that whatever we are, we are not objects and cannot adequately be represented by mechanical models. He believes humans are never devoid of choice. That is, he asserts the opposite assumption about human nature from the Calvinist tenet regarding the absence of free will. Authenticity, for Kierkegaard, requires the abandonment of the objective, mechanical view of science. The requirement that other people be treated as if they are self-determining subjects – as 'I's' – prevents the depersonalisation of relationships in impersonal social structures.

Kierkegaard thought of himself as an anti-philosopher because he believed that philosophers, like G.W.F. Hegel (1770–1831), wanted to submerge the individual in an all-encompassing system. Like Schopenhauer (who hated Hegel), Kierkegaard blamed the German idealist for dehumanising the intellectual lives of individuals and reducing them to insignificance. He attributed this dehumanisation to Hegel's 'dialectical logic' in which the Principle of Identity (A=A) is denied in favour of the view that every A is also its opposite (A=not-A). Hegel had argued that, for example, Greek democracy was consistent with Greek slavery, and hence it was its own opposite. But if the Principle of Identity is rejected so too is the coherence of thinking and thus the stability of the individual. Humans will simply be swallowed up in the great stream of chaos and flux much beloved by the more unrestrained Romantics. Psychologically, this is catastrophic and leads to widespread apathy, demoralisation and anguish. By denying the basic means by which we make decisions – in terms of either/or choices – such a philosophy effectively denies human freedom which is, for Kierkegaard, the defining characteristic of human existence. His work is, in part, an attack on Hegel's philosophy and an expression of an attitude to life based on the fact of human freedom and individuality.

Hegel's philosophy, with its central idea that 'the real is rational and the rational is real', had abolished the difference between epistemology and ontology, by claiming that 'existence' and 'thought' are identical. The task of philosophy is, by dialectical means, to move from consciousness to self-consciousness to absolute thought (that which culminates in the philosophy of Hegel). Kierkegaard argued that existence cannot be thought because thought is an abstraction: 'to think is one thing, to exist another.' Existence must be lived. And living involves passion, decision, action and commitment. But decision-making entails the freedom to choose and the responsibility which accompanies it. Awareness of my freedom (including the freedom to kill myself) and the related responsibility creates a sense of dizziness and anguish which I am tempted to relieve by denying responsibility and/or freedom. But in vain. I cannot escape the subjective truth of my existential condition that I am a free-choosing individual who understands my life backwards, but lives it forwards. I am free and so I am different from and superior to objects which, in Kierkegaard's language, do not exist. An object is, a human being exists.

Descartes was right to begin philosophy with the *Cogito* – 'I think therefore I exist'. But he was wrong, as was Hegel, to associate 'I' with thought. While I can describe myself in diverse ways, there is one thing remaining that cannot be thought – I EXIST – and this fact must be lived through passion, decision and action. Objective thought must be supplemented with subjective thought for which there exist no objective criteria of truth. Objective truths are existentially indifferent whereas subjective truths are concerned with personal values, faith and commitments. Values are not mere feelings or abstract concepts floating in another world; values are committed actions and I judge values by what I freely commit to. This is the heroic element in existential thinking – I am what I do and what I do is based on decisions which cannot be grounded in certainty and so are accepted on faith (rather than pleasure or power). But faith is demanding and is accompanied by anxiety, and even despair. The confrontation with the despair of everyday existence leads me to the 'yawning abyss of eternity' from which I may emerge with a stronger sense of 'I'. Such an 'I' will be unhindered by social roles, pointless projects, material obsessions and power games.

Kierkegaard encourages me to develop my own dialectic in which I move through three stages of existence: from an aesthetic to an ethical stage, and on to an existential stage characterised by faith. The aesthetic stage of existence is grounded by preferences, the road to truth is governed by sensations, feelings and pleasures, and judgements are based on pleasurable feelings. Here, as in the life of Don Juan, there is an absence of fixed universal moral standards, a lack of form and discipline in life, and a striving for personal freedom from restraint. The second, ethical stage is grounded by problems and their solutions, the road to truth is governed by universal reason and judgements are based on social utility. Here, as in the life of Socrates, one listens to the voice of reason, enters into obligations (marriage) and attempts to achieve moral self-sufficiency.

Kierkegaard, however, encourages me to accept the challenge of progressing to a third, existential stage which is grounded by principles, where the road to truth is governed by faith in ideals and where judgements are based on what is right. At this stage I affirm myself as 'I'. Since this stage takes me beyond reason it involves me in a 'leap of faith' into personal truth. If I accept the challenge and 'leap' I am one of Kierkegaard's Knights of Faith because I am great in my own way and in proportion to my expectation. As a Knight of Faith I become great by expecting the possible and the eternal, but I become even greater by expecting the impossible. I achieve final victory by overcoming myself because I have grasped the absurdity and contingency of existence and overcome it with an act of will. Faith is a 'divine madness'.

Arguably the most famous existentialist was Jean-Paul Sartre (1905–1980), who took from Kierkegaard the idea that human beings are condemned to be free and are responsible for what they do with their freedom. This was a particularly poignant idea in Nazi-occupied Paris in the early 1940s when existentialism became popular with members of the Paris resistance movement and their fellow-travellers. Each day Parisians faced agonising decisions: will I collaborate with the Germans? Will I join the Resistance? If I am caught and tortured will I betray my comrades? In normal times I am rarely placed in such situations and so I lose a clear sense of the power of my freedom to make life and death choices. But when the need to make such life and death choices arises, I become acutely aware of my freedom to choose and the associated responsibility before myself and those people who depend on me. Sartre's philosophy is clear from his heroic speech in *The Republic of Silence*:

'We were never more free than during the German occupation. We had lost all our rights, beginning with the right to talk. Every day we were insulted to our faces and had to take it in silence. And because of this we were free. Because the Nazi venom seeped into our thoughts, every accurate thought was a conquest. Because an all powerful police tried to force us to hold our tongues, every word took on the value of a declaration of principles. Because we were hunted down, every one of our gestures had the weight of solemn commitment. The circumstances, atrocious as they often were, finally made it possible for us to live the hectic and impossible existence that is known as the lot of man'.

Sartre emphasises the gulf between scientific and philosophical thinking, the non-conscious material world and the conscious human world. Like Kierkegaard, he argues that human beings are never devoid of choice. To those who would argue that this is unrealistic – that indeed our choices are often limited – Sartre's reply is that this is an illusion fostered by a cowardly wish to be encapsulated in the social order. To those who would then object that total freedom makes us wholly responsible for ourselves, with no external supports whatever, Sartre retorts that such supports are both delusory and debilitating. Shearing away these external supports means that I cannot refer my decisions to outside agencies. I must face nothingness if I am to learn to face myself and my problems. If I fall into the cliché of believing I have no choice, the solution must be through a raising of consciousness to the point where I recognise that I do have a choice.

As far as authority is concerned, in existentialism this has virtually become wholly a matter of personal 'values' without reference to impersonal systems. Sartre and other existentialists maintain that to treat individuals in the objective mode – as role players or bundles of personality traits – is to deprive them of their essential humanity, to belittle their individuality by allotting them the status of predictable objects. On the contrary, individuals should be accorded the respect which is due to their being the incalculable seed of unlimited future possibilities, creative and spontaneous – an attitude which emphasises the poetry of an unbounded future. To relate to others in this way is to be 'authentic', a state in which such features as dominance and coercion have disappeared from personal relationships. Authenticity requires the abandonment of that objective view of humans which is striven for in science and needed where people are to be restricted in their behaviour by social roles.

Existentialism in the middle 20th Century came to be associated with its atheistic wing, represented most prominently by Sartre, Simone de Beauvoir (1908–1986) and Albert Camus (1913–1960). In his famous lecture *Existentialism is a Humanism* delivered in Paris in 1945, Sartre answers the question: what is existentialism? He notes that the question is complicated because there are two kinds of existentialists. There are on the one hand, Christians (Jaspers and Marcel), and on the other hand, there are atheistic existentialists. What they have in common is simply the fact that they believe that 'existence precedes essence'. By this existentialists mean that individuals first of all exist, encounter themselves and define themselves afterwards. For humans 'in the beginning there is nothing' – no fixed human nature – and out of this nothingness individuals make themselves. So the first principle of existentialism is: human beings exist and are nothing else but that which they make of themselves. I exist as a human being because I am conscious and can propel myself into the future. I am a 'project' who possesses a subjective life – a life 'for-myself'.

Now if it is true that existence precedes essence, I am responsible for what I am. So the first corollary of existentialism is that it puts me in possession of myself and so places the entire responsibility for my existence on my own shoulders. But Sartre goes further when he says (with poetic licence) that I am responsible for my own individuality and 'for all mankind'. My responsibility is thus much greater than I normally suppose, for it concerns mankind as well. If I choose to marry, I choose for myself, for my bride and for the institution of marriage. If I marry in a church, even though I am an atheist, I choose for the continuing existence of churches (at least as places in which marriage ceremonies are conducted).

Recognition of my freedom and my profound responsibility is an anxious burden. As anxiety increases in the face of my responsible freedom I am sorely tempted to deny my freedom and/or responsibility – to enter into bad faith. But in vain. I am condemned to my freedom, and since I am free, I am responsible for what I freely choose to become. Freedom is for Sartre, as it was for Fichte, an irreducible datum; indeed it is the primary datum of human existence. But freedom without responsibility is self-contradictory and therefore there is 'no exit'.

I am never able to explain my actions by reference to specific human nature or any other form of determinism. I am alone with no excuses. That is what Sartre means when he says that I am condemned to be free. Condemned because I did not create myself, yet I am free, and from the moment that I am thrown into the world I have the power of choice. Sartre will not accept that my power of choice is compromised by the power of passion. He refuses to regard a strong passion as a destructive torrent which overwhelms me and is therefore an excuse. I am responsible for my passions.

Sartre's is a philosophy of consciousness, and consciousness is always of something. It is like a wind blowing towards an object – it is exhausted in intending what is outside itself. This notion of consciousness is taken from the inventor of phenomenology, Edmund Husserl (1859–1938), who argues that it is 'intentionality' that characterises consciousness. By intentionality Husserl means the unique peculiarity of experiences to be conscious of something. So consciousness is not a fixed essence or substance, but is best thought of as a moving flux of intentions. Consciousness, for Sartre, has no contents because content is on the side of the objects of the world. Consciousness is a spontaneous activity and so there is no 'I' in consciousness, as there was for Husserl – 'I' is not the owner of consciousness but is consciousness.

Sartre believes that the orthodox view that the 'Me' is an object of consciousness and 'I' the subject of consciousness is incorrect if, by the latter, we mean that 'I' inhabits or owns consciousness. On the contrary, 'I' is consciousness, or at the very least, 'I' and consciousness arise together. Sartre calls consciousness a nothing, or a nothingness, because all physical and psychological objects, all truths, all values are outside it. It is this nothingness which provides man with his freedom. Freedom is made possible by the nothingness which is consciousness. But our freedom is always threatened by the non-conscious world of things.

In his celebrated novel *Nausea* Sartre describes the various ways in which the material world threatens personal freedom. The anti-hero, Roquentin, becomes aware of his freedom in its negative aspects. He discovers freedom by the demands which it thrusts upon him by its nihilating possibilities. 'I glance around and a feeling of disgust comes over me. What am I doing here? I want to leave, but my place is nowhere. I feel like vomiting – and then, there it is: the nausea. A really bad attack: it shakes me from top to bottom. So this is the nausea: this blinding revelation? To think how I have racked my brains over it! Now I know: I exist, but I don't care. I want to let myself go, to forget, to sleep – but I can't. I'm suffocating: existence is penetrating me all over. And suddenly, the veil is torn away, I understand. I can't say that I feel relieved or happy: rather I feel crushed. But I have achieved my aim: I know what I wanted to know; the nausea hasn't left me. But it is no longer an illness: it is me. And then I have a revelation which takes my breath away. Never until these last few days had I suspected what it means "to exist". Usually existence hides itself – it is there, around us, in us, it is us. You can't say a couple of words without speaking of it. There was just one word in my head – the word "to be". There is no half-way house between non-existence and this rapturous abundance. If you exist, you have to exist to the point of mildew, blisters, obscenity. We are a heap of existents, embarrassed by ourselves, and we haven't the slightest reason for being here. Vaguely ill at ease, we feel superfluous. The essential thing is contingency – existence is not necessity. Some people understand this – but they try to overcome this contingency by inventing a necessary being. But no necessary being can explain existence – everything is gratuitous. When you realise this, everything starts floating – that is the nausea. When I say "I" it seems hollow. The only real thing left in me is an existence which can feel itself existing. Antoine Roquentin exists for nobody – that amuses me. And exactly what is Antoine Roquentin? An abstraction – a pale little memory of myself wavers in consciousness, and suddenly the "I" pales, pales, and finally goes out. Lucid, motionless, empty, my consciousness perpetuates itself. Nothing inhabits it anymore – this is the meaning of existence. It is a consciousness of being nothing. It dilutes itself, it scatters itself, it tries to lose itself. But it never forgets itself – that is its lot. There is a consciousness of this body walking slowly along a dark street. It walks but it gets no further away. The dark street of consciousness does not come to a end. It loses itself in nothingness.'

Nausea is a great philosophical novel about an encounter with nothingness. It is a philosophical enema which flushes everything out of consciousness. Its main themes – existence is inherently contingent and meaningless, only particulars exist, language cannot capture reality, logic and reason are trivial and relatively unimportant in human affairs – lead to the conclusion that the encounter with nothingness is the encounter with consciousness. Consciousness is nothingness, it is of something and so is empty of content, it is possibility, it is not what it is and is what it is not. Consciousness is freedom.

But my freedom is worth nothing until I give it meaning. I may be tempted to adopt a 'serious attitude' – that is, to attempt to hide from myself the consciousness of my freedom and try to treat myself as an object with fixed qualities. But I will fail because the consciousness of freedom is consciousness itself. Sartre is adamant that I cannot be half-free – I cannot be sometimes slave and sometimes free. Because freedom is absolute I face a boundless field of possibilities, including creating my own boundaries and obstacles. Obstacles are revealed only in terms of a project already chosen by a free person. And this includes emotions and feelings which are part of my projects.

In a *Sketch for a Theory of Emotions*, Sartre argues that emotions and feelings are not obstacles to my freedom. On the contrary, emotions are modifications of my freedom. Emotional behaviour is not a disorder at all. It is an organised system of means aiming at ends. Emotional states (such as fainting, 'losing' my temper) are freely chosen actions designed to achieve a particular goal, such as the tendency of women to cry in order to achieve specific advantages over men. Emotion is, for Sartre, a transformation of the world. The true origin of emotions is a spontaneous and lived degradation of consciousness in the face of the world. I must always consent to emotion before it can manifest itself – I put myself into emotional states. In this way, emotional behaviour can be thought of as role-playing. Indeed, Sartre wonders if real emotions are not merely false emotions badly acted. This applies especially to the 'passions' which have no weight – they have only the weight I choose to give them. Clearly then, Sartre does not accept the popular view that emotions are drives or dispositions which irresistibly overwhelm me. I make an emotion as I choose myself.

Sartre even deals with so-called psychotic states in terms of freedom. In order to escape from an intolerable environment, psychotics choose instead to change themselves in relation to it. Their bad faith is simply greater than ours. Sartre's life-long companion, Simone de Beauvoir in *The Prime of Life*, tells how he had fallen victim to a 'psychosis' following an experiment with an hallucinogenic drug. 'Sartre suddenly declared that he was tired of being mad . . . He kept his word too; henceforward, he displayed an absolutely imperturbable happiness.'

Sartre does, however, recognise a restriction on freedom in the form of 'the other' (that is, another free individual). When, for example, other people stare at me, I find the field of my possibilities somewhat limited because they can, in a sense, steal my freedom. In the other there dwells an alien consciousness which has the power to objectify me. The other reveals to me that I am, as an individual, superfluous to him, and this represents a form of alienation. Garcin, one of the three characters in Sartre's play *No Exit*, says: 'The only thing I wish for now is to convince you. The curtain's down, nothing of me is left on earth – not even the name of coward. It's you who matter: you who hate me. If you'll have faith in me, I'm saved. You say I dreamed. It was no dream when I choose the hardest path. I made my choice deliberately. A man is what he wills himself to be. But I died too soon. I wasn't allowed time to . . . to do my deeds. You say that one always dies too soon – or too late. You say that one's life is complete at the moment, with a line drawn neatly under it, ready for the summing up. You say you are your life and nothing else. So this is hell. I'd never have believed it. Remember all we were told about the torture chambers, the fire and brimstone. Old wives' tales. There's no need for red-hot pokers. Hell is . . . other people.'

Such is, in general outline, the existentialism of Sartre. Whilst many readers have, over the years, found his emphasis on radical and responsible freedom exhilarating, his philosophy of consciousness raises peculiar problems. First, it is not clear how consciousness arises in the first place. We have seen that consciousness means separation from the material world to which it is present. Furthermore, the act by which consciousness separates itself from its past constitutes its freedom. And freedom is separating myself from my past by 'secreting my own nothingness'. My essence is, therefore, what I have made of myself. And so existence precedes essence; and the acceptance of this proposition is a victory for human freedom. But is this freedom of action or of attitude? And what is it about the world that enables it to generate nothingness?

The active character of consciousness highlights a major problem in Sartre's philosophy. If Simone de Beauvoir is right in her conviction that the key concepts of Sartre's philosophy are the conscious mind as empty (*tabula rasa*) and its power of annihilation, the problem is to reconcile the emptiness with the power. It is hard to see how nothingness can do anything. And if actions are free by definition, then 'free' adds nothing to 'action' in the term 'free action'. It is easy to see why critics concluded that whilst Sartre needs consciousness to be other than a thing – because if it were a thing it would have causal relationships with other things and so would not be free – it is difficult to imagine how it can have the power to do anything at all. Critics have accused Sartre of building his philosophy on an egregious reification of consciousness. It is understandable that a philosopher of freedom resists the idea that consciousness is a 'thing', but some critics are not convinced that the solution is to claim consciousness is, therefore, a no-thing, and then give it the power to act.

Sartre's existentialism has also been criticised for its pessimism. But surely it is one of the most optimistic of philosophies. It sees human beings as free to choose themselves, responsible for their choices and defined by their actions. Far from being a pessimistic description of human existence, existentialism is optimistic because the destiny of individuals is placed within themselves. When existential writers portray a coward, for instance, they show him as responsible for his cowardice because he has made himself cowardly by his actions. There is no such thing as a cowardly temperament – no one is born a coward. Nor is cowardly behaviour the result of environmental conditioning, group pressure, or an unconscious motive to self-abuse. A coward is defined by the deeds he has done. Existentialists believe that cowards make themselves cowardly, heroes make themselves heroic; and there is always the possibility for cowards to give up cowardice and for heroes to stop acting heroically.

Sartre's existentialism is a philosophy of action and self-commitment. It is vehemently opposed to all doctrines which deprive me of my dignity by turning me into an object. I make myself. I am not found ready-made. And if I take refuge behind the excuse of my passions, or by inventing some deterministic doctrine, I act in bad faith. Freedom is the foundation of all values and if I deny my freedom I deceive myself. Now if freedom is the foundation of all values – the primary datum of human existence – I cannot not will the freedom of others. Sartre does not pull any punches when he says that in the name of that will to freedom which is implied in freedom itself, he can judge those who seek to hide from themselves the voluntary nature of their existence and its complete freedom. Those who use deterministic excuses to escape from freedom, or those who try to show that their existence is necessary, when it is merely an accident of the appearance of the human race on earth, are psychological cowards.

Sartre agrees with Kant's declaration that freedom is a will both to itself and to the freedom of others. But whereas Kant thinks that morality is based on a universal principle, Sartre believes that principles which are too abstract break down when I come to judging actions. In the end, I am what I do. And I shall be judged by what I do and what I commit to. Sartre placed the existential choice as one between being and non-being. Once the choice is made I am committed to the course of action resulting therefrom and I am responsible for it. To choose and not to become committed represents non-being. In this way values are created by choices – they are self-created. Similarly, 'I' is not to be found by scientific or introspective means. 'I' is created because the act of choosing entails responsibility. For Sartre, I am what I make of myself, I choose the man I want to be and there is not a single one of my acts which does not create an image of myself as I think I ought to be. To choose is to affirm the value of what I choose. It has been said of existentialism that it is as though I am following various signposts on the road which read: 'this way to the signpost', knowing all the while that when I arrive at the signpost I will find a sign pointing directly at me.

Many of the existential problems I experience arise because I can see no good reason why I should regulate my behaviour according to apparently arbitrary values. Is it even possible to be rational about values? Every philosophy begs the question: 'How may any value be justified?' Can existentialism help me justify my values?

The most common answer to the question of how I may judge a value is to determine the normal expectation of that value. If most people in a society could be expected to hold the same value in similar circumstances it will probably be judged rational. This answer is not satisfying to critical thinkers but it seems to have been enough for the transmission of culture over millennia before the human race thought of philosophy.

Religions have typically sought to justify values by reference to authorities which reveal the will of spiritual beings. This may work for religiously-minded folk but since I have no experience of communication with spiritual beings, I must decline any view which presupposes that type of experience.

In everyday life many people typically seek to justify values by referring to some higher value which is either held in common or is advanced as being self-evidently true. For example, when asked why she opposes nuclear weapons a demonstrator said that she does so because they might annihilate the human race. When pressed as to why she considered that the interests of the human race placed her under an obligation to act, she replied that there is no need to justify the value of human life, its value is self-evident. But how can she justify that view given the history of human greed and stupidity, mass homicide and destruction of the planet? What possible justification is there for such a bungled and blotched species? How can its survival be a fundamental value?

Scholars point out that moral propositions are usually justified by an appeal either to 'intuitive' knowledge of right and wrong or to empirical facts. In both cases the philosophical arguments advanced purport to provide some reasoned, deductive support for the moral propositions in question. A traditional moral position is usually expressed in the injunctive form (thou shalt . . .) and is then viewed as implying an obligation to people to behave accordingly. Many people believe that 'obligation' is the essential element of morality and consider that any value system which does not create some kind of cosmic onus is less than moral. I describe this view as the 'big stick' approach to morality. Yet it is hard to find a description of this idea which is both clear and meaningful other than descriptions in terms of my 'feelings' of obligation or habits of obedience. Can I be rational about morality?

'Morality' brings to mind codes of rules, community

judgements, a sense of rightness and wrongness, reward and punishment and the emotions of 'guilt' and 'self-righteousness'. 'Rationality', in contrast, suggests ideas of self-interestness, reasonableness, success or failure, relative costs and benefits. Morality carries a much stronger emotional colouring and seems to demand a higher degree of selfless dedication. These differences between what are seen as moral and rational are accountable in terms of our common heritage of the 'big stick' view of morality, and of moral assumptions about altruistic motivations. The false dichotomy between the rational and the moral has led to the view that rationality should be judged in terms of rational self-interest. There has also been an under-lying attitude that altruistic beliefs are irrational and unjustifiable.

If I were a truly rational person I would not experience the kind of tension that is engendered in the moralist who undertakes his altruism as an emotional sacrifice to an ineffable principle. I would not act on altruistic principle unless I genuinely identified the altruistic purpose as truly my own purpose. I would only favour the interests of 'the other' in action if in fact the interests of 'the other' were my own dominant concern. In that case, I assess the risks, the costs and benefits, realistically according to my own genuine purposes and do not accrue the resentment that develops in the person for whom morality is a handicap imposed on his truly rational purpose. Conflicts in the person whose rationality and morality are divided are a sign of the false dichotomy of those concepts. The phenomenon is symptomatic of Sartre's 'bad faith', which is moral cowardice displayed by the person who has been intimidated by the 'big stick' conception of morality and who acts out a role to which he is not committed.

The other side of this coin leads to false ascriptions of motivation and to a related denial of the possible rationality of altruism. For example, in the face of extreme provocation from a colleague, I may keep my cool and explain to my colleague only later what my feelings were. It is possible to see my behaviour as motivated by the moral precept that I should 'turn the other cheek'. This would, however, be to ignore the wealth of rational motivation which could explain my behaviour. I may be determined to provide my colleague with a model of dignity or to instil in him the importance of politeness. These are genuinely rational objectives.

There are two other elements in the common conception of rationality. One is associated with standards of information and logic. The other is 'reasonableness' (an ideal defined in law in terms of what a competent, caring and self-disciplined person could be expected to do). Reasonableness is an expression of social interest as distinct from the self-interest of the rational agent. If rationality implies reasonableness, and reasonableness means being competent, caring and self-disciplined, then rationality implies some degree of social definition and denotes some quality of social interaction. Such a quality could be justified by rational self-interest but no demonstration of rational self-interest is at all necessary to the legal concept of reasonableness. The law clearly sees reasonableness as a standard or expectation the community imposes on its members regardless of their individual concerns. This is also a fair representation of the idea of reasonableness in the concept of rationality. There is no necessary reason to regard rationality as primarily a self-centred ideal. It is therefore quite reasonable to conclude that a genuinely altruistic purpose may be a rational purpose, conceived from my perspective, provided only that I conceive it as springing from my free desire rather than from some external purpose with which I do not fully identify.

Morality is concerned with preferences. To say a thing is good is equivalent to saying that it is preferable or serves some purpose. A moral position can therefore be justified only by demonstrating that it is a position which serves to satisfy some preference or advance some purpose. In effect, goodness is a kind of functionality. Any purpose may be judged for functionality from the perspective of any other relevant purpose. Purposes are relevant to each other if the frustration or fulfilment of one has some consequences bearing on the frustration or fulfilment of the other.

The process of moral judgement as applied to an action or purpose is seldom simple. To an extent, though, I can judge an action or purpose according to the knowledge of a consensus of human purpose and quickly reach a satisfying appreciation of the significant issues involved. In the final analysis I can determine my overall attitude to the action of purpose in question only by determining which purposes I judge to be significant. Moral judgements are not empirical, they are existential. In short, I may choose.

The act of choosing is an expression of purpose or evaluation. When pressed for a justification of some value, such as 'a value for human liberty', I may find myself hard pressed to advance an abstract reason. There is, however, no valid reason why I may not advance the fact of deliberate choice in justification of a moral value. Many critics of existentialism argued that 'choice' is not a satisfying foundation for moral justification. First, it could be objected that to say 'I hold x value because I choose to' is a tautologous statement and therefore meaningless. If it does not mean anything more than 'I choose to hold x value because I choose to hold x value' then this objection is valid on the charge of tautology. It seems clear, though, that the proposition, in the instant of its conception, is not empty because it conveys a psychological fact, the fact of the event of my resolve. It is probable that my conscious choice is actually made as a consequence of a history of previous choices on the issue. Whilst the criticism of tautology could conceivably be valid in the instant of choice, it cannot be extended to any future occasion on which x value is applied.

Secondly, it could be objected that choice is not a satisfactory kind of moral justification on the grounds that it may be an isolated and idiosyncratic event. This kind of justification could encourage irresponsible individualism. An idiosyncratic choice of value which was not justified on any additional grounds would, admittedly, be weakly justified. Strong moral justifications are the product of a convergence of purposes. Also, whilst some such choices may be subjective and indiscriminate, there are many instances in human history where such a point of resolve has been the impetus to a career of high distinction. In these days of religious fundamentalism

I can surely recognise the potential power of a seminal choice of value.

The implications of existential morality for philosophy, science, psychology and everyday living are endless. It suggests that the real questions to be addressed are: which goals, desires and purposes typify human existence? Which are most important to us? Which of those goals, desires and purposes can be attained and at what costs in relation to the other typical purposes? How can we maximise our individual and social effectiveness in fulfilling our purposes?

Psychologists have typically studied the psychological and social reality as though people are automata. They have failed to realise that human experience is existential. It is not possible to conceive of human experience devoid of evaluative and intentional dimensions. For scientists to suggest that their intellectual faculties are capable of making sense of a universe which is external to their intellectual experience by means of their intellectual experience, and at the same time to deny any significance to their existential experience, is arbitrary and inconsistent. For scientists to deny the significance of existential experience in explaining human behaviour when in fact they can explain their own behaviour intelligibly, only in existential terms, is obstinate obscurantism.

Humanity's privileged perspective on its own experience reveals that human existence is purposive and this means coming to grips with what people actually want and elucidating the conflicts of purpose that exist. That course will necessarily indicate situations where the convergence of purpose presents some challenge to human cooperation. To this extent an existential philosophy will necessarily be revolutionary in Nietzsche's view of imposing a regime of change. Existential morality is vastly different from traditional morality which involves ideas of guilt, obligation, blind obedience, reward, punishment and self-righteousness. These ideas play no part whatsoever in existential morality which emphasises the freedom to choose one's values. Freedom in its common usage implies choice and responsibility, which is consciousness of being the incontestable author of an event. In this, Sartrean sense, responsibility is a 'moral glue' and presupposes freedom and choice. We are condemned, therefore, to be responsible for ourselves.

Existentialists are united in their belief that individuals are not biologically or socially conditioned robots. Individuals exist, create their nature, experience freedom and the frightening responsibility that accompanies it. In order to avoid their responsible freedom many turn to science. But scientific facts are no panacea for psychological problems – in fact they are probably very little help at all. On the larger canvas not the physical sciences, nor scientific training, nor counselling can reach the jungle of invalidated beliefs for which humans seem so bent on sacrificing themselves, their families and species. Human reasoning is obviously flawed. The main way to get to the heart of the problem of human existence would seem to be to educate people to use stricter criteria for what they are prepared to believe. In France those who are prepared to educate in this fashion are called 'moralistes', and one of the 20th Century's best known representatives of this literary tradition is the French/Algerian, Albert Camus (1913–1960).

Albert Camus, an existential writer if not an existentialist, suffered certain doubts about Kierkegaard's Leap of Faith. Taking his lead from Nietzsche, Camus believed that the eccentric German philosopher had rightly predicted the rise of nihilism – the view that the modern world has no meaning. While it is up to humans to give meaning to the world, Camus did not believe that Kierkegaard's Knight of Faith could stem the tide of anxious meaningless that was flooding across Europe in the first half of the 20th Century. Nietzsche had struck the right note when he announced that God is dead and so absolute values had disappeared from human life. But if there are no absolute values, everything is permitted, and chaos will result in society and in the hearts of individuals. Humans need order, security and metaphysical assurances which had been provided by religious leaders, scientists and systematic philosophers. But these systems had turned on and devoured each other leaving modern men confused, anxious and empty. Reason had failed, ennui has triumphed. The Knights of Faith had turned into modern cynics.

The world is not rational and when we realise this there arises a feeling of the absurdity of human existence. For Camus the absurd arises from this confrontation between man's appeal and the irrational silence of the world. The feeling of the absurd can arise in various ways: the perception of nature's indifference to man, recognition of the pointless of life and the inevitability of death. This uncomfortable feeling can arise suddenly in the midst of the normal monotony of life when I stop and ask WHY and my existence becomes 'a weariness tinged with amazement' and reason cannot help me.

Many people, like Kierkegaard, escape the feeling of the absurd by leaping into faith in a desperate attempt to anchor themselves in a floating world. This form of escapism does not appeal to Camus who, like Nietzsche, wants us to look the absurdity of human existence in the face and stare it down. It is up to the individual, not a group, sect or religion, to give meaning to the world. And this is achieved by embracing life on its own terms, because the absurd frees man from all moral codes, annihilates the future and leaves only one certainty – the sensation of being alive. The feeling of the absurd can, however, be used to justify any action, including murder, because if I believe in nothing, if nothing makes sense, if I can assert no value whatsoever, everything is permissible and nothing is important. I am then free to stoke the crematory fires or to give my life to the care of lepers. In *The Myth of Sisyphus* he says that one must imagine Sisyphus (who was condemned eternally to roll a stone up a hill) happy. But one can, in his absurd confrontation with the world, happily kill innocent children. And so Camus moves from an early concern with 'cosmic absurdity' to a philosophy of revolt which insists on freedom and justice for all.

Camus is a writer of revolt who maintains an existential concern for human existence. He is modern in his loss of faith in God and universal reason. Absolutes have lost their meaning for him. And they cannot be recovered by such poor substitutes as science or materialism. Philosophically, Camus moves from absurdity to rebellion against absolutes, even absolute freedom, because that leads to the right of the strongest to dominate. And absolute justice is likewise dangerous because it is achieved by the suppression of dissent: therefore it destroys freedom.

Camus finds his values in I-consciousness, in the lucid awareness of one's concrete existence in the world. His is a philosophy of life, a sort of Nietzscheanism stripped of the elitist elements. Like the Greeks, Camus believes in nature and beauty although he is acutely aware of man's basic duplicity – of the tension between man's rational attempt to control nature and his aesthetic contemplation of its beauty. Nature is without notions of good and evil and Camus wrestles mightily with issues of oppression, social justice and the fight against moral absolutes. We have to abandon absolutes and embrace moderation and toleration, sensuality rather than rationality. He was, however, haunted by the darkness at the heart of man and in *The Fall* has his central character refer to 'the basic duplicity of the human being' as though man is basically evil. Such a view of human nature is inconsistent with his attitude to social justice and suggests that he never fully abandoned his philosophy of the absurdity of human existence.

He was awarded the Nobel Prize in 1957 but it did not help him solve the riddle of the absurd. The Swedish ambassador said he was awarded the prize because he is a man who belongs to the Resistance, a rebel who was able to give a meaning to the Absurd and to sustain from the depths of the abyss the necessity for hope, by giving back to creativity, action, and human nobility their rightful place in this senseless world. He died, absurdly, in a car crash in January 1960. After hearing of his death Sartre said that he had been for him the admirable conjunction of a person, an action, and a work. He summed up in himself the conflicts of the age and he surpassed them through his ardour to live.

There is in Camus's work a consistent heroic emphasis on fighting for human freedom and responsibility. The aim of life, he writes in *Resistance, Rebellion and Death*, can only be to increase the sum of freedom and responsibility to be found in every human being and in the world. It cannot, under any circumstances, be to reduce or suppress that freedom, even temporarily. His defiance of the fates still evokes feelings of admiration because he reminds me that I have a crucial choice in the way I live my life: the choice of nihilism, which is the belief that everything is futile; the choice of revolt, which is the belief that though everything is ultimately futile, I should behave as though it were not. Camus chose the latter – the path of heroic defiance. In order to be a man, I must refuse to be a God.

Camus pursued an existential project in which he sees human beings as animated by a vital force which enable us to move from philosophical nausea to happiness, from Christianity to neo-paganism, from self-reflection to sensuality, from revolution to rebellion. He pursued and developed a dramatic conception of human existence grounded on the fact of human freedom, the contingent nature of human existence, the impotence of reason in the face of 'the bloodstained mathematical certainties that rule the human lot', the importance of potentiality and possibility, the instability of human relationships, and the ever-present threat of alienation from others and from oneself, the need to live with the prospect of death before us, the importance of solitude and the threat of nihilism.

Like Seneca, Erasmus, Montaigne, Voltaire and Russell he believed in freedom, responsibility and toleration which placed him in the grand tradition of the 'moraliste'. He wrote that modern men, having turned their backs on the present, have sacrificed the fate of humanity for the delusion of power, the misery of the slums for the mirage of the eternal city; they despair of personal freedom and dream of empty promised lands. In short, the secret of modern men is that they no longer love life.

Sartre said of him that he represented the last example of that long line of 'moralistes' whose works constitute the most original element in French literature. His obstinate humanism waged war against the Machiavellians and the realists who replace moral issues with crass pragmatism. He never stopped questioning the political act so that one had to avoid him or fight him. Sartre fought, but respected him because he was indispensable to that tension which sustains intellectual life. The accident that killed Camus was a scandal because it highlights the contingency of life and the absurdity of human existence. At the age of 20 Camus is struck down with tuberculosis and discovers the absurd – the senseless negation of man. He struggled with it, and successfully triumphed over it. And then that cured invalid is annihilated by an unexpected death from the outside. What better example could there be of the absurdity and fragility of human existence?

Existentialism presents itself as the antithesis to the psychological conditions that have developed in modern industrial society following the impact of the Protestant Ethic. There is no doubt that it clearly reveals the relationship between basic assumptions about human freedom to moral exhortation about behaviour, and in this respect existentialism is much more revealing than was the Protestant Ethic. Compared with the latter existentialism is anti-materialistic and offers few prescriptions about how we are to deal with the material conditions of existence. It reveals, therefore, the fact that 'I' is a highly abstract concept when viewed from a scientific perspective, perhaps the ultimate abstraction, since it cannot be described in material terms at all. Existentialism is, then, a collection of philosophies springing from the idea that human beings are essentially nothing – formless and totally alone in the world with themselves to make, and it forces me to see that my favoured moral judgements are personal acts of choice.

When I am faced with a choice about beliefs concerning human existence, two main options confront me. I can agree with Descartes that it is freedom which I find so great in me that I can conceive the idea of nothing greater. This is the road to existentialism and libertarianism. Alternatively, I can deny what was for Descartes a self-evident truth and embrace the doctrine of 'psychological determinism' which claims that I am controlled by internal and/or external forces. But if I deny freedom and adopt psychological determinism, it is pointless to talk of personal responsibility. This is the road to scientific psychology and psychiatry.

While the rejection of scientific psychology is liberating for those who see it as inconsistent with human freedom, existentialism is too tough-mindedly optimistic for others because the tough-minded emphasis on responsibility compromises the optimistic emphasis on freedom.

Since freedom implies options and responsibility implies obligations, there is a strong tendency for people to maximise their freedom and minimise their responsibility. Such people expect from psychology and psychiatry a determinism which absolves them of their personal responsibilities. It is against this bad faith that existentialists and libertarians stand and fight. Once the pernicious doctrine of psychological determinism is rejected, the idea of personal responsibility follows logically. If I am free to choose, and I choose, I am responsible for my choice. I might not always like the consequences which may accrue, but that is the way it is. Whether people will take to the streets and chant for more responsibility is another matter.

Existentialists' assertion of free will is potentially as libertarian as any previous individualistic moral code. The emphasis on freedom, choice, responsibility is an assertion that human beings are never, necessarily, victims of their own created orders.

Epilogue:
An I for An Eye

Now that eleven of my I's have written their chapters, and my eye has kept an eye on them, it is appropriate to ask whether there is an I which was overseeing them all. Am I the author of this book?

Postmodern anti-philosophers maintain that the author and 'I' are dead. So I am dead. But since I am composing this Epilogue I cannot be dead. So I must be alive. Can I be alive with a dead I? If 'I' is dead how can I own my actions, since 'I' implies that I am the author of those actions? Is it possible that my actions are not owned by me? If so, who owns them? If nobody owns them, how can they be said to be actions? Should I take seriously the ravings of authors who say they are dead while writing books telling me that they and I are dead? I think not.

Someone said that the cure for postmodernism is the illness of Romanticism. Postmodernism does not need to be cured – it needs to be allowed to die of its logical deficiencies and terminal illiteracy. Among the fantasies of the 21st Century is the one which holds that postmodernism has improved the health of the many fields it has infected. Among the many things I – the author of this book –

cannot believe, this is the chief. I cannot believe that post-modernists will reach so far as to deprive us of our universal madness. If they did, we would no longer be recognisable as the same animal. In the support they have received in their battle against rationality postmodernists have shown that human beings are, as they have always been, stark-raving mad.

Given the history of humankind it is impossible to maintain that sanity is the norm. The truth is that sanity is an extremely rare state that we might not recognise if we were to encounter it. Human reasoning is fatally flawed because of its tendency to 'believe'. It believes – or believes in – heavens, gods, devils, witches, ghosts, spirits, souls, minds, mental illness, reincarnation, prophets, saviours, life after death, universal determinism, the death of truth. For any kind of nonsense believers can be found. And the effect of (rational) philosophy on the massive unreason of the world appears, sadly, to have been quite negligible.

That rational philosophy has died is regarded as a fact by many people who don't believe in facts. It is an historical truth that many writers in the 1970s felt that whatever philosophy was, it wasn't rational. Anti-philosophers wrote with great feeling to remind us that logic, facts and truth are discursive fictions, and argument is just plain nasty. The impact of the attack upon Western rationality launched by the better-washed Hippies cannot be over-estimated since it led to a progressive paralysis of thought. The war cry was jejune: feelings are the true reality (thinking led to patriarchy, Auschwitz, Hiroshima, etc.) Thinking must be replaced by feeling – I feel it is so, ergo it is so. Rational philosophy was, therefore, subjected to a critique which left it, if not dead, battered. And so it remains today – a battered, bruised bullshit detector.

But rational thinking does manage, occasionally, to penetrate the fog of postmodern pretentiousness. The Romantics, even in their radical moments, kept one foot firmly in the classical tradition for fear that without a mild dose of rationality chaos would result. From Beethoven to Friedrich, Rousseau to Schopenhauer, romantic images and ideas were grounded on classical forms without which there would be no form. If Romanticism was an illness, it was one from which people of strong will and reasonable intelligence recovered with a mixture of classical ideas and romantic voluntarism.

Reading the classical Greek philosophers, I am struck by how sane they were, and how long they lived. Even such eccentrics as Diogenes and Crates seem incredibly rational judged by postmodern standards. Their passion to understand the world and themselves was guided by their belief in truth and their love of rational argument. They never stopped arguing, preferring to give reasons to support their assertions rather than to share their feelings with each other. To argue rationally was to argue logically; to be reasonable was to be rational. Today we tell people who spout nonsense that, well, I don't feel the way you do, but, well, your feelings are, well, reasonable. But feelings are feelings, they are neither true nor false. Sharing feelings with others may be good psychotherapy (and it may not), but it is not good philosophy. When Socrates challenges me to 'know myself', he is not suggesting that I 'get in touch with my feelings' on a Californian-style self-discovery tour. Rather, he is encouraging me to use my mind that I may know my place and accept my fate.

As I speak to myself I am minded to say that I have no mind. I like to think that I think rationally by talking to myself in a logical way. I like Homer because he taught me that I can talk to myself without using words like 'mind', but at the price of accepting his gods. The price is too high – I do not believe that 55 gods are needed to guide me through life. I don't need a mind to do that, but I do need I, otherwise I am not my own guide. If I am my own guide, I need a notion of what separates me from other people and from gods. That notion is I. Homer assumes 'I' and simply takes it for granted. He does not write of 'I' preferring a language of action viewed from outside the actor. Indeed, there is no actor, only actions described in a no-nonsense language which has no need of spiritual concepts. More strength to Homer's stylus. He describes actions as patterns in the stream of movement seen from the outside as focused on producing an effect – the final element in the pattern. To be convincing the author needs no assumption other than that his readers can detect such patterns, and there is ample evidence to justify such an assumption. From Socrates to Sartre, philosophers write of patterns in human affairs, and especially cause-effect patterns.

One of the most important patterns I perceive and use involves cause-effect relationships, and I have learned to label my activities as causes and all the results as effects. Since all the causes have a single source in me, I label it I. My activities are, therefore, causative enterprises originating in me. I have developed an awareness of I through a process that requires little more than perception of simple patterns. But I have also become a practicing philosopher because I am now armed with the cause-effect concept and have learned its use; and I have also learned about the use of concepts to describe what is quintessentially human about me. Once I become conscious of I, I hold myself responsible for consequences of my actions which I can foresee. I can therefore choose my actions and hold others responsible for the effects of their actions insofar as they were aware of the consequences beforehand. So the ability to utilise the concept of cause and effect has led me to a concept of I, personal responsibility and the power to choose my actions. These attributes distinguish me from other animals and all must be taken into account in a viable philosophy of life. If philosophy is going to study what it means for me to live as a human being, (and what else could it study?), it must accept some assumption which allows 'I' to exist and, with it, the power to choose my actions.

But this view opens the way for sceptical philosophers to argue that 'I' is an admission that there is a little person inside the head directing actions, and to dismiss it with this derisory caricature of an homunculus – an ancient superstition, harking back to the way monks in the Middle Ages drew pictures of the soul inhabited by good angels and evil devils. It has no substance because 'I' is not a substance, although it is the very source of the notion of responsibility which I apply to adult humans but not to other animals. 'I' is, then, a concept which is needed to deal with human beings, but not with dogs or dolphins.

Such a view of responsibility is easily compromised when metaphysical speculation about an immaterial soul is allowed to intrude into philosophical reasoning. Aristotle, for instance, believed: 'From the hour of their birth, some are marked for subjection, others for rule.' This view of an unchanging, predetermined 'I' was maintained through the many centuries of Christian dogma which stated that the soul was immortal. With the separation of 'I' from the the world of facts comes a tendency to shut out the perception of everyday patterns and seek a withdrawal from the world as 'I' searches for immortal 'truths'. Judaism and Christianity promote world-rejection as a step towards searching within oneself for knowledge of the principles which lie beneath the perception of patterns, and this establishes 'I' over and against the fragmentary nature of everyday experience. While religions promise me that I can understand the true structure of reality and participate actively in it, the risk of failure is great. On the religious acccount 'I' is a fiction which arises from my attempt to separate myself from the world and must be created in the future. I am thus licensed to construct my own myths about the nature of the world and there are as many worlds as there are models of understanding them. Life has become an infinite possibility and 'I' is infinitely revisable because it is made by me through my religion. I can transform my 'I' and therefore remake the world. Of course, the world is indifferent to these paranoid ravings.

Clearly, philosophers who did not see themselves as religionists needed to account for the unusual properties of 'I' and Hume, ever the daring thinker, proposed one. Hume, like Nietzsche after him, compares 'I' to a republic in which the members are united by the reciprocal ties of government and subordination. As an individual republic may change its members and laws, so a person may change his character and disposition, without losing his identity. Hume, a man of science, was expressing a decidedly non-scientific view. Without realising it, he was preparing the ground for the Romantics who attacked and dispensed with the idea that 'I' is a thing. If 'I' is not a thing, it is not an 'it' but a process. 'I' is no longer the ancient notion of an unchanging essence, nor is it the medieval idea of a soul which is born into the world with the body. Neither soul nor mind, 'I' is an ongoing process in which the boundary between I and not-I becomes increasingly blurred. As that man of strong 'I', Max Stirner, said: 'I take the world as what it is to be mine; I refer all to my I.' This is not an exercise in narcissism because the narcissist is in love with his cozy 'I', whilst the Romantic actively projects 'I' into the world. A Romantic like Fichte is concerned with exhausting 'I' through action and speech. 'I am at once agent and the product of action; the active and what the activity brings about.' For the Romantics I is will: Schopenhauer's will to life; Nietzsche's will to power; existentialists' will to freedom. And Wittgenstein, a sort of Romantic, admitted that if there were not will, then there would not be that centre of the world which I call 'I'.

The Romantics' emphasis on will is an acknowledgement that I am a spontaneous mover and always in motion. Consequently, there is no need to explain why I behave but rather to show why my actions take the direction they do. If I fail to move at all except under the influence of external forces then I fail to come within the scope of philosophical discourse. Dead bodies are therefore excluded. As a live body I am throughout my life a perceiver of patterns, especially patterns of cause and effect and I use knowledge of causes to control effects and to avoid being affected myself. Above all, I am a perceiver of pain and pleasure and the difference between them, and I use this perception as a basis of choice.

My capacity to experience pleasure and pain and to perceive patterns in the world enables me to develop a value hierarchy which is based partly on learning by trial and error elimination, and partly on the values of my community. Philosophies offer me alternatives to these values and help me make more trials and thereby commit more errors. The elimination of error helps me develop my powers of critical thinking and so take more philosophical risks by employing an array of hypothetical constructs such as purpose, intention, choice, responsibility, which indicate the special types of pattern perception that are hypothesised under different conditions.

Philosophies can be lived because they explore fields of phenomena, attempt to discover patterns therein and explain these patterns by describing a possible causal mechanism that produces them. Homer uses his gods as causative agents which affect the behaviour of his warriors. Plato analyses the causative properties of the 'soul'. Religionists see their gods as the prime mover – the ultimate cause in the pattern of human activities. Astronomy commences from perceived patterns of movement among the heavenly bodies for which various causative mechanisms have been proposed. Newtonian mechanics started from Newton's realisation that motion involved the perception of a regular pattern. And Hume pointed out that causation is based on perceiving regularity in events. Darwin, Einstein and other scientific innovators belong in this list, in that their initial contribution lay in discovering a pattern in the phenomena under investigation. Some of these patterns are later reduced to the simplest of them – causation – and it is this process which establishes a science, or a philosophy.

The core of philosophy lies in patterns implicit in our perceptions of the world but not explained by science. And this is where the distinction between 'I' and 'Me' is important. If I accept that 'Me' is the object of thinking then it can be studied scientifically, much like the method used by scientifically-orientated psychologists. Now since 'I' is not an object of thinking, not even in principle, it cannot be studied scientifically. Indeed, it cannot be studied at all. 'I' is an abstraction, perhaps the ultimate abstraction, since it cannot be described in material terms, and this is reflected in its status as a pronoun. Should I conclude, then, that 'I' is a fiction?

Such a conclusion ignores the existentially obvious nature of human beings who regard themselves as having choice, and this perception is self-fulfilling in that it leads them to choose and to regard themselves as responsible for the results of that choice. This lends them some degree of freedom and consequently entitles them to respect as persons. We cannot abandon the notion of 'I' without abandoning the concepts of freedom and responsibility for the former is by definition the carrier of the latter. To abandon these notions is to abandon the basis of rational explanation and to suggest that we have been radically in error about ourselves for millennia. If we cannot provide a philosophically viable account of human existence which takes into account the existential fact of 'I', then so much the worse for philosophy.

I use I to indicate that I am aware that I am the author of the actions I perform, and the author of this book. I own the strategies I have used (hopefully) to entertain and educate readers. Similarly, I own the values which guide the choices of my actions. I has some coherence in the way that this book has some coherence because of the logic of writing, the cultural tradition in which such writing is performed and my value hierarchy. Nevertheless, I remains an elusive quasi-pattern, always subject to change while I am alive. Of one thing I am certain: whilst my eye cannot see my I, eye is for I.

Index

Adler, Alfred 235
Aeschylus 30–1
Anaxagoras 41
Anaximander 41, 286
Anaximenes 41
Antisthenes 71–3
Aquinas, Thomas 144, 158
Aristophanes 41
Aristotle 62–8, 110, 143–4, 146,
    164, 172, 182, 220, 224, 286,
    295, 352
Augustine 141–2, 158, 161, 286
Bacon, Francis 161, 223–4, 287
Banks, Joseph 288
Barthes, Roland 247
Beethoven, Ludwig van 251, 261,
    349
Berlin, Isaiah 250
Bierce, Ambrose 11, 97–104, 131,
    187, 313
Borgia, Cesare 163, 167
Boswell, James 231
Buddha 39
Burke, Edmund 161, 172, 181–6
Butler, Samuel 294–5
Calvin, John 90, 148–50, 153–4,
    317
Camus, Albert 322, 339–344
Carroll, Lewis 243
Chekhov, Anton 96
Christianity 138–46, 165–6,
    188–9, 263–4, 272–3, 274, 296,
    352
Condillac, Etienne de 251
Condorcet, Marquis de 251
Copernicus 150, 191
Crates 70, 78–82, 108–9, 349
Cuchulain 12

Cynics 70–83, 95–7, 108–10
D'Alembert, Jean 251
Dante 10
Darwin, Charles 283, 285–6, 289,
    290–8, 300–1, 355
Darwin, Erasmus 288–9, 297–8
de Beauvoir, Simone 11, 260, 322,
    328–9
de Maistre, J.M. 95
Democritus 41
Dennett, Daniel C. 213
Derrida, Jacques 245, 247
Descartes, René 101, 187–96, 207,
    222, 224–5, 254, 260, 279, 285,
    287, 300–1, 318, 345
Devitt, Michael 248
Dewey, John 196
Diogenes the Cynic 70, 72–9, 80,
    82, 95, 109–10, 276, 349
Diogenes Laertius 42, 72, 218
Dworkin, Andrea 247
Einstein, Albert 235, 355
Ellis, Albert 107–8, 120–30
Empedocles 41, 286
Engels, Friedrich 262
Epictetus 79, 105, 107–8, 112–19,
    120–1
Erasmus, Desiderius 344
Euclides 73
Euripides 31–3
Feyerabend, Paul 238–41, 247
Fichte, Johann 251, 258–61, 264,
    267–9, 316, 323, 353
Flavius, Arrianus 112
Foucault, Michel 245–7
Frazer, James 133–4
Freud, Sigmund 105, 176, 235, 245,
    268, 272, 314

Friedrich, Caspar David 251, 261–2, 349

Galileo 150, 172, 187, 191, 292

Galton, Samuel 288

Geertz, Clifford 303–6

Gilgamesh 13, 14–19

Goethe, J.W. 259

Golding, William 306

Gorgias 43, 71

Harding, Sandra 247–8

Hardy, Alister 298–300

Harvey, William 191

Hegel, G.W.F. 251, 317–8

Helvetius, Claude-Adrien 251

Heraclitus 41, 110

Herder, J.G. 251

Hipparchia 78–81

Hobbes, Thomas 172–7, 180, 183

Hoffmann, E.T.A. 261

Homer 12–15, 19–40, 52, 59, 273, 275, 350, 354

Hooker, John 290

Hughes, Robert 36, 281

Hume, David 94, 217, 224, 226–33, 240, 242–3, 252–5, 259–60, 352–3, 355

Husserl, Edmund 324

Hutton, James 287, 290

Huxley, T.H. 285, 291–4

Ibsen, Henrik 264

Irigaray, Luce 247

Isaiah 39

James, William 196

Jaspers, Karl 322

Joan of Arc 11

Judaism 134–40, 176, 184

Jung, Carl 268, 272

Kant, Immanuel 251, 253–9, 270, 287, 331

Kepler, Johann 150

Kierkegaard, Soren 260, 315–21, 340–1

Kraus, Karl 285

Kristeva, Julia 247

Lamarck, Jean-Baptiste de 288–9, 297–8, 300–1

Leonardo da Vinci 161, 222–3, 270

Lessing, G.E. 251

Lewin, Kurt 66

Locke, John 84, 101, 111, 172, 177–81, 184, 224–6, 259

Lucian 82

Luther, Martin 146–8, 150

Machiavelli, Niccolo 83, 161–72, 223, 263

Malthus, T.R. 290–1, 301

Marcel, Gabriel 322

Marcus, Aurelius 83, 108, 112, 117–20

Marx, Karl 157–8, 185, 235, 262, 314

Maupertius, P.L.M. de 287

Maxwell, J.C. 293

Mead, George Herbert 196–203, 214

Michelangelo 261, 270

Mill, John Stuart 264

Montaigne, Michel de 208, 344

Montesquieu, Baron de 251

Newton, Isaac 84, 103, 151, 252–3, 257–8, 354

Nietzsche, Friedrich 3, 5, 7, 14, 38–9, 245–6, 255–6, 259–60, 263, 268, 271–84, 295–7, 299, 314, 339, 340–2, 352–3

Novalis 250

Owen, Richard 292

Parmenides 41, 58–60

Paul 161

Peirce, Charles Sanders 196

Peregrinus 82–3

Petrarch 208

Plato 26, 33, 38–9, 45–7, 49, 53, 56–65, 68, 71–3, 104, 108, 110,

173, 179, 184, 220–1, 224, 225, 235–6, 254, 273, 278, 295, 354

Popper, Karl 60, 130, 232–41

Priestley, Joseph 288

Protagoras 41–3, 56

Puritanism 148–54, 159

Pyrrho 217–20

Pythagoras 41

Raphael 161

Rousseau, Jean-Jacques 83–4, 90–6, 181, 232, 256, 349

Royce, Josiah ix

Russell, Bertrand 63, 107, 120, 142, 162, 181, 187, 221, 230–2, 271, 344

Ryle, Gilbert 181, 195

Sartre, Jean-Paul 4, 5, 10, 259, 260, 320–32, 334–5, 339, 342–4, 350

Sceptics 217–22

Schaler, Jeffrey 204, 212

Schelling, Friedrich 251

Schiller, J. von 251

Schlegel, Friedrich 261

Schopenhauer, Arthur 267–71, 273, 287, 317, 349, 353

Searle, John R. 213

Sedgwick, Adam 292

Seneca 21, 108, 112, 344

Sextus, Empiricus 222

Sloterdijk, Peter 97

Smith, Adam 231

Socrates 7, 8, 33, 38, 43–63, 71, 108–112, 208, 217, 221, 224, 234–5, 273, 319, 349–50

Sophists 41–4, 53, 104, 217

Sophocles 31

Spinoza, Baruch 287

Stirner, Max 5, 260, 262–7, 353

Stoics 68, 82, 105–120, 279, 315

Stove, David 240–2, 248–9

Szasz, Thomas 203–16

Tennyson, Alfred 289

Thales 40–1

Timon 220

Vico, Giambattista 208

Vidal, Gore 203

Virgil 5

Viroli, Maurizio 162

Voltaire 83–90, 94–8, 251, 344

Wagner, Richard 270, 273

Wallace, Alfred Russell 291, 293–5, 300–1

Watt, James 288

Weber, Max 133, 152–60

Wedgwood, Josiah 288

Wesley, John 154

Wilde, Oscar 96

Wittgenstein, Ludwig 4, 243–4, 353

Zarathustra 39

Zeno 108–113, 118

Zoroaster 39